CRIME AND PUNISHMENT
IN THE JIM CROW SOUTH

CRIME
AND
PUNISHMENT
IN THE
JIM CROW SOUTH

Edited by
AMY LOUISE WOOD AND
NATALIE J. RING

UNIVERSITY OF
ILLINOIS PRESS
Urbana, Chicago, and Springfield

Library of Congress Cataloging-in-Publication Data
Names: Wood, Amy Louise, 1967- editor. | Ring, Natalie J., editor.
Title: Crime and punishment in the Jim Crow South / edited by Amy Louise
  Wood and Natalie J. Ring.
Description: Urbana: University of Illinois Press, [2019] | Includes
  bibliographical references and index.
Identifiers: LCCN 2018045776| ISBN 9780252042409 (cloth : alk. paper) |
  ISBN 9780252084195 (pbk. : alk. paper)
Subjects: LCSH: Discrimination in criminal justice administration—Southern
  States—History—20th century. | African Americans—Social conditions—
  To 1964. | African Americans—Southern States—History—20th century. |
  United States—Race relations—History—20th century.
Classification: LCC HV9955.S63 C75 2019 | DDC 364.97509/041—dc23
  LC record available at https://lccn.loc.gov/2018045776

Ebook ISBN 978-0-252-05124-1

CONTENTS

Acknowledgments

Introduction   1
Amy Louise Wood and Natalie J. Ring

PART I: CRIME

1   The Trials of George Doyle: Race and Policing
in Jim Crow New Orleans   17
K. Stephen Prince

2   "Many People 'Colored' Have Come to the
Homicide Office": Police Investigations of
African American Homicides in Memphis, 1920–1945   34
Brandon T. Jett

3   Forced Confessions: Police Torture and the African American
Struggle for Civil Rights in the 1930s and 1940s South   58
Silvan Niedermeier

4   The South's Sin City: White Crime and the Limits of Law
and Order in Phenix City, Alabama   79
Tammy Ingram

PART II: PUNISHMENT

5   Testimonial Incapacity and Criminal Defendants
in the South   107
Pippa Holloway

6 Sewing and Spinning for the State: Incarcerated
   Black Female Garment Workers in the Jim Crow South   130
     Talitha L. LeFlouria

7 Cole Blease's Pardoning Pen: State Power and
   Penal Reform in South Carolina   147
     Amy Louise Wood

8 Hanging, the Electric Chair, and Death Penalty Reform
   in the Early Twentieth-Century South   170
     Vivien Miller

9 The Making of the Modern Death Penalty
   in Jim Crow North Carolina   192
     Seth Kotch

Contributors   215

Index   219

ACKNOWLEDGMENTS

Dawn Durante at the University of Illinois Press has been a great pleasure to work with, and we are grateful for the enthusiasm and care she has shown for this project from the start. Illinois State University and the School of Arts and Humanities at the University of Texas at Dallas provided financial support. We would also like to thank the three anonymous readers who read our proposal and the completed manuscript for their insightful suggestions. Carole Emberton reviewed our introduction at a critical time, and we appreciate the sound advice she offered throughout this process. Finally, we would like to thank all our contributors, who responded to our suggestions and critiques patiently and cheerfully.

CRIME AND PUNISHMENT
IN THE JIM CROW SOUTH

INTRODUCTION

Amy Louise Wood and Natalie J. Ring

In recent years, we have seen renewed attention paid to problems that pervade the criminal justice system in the United States. The prison population has grown exponentially since 1980 due to the war on drugs, minimum sentencing laws, and other crime control measures instituted in the 1980s and 1990s. The United States now incarcerates more people than any other nation in the world, currently over two million. African Americans constitute nearly half of those prisoners. People on both sides of the political spectrum have become more attuned to the terrible consequences of mass incarceration: the problems of overcrowding, the school-to-prison pipeline, and the abuse of solitary confinement as a disciplinary mechanism. Mass incarceration has also devastated many African American communities already burdened by poverty and lack of employment opportunities. The Obama administration began to reform federal prison policy and worked with Congress to pass the Fair Sentencing Act in 2010, which reduced the disparity in sentencing between crack and powder cocaine. But other sentencing reform legislation remains stalled in Congress.[1]

Mass incarceration has had significant political effects. With the exception of Vermont and Maine, all states impose some form of voting restrictions on convicted felons, ranging from bans on voting while incarcerated, while on probation or parole, or even after the completion of their sentences. The number of people who have been denied the right to vote through these laws has skyrocketed in the past forty years, from 1.17 million in 1976 to 6.1 million as of the November 2016 election. As a result, one out of thirteen African Americans have been disfranchised. In recent years, a number of states have passed reforms to reinstate some or all voting rights for convicted felons who have been released, especially those convicted of nonviolent offenses. But as governorships or legislatures have changed parties, some of these reforms have been overturned.[2]

Increased policing, especially the rise of "stop and frisk" practices over the past twenty years, has fueled more cases of police brutality against African Americans. Each day, it seems, we are met with another story of a black man or woman struck down by police with little or no provocation. In response, more cities are requiring officers to wear body cameras, and in 2015 the Federal Bureau of Investigation announced that it would expand its tracking of police fatalities. Still, in the past ten years, only a handful of officers have been convicted for murders committed in the line of duty.[3]

Finally, debates surrounding the death penalty continue to hover over our criminal justice system. The United States is the only advanced industrial nation to still practice capital punishment, and, again, the application of the death penalty affects African Americans disproportionately: over 40 percent of prisoners on death row are black. Increased public awareness of the racial disparities in sentencing, as well as the use of DNA testing to exonerate death row prisoners, has led to the abolition of the death penalty in six states since 2007. Another thirteen states, as well as the federal government, have put moratoriums on the practice due to problems surrounding lethal injection. States are facing a shortage of the necessary drugs, especially since the European Union began banning exports of those drugs in 2011, which has led to excruciating incidences of botched executions and subsequent legal challenges.[4]

We are in a moment, then, when Americans are primed for a real reckoning with these aspects of the US criminal justice system: incarceration, policing, and capital punishment. This collection contributes to that accounting by providing a historical perspective on these practices as they developed in the Jim Crow South from the 1890s through the 1950s. After all, our metaphors for understanding present-day problems in the criminal justice system are rooted in the Jim Crow period. Present-day mass incarceration has been deemed, to use Michelle Alexander's phrase, "the new Jim Crow." Similarly, capital punishment is commonly referred to as "legal lynching," and recent cases of police brutality have also been likened to a form of state-sanctioned lynching.[5] These analogies are not without reason. The history of criminal justice in the Jim Crow South can illuminate much about our present-day system: its brutality and the racial injustices endemic to it; its emphasis on retribution over rehabilitation; its concerns with profit over state responsibility.[6] In fact, many of the problems in our current system are concentrated in southern states. Seven out of the ten states with the highest per capita incarceration rates are in the South.[7] Three out of the four states that permanently disfranchise convicted felons are also southern.[8] And since the death penalty was reinstated in 1976, southern states have executed the majority of prisoners by a large margin. As of May 2018, 1,206 individuals have been executed in the South compared to 181 in the Midwest, 85 in the West, and 4 in the Northeast.[9] Yet most histories of penitentiaries, policing, and capital punishment in the United States have relegated southern penal practices to the margins of the story.[10]

At the same time, it is important to question analogies that assume a direct trajectory from slavery to Jim Crow to modern-day criminal justice practices without recognizing the ebbs and flows of historical change. The essays in this collection explore the complexities of Jim Crow criminal justice as it came into being and as it changed over time, particularly in light of protest and reform efforts. In doing so, they make a case for regional distinctiveness. In recent years, historians of the South have come to question the idea of southern exceptionalism or, in particular, the notion that southern racial practices diverged dramatically from those in the rest of the nation.[11] Likewise, scholars of criminal justice have recently emphasized that extralegal practices like lynching were nationwide or that the brutalities we associate with southern prisons were not confined to the South. To treat southern penal systems as exceptionally barbaric, Heather Ann Thompson notes, is to dangerously conceal the racial disparities and abuses that have plagued systems in nonsouthern states.[12] The idea of the South as a distinct problem in need of rehabilitation gained more prominence in the national imagination in the late nineteenth and early twentieth centuries, when the region became a convenient repository for the presumed ills plaguing modern society.[13] The inclination to assume the South was backward, degraded, and uncivilized produced a powerful mythology that has been difficult for Americans to abandon.

Yet, discarding the concept of southern distinctiveness might obscure real regional differences and might flatten the nuances and contingencies of history, just as transhistorical analogies between present-day practices and the past risk doing. Many of the essays here demonstrate that criminal justice in the Jim Crow South looked quite different than it did in the North, at least until the mid-twentieth century. But to make that argument is not to claim that Jim Crow criminal justice was marginal or incidental to the national system. Nor is it to claim that other regions did not have their own discrete features and histories.

In the Jim Crow South, criminal justice was inseparable from white southerners' imperative to establish and maintain racial control. Indeed, it stood at the core of Jim Crow regimes. White supremacy and the rise of Jim Crow were predicated upon white fears about black crime. Southern whites tended to interpret African Americans' claims to their civil rights as acts of aggression, and political assaults on white supremacy were read as literal assaults upon white bodies and homes. Stories of black criminality proliferated in southern newspapers, fueling white beliefs in black inferiority and brutishness and the possibility of a "race war." The mechanisms of white supremacy that constituted Jim Crow—segregation, disfranchisement, and lynching—were justified as necessary to control an unruly and criminal black population. As the essays in this collection show, policing, incarceration, capital punishment, and other forms of crime control served alongside these mechanisms to reduce African American political and social power and shore up white supremacy.

Criminal justice in the South developed in distinct ways not only because of these demands for racial control but also because of white southerners' suspicions of centralized state power, even as they relied on state power to defend the racial hierarchy. In the antebellum era, southern states were late to establish penitentiaries, and southern cities lagged behind in forming professional police departments, largely because the institution of slavery controlled the population white southerners most feared. Where penitentiaries did exist in the Old South, they looked not much different from their counterparts in the North, but resistance to them was stronger. Southern critics saw them as a threat to local jurisdiction over criminal punishment and to traditions of retributive justice. Punishment, they believed, should be based in biblical demands for vengeance and vindication, not rehabilitation.[14] These same attitudes fueled the rise of lynching as a southern, racialized phenomenon in the late nineteenth century. About 90 percent of lynchings took place in the South in this period, and white southerners justified them not only through the specter of black criminality but also through the concept that communities had a right to avenge crimes committed against them, and avenge them swiftly and harshly. Black criminals, defenders of lynching argued, did not deserve the due process rights that the state supposedly guaranteed.[15] Similarly, as Vivien Miller and Seth Kotch in this collection show, southern states centralized capital punishment later than states in the rest of the country, as local sheriffs retained control over hangings, often still public, until the 1910s and 1920s. In Mississippi and Louisiana, executions were still local events until the 1940s.

The convict leasing system, which developed during Reconstruction, was also particular to the South. Indeed, it was arguably the defining feature of southern criminal justice in the late nineteenth century. The histories of incarceration and other forms of crime control covered in this collection emerged in the wake of convict leasing and bore its imprint. Although northern prisons contracted prison labor to private industries, prisoners remained housed in state penitentiaries. Southern states, however, leased their prisoners to private companies, which took over the management of the prisoners in exchange for their work. This system resolved many white southerners' discomfort with centralized, taxpayer-funded state penitentiaries.

Convict leasing also helped to foster the criminalization of the black population in the South after the Civil War. Over 90 percent of convicts in most places were African American, leading many historians to view convict leasing as a functional replacement for slavery. In other words, it ensnared emancipated African Americans back into conditions that mirrored enslavement, forcing them to labor on private plantations or industries under brutal conditions for no pay.[16] Crime control cannot be understood separately from this racial imperative. Some historians have argued that crime rates were increasing amid the social turmoil and economic upheaval after the Civil War and as towns and cities developed in the late nineteenth century.[17] Yet, as others have pointed out, the desire to control a newly freed slave population contributed to or even caused those rising crime rates. During the 1870s and 1880s, courts and legislatures turned misdemeanors associated with African Americans, such as petty larceny, into felonies in order to increase sentences. Or laws were applied so arbitrarily that African Americans faced long sentences for petty crimes while white crimes went overlooked. The profits to be made from convict leasing provided further incentive for states, effectively, to create criminals.[18] The postwar criminalization of African Americans had lasting effects. In the late nineteenth century, criminal justice legislation coincided with Jim Crow when southern states stripped convicts of their right to vote, even after release, in the same constitutions that established other racialized voting restrictions.[19] And whites continued to believe that black crime constituted a pervasive threat even when, in the twentieth century, black crime rates decreased.[20]

To view convict leasing as simply an extension of slavery may be too easy, however. Convict leasing was decidedly a product of the postbellum era and met the economic and social needs of its time. In particular, it provided cheap labor for the newly industrializing South as convicts across the region were sent to work building railroads or, by the 1880s and 1890s, in mines.[21] Convict leasing had ended across the South by the early twentieth century due to protests from labor advocates, humanitarian reformers, and those who thought the state, not private industry, should benefit from convict labor. It was initially replaced in some states by contract labor, whereby the state housed and managed prisoners while allowing private contractors to operate factories on prison grounds. But by the 1910s and 1920s most southern states had turned to using convict labor for state projects, whether on state penal farms or on county chain gangs, building roads and bridges to improve state infrastructure. As states centralized prison management, the prison population swelled, creating a new host of problems associated with overcrowding: disease, abuses, and prisoner rioting and resistance.

The centralization of criminal punishment in this period shifted legal and political authority that had belonged to private businesses or local jurisdictions to state entities and bureaucracies. This expansion of state power was part of a larger process of southern modernization, that is, increased urbanization and industrialization, as well as progressive-minded reforms of state infrastructure, education, and public health. Southern cities, for instance, saw the rise of professional police departments, with uniformed "beat" officers and detective units. Modernization, however, did not lead to more enlightened policies that would challenge entrenched white supremacist beliefs and traditions. Rather, Jim Crow was a modern invention established to resolve the racial uncertainties that modern life had wrought. The rise of towns and cities had brought blacks and whites in close proximity, away from the racial customs and habits that dictated rural life. Industrialization and consumerism also threatened to place the races on an equal footing. As many scholars have pointed out, Jim Crow was a fragile and often inconstant institution that required continual reinforcement.[22] Criminal justice served to bolster the racial hierarchy in the face of these changes associated with modernity.

The essays in this volume address these relationships between the modernizing state, white supremacy, and crime control. The development of a modern criminal justice system in the South, this collection shows, was part and parcel of Jim Crow. At the same time, these essays, as a whole, provide a more nuanced portrait of the dynamic between state power and white supremacy in the South beyond a story of top-down social control. They reveal stories of state institutions grappling with their expanding authority, stories of political leaders and reformers anxious to render that power modern and efficient, and stories of African Americans appealing to the regulatory state in order to push back against racial injustice and demand state protections.

This collection is organized into two parts largely conforming to the broader categories of "crime" and "punishment." The first part addresses issues of crime and law enforcement in the South, while the second part concerns legal forms of punishment, including incarceration and postincarceration restrictions, as well as capital punishment. The first three essays explore issues surrounding policing and police departments that arose as part of bureaucratic expansion in New South cities. With the decline of extralegal crime control in the twentieth century, the police, as agents of state power, played an increasingly important role in maintaining social control and the racial order. The role of the police in enforcing Jim Crow laws, as well as law enforcement's neglect to investigate crimes in black communities, is well understood. These three essays, however, present a more complicated picture of the relationship between police departments and African American communities, a relationship that was based in fear, distrust, and brutality but also one that entailed adaptation and resistance.

In "The Trials of George Doyle: Race and Policing in Jim Crow New Orleans," K. Stephen Prince explores the gradual exclusion of African Americans from the New Orleans police force. Although African Americans in New Orleans had been stripped of their civil rights through disfranchisement and segregation, the police force remained integrated until the 1910s, a holdover from Reconstruction. Prince draws particular attention to the experience of George Doyle, a black off-duty police officer who shot a white man in a saloon in 1905. Doyle's story demonstrates the problems black police officers posed for white New Orleanians as they instituted a Jim Crow regime. It also shows how elemental all-white police departments were to that regime; in denying African Americans the ability to police their own communities, white New Orleans stripped from them a fundamental right.

The next two chapters show the consequences of all-white police departments for African American citizens. Brandon T. Jett, in "'Many People "Colored" Have Come to the Homicide Office': Police Investigations of African American Homicides in Memphis, 1920–1945," uses black-on-black homicide reports from the Memphis Police Department in the Jim Crow era to reveal the complex interactions between the police and black Memphians. Rather than neglecting black-on-black crime, the police began to investigate these crimes extensively, especially in light of the white public's outcries about crime rates. Jett demonstrates that this was not a simple matter of white social control. African Americans worked actively to aid the police in these efforts, collecting evidence, acting as witnesses, and providing information to track down suspects. They did so not because they trusted the police to protect their neighborhoods but precisely because they did not. Their involvement, Jett argues, allowed them to grasp some leverage in a system under which they otherwise had very little power.

Like Jett, Silvan Niedermeier explores black responses to police authority in "Forced Confessions: Police Torture and the African American Struggle for Civil Rights in the 1930s and 1940s South." He studies two high-profile cases in which police officers used torture to extract confessions from black criminal suspects. In these cases, African Americans, aided by prominent white allies and the National Association for the Advancement of Colored People, appealed to the courts to protest acts of torture, contest the alleged confessions, and challenge legal discrimination. Niedermeier places these protests within the context of the "long civil rights movement." In doing so, he illuminates the tensions between the demands of white supremacy and the demands of a "color-blind" law characteristic of the modern bureaucratic state.

This part ends with Tammy Ingram's study of white criminal activity in the South in the late Jim Crow era and its relationship to state power and white supremacy. Her essay, "The South's Sin City: White Crime and the Limits of Law and Order in Phenix City, Alabama," examines the little-known phenomenon of organized crime in the South, focusing on Phenix City, Alabama, which became notorious for its high concentration of gambling dens, illegal bars, and prostitution rings. Crime and vice flourished in Phenix City because corrupt public officials not only tolerated mobsters but also cooperated with them and ensured their immunity from arrest and prosecution, a fact Ingram attributes to white desires for local sovereignty and racial order. "The decriminalization of whites," she argues, "was as important a function of [Jim Crow] governments as the criminalization of African Americans."

The second part of the collection brings us off the streets and out of police departments to focus on postconviction punishments. This part opens with Pippa Holloway's essay, "Testimonial Incapacity and Criminal Defendants in the South," which highlights the tensions between the demands of modern law and white supremacy by studying the rights of convicted criminals in court. Holloway shows how many southern states, for racial and partisan ends, used criminal convictions to strip convicts of their right to testify on their own behalf in court. While states in the rest of the country had revoked such limitations on courtroom testimony by the late nineteenth century, southern states maintained them. They served as an extension of Jim Crow laws, Holloway argues, used to deny African Americans full citizenship, much as felon disfranchisement laws did.

The next two chapters address southern penitentiaries, covering the lived experiences of convicts in southern prisons and the dynamics of prison reform in the South, respectively. Talitha L. LeFlouria, in "Sewing and Spinning for the State: Incarcerated Black Female Garment Workers in the Jim Crow South," details the experiences of African American women prisoners in contract labor systems in Tennessee and Alabama. They were put to work making garments for the apparel industry, an industry from which they were excluded outside prison walls. Her essay demonstrates that the state could tolerate the crossing of racial boundaries as long as such transgressions were managed within penal institutions and served the economic demands of those institutions. LeFlouria also shows that black female convicts' labor was essential to the economic prosperity of the Jim Crow penal system and that it contributed to the economic modernization of the New South.

Amy Louise Wood, in "Cole Blease's Pardoning Pen: State Power and Penal Reform in South Carolina," examines prison reform efforts that arose out of the expansion of the regulatory state in the early twentieth century. She focuses on Cole Blease's governorship of South Carolina from 1911 to 1915 to reveal how, due to southern class and racial politics, this reform played out in distinct ways in the South. Although Blease was an infamous race-baiter, he also advocated for modern prison reform and pardoned or paroled more convicted criminals, many of them African American, than any previous governor. His use of executive clemency, however, had much more to do with imposing an authoritarian and premodern form of power onto state bureaucracy than it did with progressive ideals about the promise of the modern state. Blease's approach to prison reform illuminates the tensions that existed within southern progressivism more broadly.

Finally, the last two essays in this part examine southern states' centralization of legal executions in the early twentieth century, when electrocution, conducted at state penitentiaries, replaced local hangings, overseen by county sheriffs. Vivien Miller, in "Hanging, the Electric Chair, and Death Penalty Reform in the Early Twentieth-Century South" examines the moment when southern states adopted the electric chair by studying Florida's fraught and uneven transition in the 1920s. Compared to the amateurish and messy practice of hanging, the electric chair offered efficiency, professionalism, and privacy, leading state officials to celebrate it as a form of "penal modernism." This modernism, however, shifted authority of criminal justice from local communities to a centralized state bureaucracy. Miller highlights the effects of this shift on long-standing execution rituals, which came to be imbued with new class, gender, and racial constrictions that were, in Miller's words, "emblematic of the modernizing industrial state."

Seth Kotch, in "The Making of the Modern Death Penalty in Jim Crow North Carolina," focuses on this same transition from local public hangings to state-controlled electrocutions in North Carolina. Kotch, however, focuses on the impact of this shift on African American communities. Although the death penalty had long served as an instrument of racial control, the ritual of a local hanging nevertheless had allowed the condemned and black witnesses, particularly black women, a public space to express religious convictions and honor the condemned's suffering. Once the state seized control of this ritual, African Americans were largely excluded as witnesses. In this way, Kotch argues, the modern death penalty came to more starkly represent the racial subjugation of Jim Crow; indeed, it came to have more in common with lynchings than legal public hangings had.

These essays as a whole focus on the rigid black/white hierarchy that defined the South in the Jim Crow era. White southerners' need to enforce that hierarchy shaped other sentiments that had a bearing on criminal justice, such as a fierce commitment to federalism and localism, a skepticism toward any penal or police reforms that might equalize the races, and a prioritization of the lives and safety of white citizens over those of black citizens. These sentiments rendered southern practices of policing, incarceration, and capital punishment from the 1890s through the 1950s distinct, even as forms and methods of enforcement varied across the region, and even as many nonsoutherners might have shared many of these sentiments.

As noted earlier, this legacy still persists in the South. Yet many of the problems endemic to our criminal justice system, enumerated at the start of this introduction, are also national ones. Mass incarceration is a nationwide phenomenon; thirty-one states each, separately, imprison more people per capita than El Salvador, the nation with the second highest incarceration rate after the United States. Thirty-four states in every region of the country restrict the voting rights of released felons. And police brutality is not limited to the South.[23] Of the ten states with the highest numbers of fatal police shootings from 2016 to 2018, the majority are outside the South, and high-profile cases have occurred in Chicago, Illinois; Cleveland, Ohio; Sacramento, California; and Ferguson, Missouri.[24] One could argue that as African American migration to northern cities increased in the mid-twentieth century and as southern conservative politics migrated north in the late twentieth century, so too did southern approaches to criminal justice, albeit in often altered guises. For that reason, our contemporary system evokes a southern past.

NOTES

1. US Department of Justice, Bureau of Justice Statistics, www.bjs.gov/index.cfm ?ty=tp&tid=11 (accessed August 16, 2017); the Sentencing Project, "Criminal Justice Facts," http://www.sentencingproject.org/criminal-justice-facts/ (accessed August 16, 2017); US Department of Justice, Gary G. Grindler, Acting Deputy Attorney General, Memorandum for All Federal Prosecutors, Fair Sentencing Act of 2010, August 5, 2010, www.justice.gov/sites/default/files/oip/legacy/2014/07/23/fair-sentencing-act

-memo.pdf (accessed August 16, 2017); *New York Times*, September 16, 2016, www
.nytimes.com/2016/09/17/us/politics/senate-dysfunction-blocks-bipartisan-criminal
-justice-overhaul.html?_r=0 (accessed August 16, 2017).

2. The Sentencing Project, "Felony Disenfranchisement: A Primer," May 10, 2016,
http://www.sentencingproject.org/publications/felony-disenfranchisement-a-primer/
(accessed June 22, 2018); the Sentencing Project, "Felony Disenfranchisement Laws
in the United States," April 28, 2014, http://www.sentencingproject.org/publications/
felony-disenfranchisement-laws-in-the-united-states/ (accessed June 22, 2018).

3. President's Task Force on 21st Century Policing, *Final Report of the President's
Task Force on 21st Century Policing* (Washington, DC: Office of Community Oriented
Policing Service, 2015); US Department of Justice, Press Release, "Department of Justice Awards over $20 Million to Law Enforcement Body-Worn Camera Programs,"
September 26, 2016, www.justice.gov/opa/pr/department-justice-awards-over
-20-million-law-enforcement-body-worn-camera-programs (accessed August 16,
2017); *Washington Post*, December 8, 2015, www.washingtonpost.com/national/
fbi-to-sharply-expand-system-for-tracking-fatal-police-shootings/2015/12/08/
a60fbc16–9dd4–11e5-bce4–708fe33e3288_story.html?utm_term=.02e4fea59e89
(accessed August 16, 2017); *New York Times*, June 16, 2017, www.nytimes.com/
interactive/2017/05/17/us/what-happened-to-officers-in-police-involved-deaths-of
-blacks.html?smid=pl-share (accessed August 16, 2017).

4. Death Penalty Information Center, "Facts about the Death Penalty," deathpen-
altyinfo.org/documents/FactSheet.pdf (accessed August 16, 2017); *Washington Post*,
May 24, 2014, www.washingtonpost.com/news/the-fix/wp/2014/05/14/how-many
-states-have-abolished-the-death-penalty-since-2000/?utm_term=.062b4ff29e73
(accessed August 16, 2017); Death Penalty Information Center, "Death Penalty on
Hold in Most of the Country," deathpenaltyinfo.org/node/5829 (accessed August
16, 2017); *Atlantic Monthly*, February 18, 2014, www.theatlantic.com/international/
archive/2014/02/can-europe-end-the-death-penalty-in-america/283790/ (accessed
August 16, 2017). See also Austin Sarat, *Gruesome Spectacles: Botched Executions and America's Death Penalty* (Stanford, CA: Stanford University Press, 2014;
republished with a new preface, 2016).

5. Michelle Alexander, *The New Jim Crow: Mass Incarceration in the Age of Color
Blindness* (New York: New Press, 2012); see also, as examples, Rev. Jesse L. Jackson
et al., *Legal Lynching: The Death Penalty and America's Future* (New York: Anchor
Books, 2003); David G. Embrick, "Two Nations, Revisited: The Lynching of Black
and Brown Bodies, Police Brutality, and Racial Control in 'Post-racial' Amerikkka,"
Critical Sociology 41, no. 6 (2015): 835–43; Keisha N. Blain, "Ida B. Wells, Police
Violence, and the Legacy of Lynching," *Black Perspectives*, July 8, 2016, www.aaihs
.org/ida-b-wells-police-violence-and-the-legacy-of-lynching/ (accessed August 7, 2017).

6. Robert Perkinson makes this point in *Texas Tough: The Rise of America's
Prison Empire* (New York: Henry Holt and Company, 2010), 4–8. In particular, he
argues that the Texas penal system served as a model for post–World War II mass
incarceration. Features of the Texas system can be found in other southern states.

7. The ten states with the highest per capita incarceration rates as of June 2018 are, in order, Oklahoma, Louisiana, Mississippi, Georgia, Alabama, Arkansas, Texas, Arizona, Kentucky, and Missouri. See Prison Policy Initiative, "States of Incarceration: The Global Context, 2018," June 2018, https://www.prisonpolicy.org/global/2018 .html (accessed June 22, 2018).

8. The four states that disfranchise convicted felons for life, even after the full completion of their sentences, are Florida, Iowa, Kentucky, and Virginia. See the Sentencing Project, "Felony Disenfranchisement Laws."

9. Death Penalty Information Center, "Number of Executions by State and Region since 1976," May 17, 2018, https://deathpenaltyinfo.org/number-executions-state -and-region-1976 (accessed June 22, 2018).

10. There has been a proliferation of studies of penitentiaries and policing in the United States in recent years, but much of this scholarship focuses on the post–World War II era and the rise of mass incarceration. It also tends to be national in scope and avoids issues of regionalism. See Deborah McDowell et al., eds., *The Punitive Turn: New Approaches to Race and Incarceration* (Charlottesville: University of Virginia Press, 2013); Kelly Lytle Hernández et al., eds., "Historians and the Carceral State," special issue, *Journal of American History* 102, no. 1 (2015); Heather Ann Thompson and Donna Murch, eds., "Urban American and the Carceral State," special section, *Journal of Urban History* 41, no. 5 (2015); Leon Fink, ed., "Labor in the Correctional State," special issue, *Labor: Studies in Working-Class History* 8, no. 3 (2011); Kali N. Gross and Cheryl Hicks, eds., "Gendering the Carceral State: African American Women, History, and the Criminal Justice System," special issue, *Journal of African American History* 100, no. 3 (2015).

11. Matthew D. Lassiter and Joseph Crespino, eds., *The Myth of Southern Exceptionalism* (New York: Oxford University Press, 2009).

12. Michael J. Pfeifer, ed., *Lynching beyond Dixie: American Mob Violence outside the South* (Urbana: University of Illinois Press, 2013); Heather Ann Thompson, "Blinded by a 'Barbaric' South: Prison Horrors, Inmate Abuse, and the Ironic History of American Penal Reform," in Lassiter and Crespino, *The Myth*, 74–98.

13. Natalie J. Ring, *The Problem South: Region, Empire, and the New Liberal State, 1880–1930* (Athens: University of Georgia Press, 2012).

14. Edward L. Ayers, *Vengeance and Justice: Crime and Punishment in the Nineteenth-Century American South* (New York: Oxford University Press, 1984), 34–72; Michael S. Hindus, *Prison and Plantation: Crime, Justice, and Authority in Massachusetts and South Carolina, 1767–1878* (Chapel Hill: University of North Carolina Press, 1980).

15. Michael J. Pfeifer, *Rough Justice: Lynching and American Society, 1874–1847* (Urbana: University of Illinois Press, 2006); Amy Louise Wood, *Lynching and Spectacle: Witnessing Racial Violence in America, 1890–1940* (Chapel Hill: University of North Carolina Press, 2009), 19–44.

16. David M. Oshinsky, *"Worse Than Slavery": Parchman Farm and the Ordeal of Jim Crow Justice* (New York: Free Press Paperbacks, 1997); Douglas A. Blackmon,

Slavery by Another Name: The Re-enslavement of Black Americans from the Civil War to World War II (New York: Anchor Books, 2009).

17. Oshinsky, *Worse Than Slavery*, 32–34; Ayers, *Vengeance and Justice*, 165–75; Donald R. Walker, *Penology for Profit: A History of the Texas Prison System, 1867–1912* (College Station: Texas A&M University Press, 1988), 18–19.

18. Mary Ellen Curtin, *Black Prisoners and Their World, Alabama, 1865–1900* (Charlottesville: University of Virginia Press, 2000), 42–55; Alex Lichtenstein, *Twice the Work of Free Labor: The Political Economy of Convict Labor in the New South* (New York: Verso Books, 1996), 26–29.

19. Pippa Holloway, *Living with Infamy: Felon Disfranchisement and American Citizenship* (New York: Oxford University Press, 2013).

20. Jeffrey S. Adler, "Less Crime, More Punishment: Violence, Race, and Criminal Justice in Early Twentieth-Century America," *Journal of American History* 102, no. 1 (2015): 34–46.

21. Ayers, *Vengeance and Justice*, 191–92; Lichtenstein, *Twice the Work*; Matthew Mancini, *One Dies, Get Another: Convict Leasing in the American South, 1866–1928* (Columbia: University of South Carolina Press, 1996); Talitha L. LeFlouria, *Chained in Silence: Black Women and Convict Labor in the New South* (Chapel Hill: University of North Carolina Press, 2015).

22. C. Vann Woodward, *The Strange Career of Jim Crow*, rev. ed. (New York: Oxford University Press, 1974); Edward L. Ayers, *The Promise of the New South: Life after Reconstruction* (New York: Oxford University Press, 1992), 132–59; Grace Elizabeth Hale, *Making Whiteness: The Culture of Segregation in the South, 1890–1940* (New York: Vintage Books, 1999); Stephanie Cole and Natalie J. Ring, eds., *The Folly of Jim Crow: Rethinking the Segregated South* (College Station: Texas A&M University Press, 2012).

23. Prison Policy Initiative, "States of Incarceration; the Sentencing Project," "Felony Disenfranchisement."

24. The *Washington Post* has tracked fatal police shootings and compiled them in an online database since 2015. See https://www.washingtonpost.com/graphics/national/police-shootings-2017/?tid=a_mcntx (accessed June 22, 2018).

PART I
CRIME

CHAPTER 1

The Trials of George Doyle

Race and Policing in Jim Crow New Orleans

K. Stephen Prince

In May 1906 a New Orleans Police Department patrolman named George Doyle was put on trial for murder. The charge grew out of Doyle's involvement in the shooting death of a bartender named John Allman. At around 4:00 p.m. on September 17, 1905, Doyle tried to arrest Allman for violating the city's ban on Sunday liquor sales. Allman resisted arrest, pulling a gun. Seconds later, Allman was dead, and Doyle's career with the NOPD was in serious jeopardy. The incident, which involved a shooting across the color line, stimulated enormous public interest in the city. As historian Jeffrey S. Adler has noted, such racially charged police shootings were far from rare in early twentieth-century New Orleans.[1] But one important factor makes this particular case noteworthy: John Allman, the bartender, was a white man; George Doyle, the police officer, was black.

George Doyle's presence on the police force as late as 1906 is, in and of itself, a significant fact. By the turn of the century, Jim Crow had come to the Crescent City. Racial segregation was the norm in most of the city's public spaces and in its famed streetcars. In 1898 the state of Louisiana approved a new constitution that effectively disfranchised the vast majority of the state's African American population. Violence was also extraordinarily common. A major riot in July 1900 both reflected and exacerbated racial tensions in the city. Yet, in spite of the prevailing trends across New Orleans and across the South, a handful of African American police officers remained on active duty in the New Orleans Police Department into the first decade of the century.

The literature has had relatively little to say about black police officers in the Jim Crow South. Black officers like George Doyle, it would seem, have been hiding in plain sight. Where attention has been paid at all, the debate has revolved around two major questions: How many black officers were there, and how long did they serve? In his study of policing in nineteenth-century New Orleans, Dennis Rousey reveals that by the end of the century, African Americans held only 5.1 percent of police positions in a city that was 27.1 percent black.[2] In his influential *Black Police in America*, W. Marvin Dulaney notes that black officers remained active in New Orleans longer than in most southern cities. By Dulaney's accounting, the last two Jim Crow era black officers died in service in 1909.[3] In his study of post–World War II policing in New Orleans, Leonard N. Moore avoids the question entirely, simply noting that two African American officers appointed in 1950 "became the first black police officers in New Orleans since the turn of the century."[4] Most recently, in a master's thesis produced at the University of New Orleans, Vanessa Flores-Robert found evidence of African American officers on the police force as late as 1913.[5]

Questions of "how many" and "how long" have much scholarly value, but there is more to be said. The trials of George Doyle—his murder trial, which produced an acquittal, and the subsequent Police Board trial, which resulted in Doyle's removal from the force—present a perfect opportunity to reflect on the significance of African American police officers in the Jim Crow South. By 1906 the idea of a black police officer was difficult for most white New Orleanians to accept. The continued presence of these officers posed major political and intellectual problems for New Orleans's nascent white supremacist regime. The city's civil service laws, however, made it illegal to unilaterally remove African American officers. This tension played itself out in a remarkably public manner during Doyle's trials.

Since C. Vann Woodward, historians have recognized that the growth of Jim Crow was uneven, unsteady, and contested.[6] In an attempt to advance and complicate the "Woodward thesis," the contributors to *The Folly of Jim Crow*, a 2012 edited collection, urged scholars to engage with the "exceptions, contradictions, and unintended consequences" that attended the growth of the Jim Crow system. Such moments remind us that the "ideology of segregation" and the "day-to-day practice" of white supremacy were never perfectly aligned.[7] The former was closed, absolute, and all-encompassing; the latter was messy, unpredictable, and constantly negotiated.[8] The surprising presence of black police officers in early twentieth-century New Orleans would certainly qualify as such an "exception." According to the logic of Jim Crow, George Doyle should have been stripped of his position on the police force long before 1906. But in spite of these expectations, the NOPD remained integrated into the twentieth century. These events remind us that Jim Crow encroached upon southern life gradually, making its presence felt in different institutions at different times. In the New Orleans Police Department, at least, segregation was unexpectedly slow in taking root.

Finally, a word on New Orleans exceptionalism. Though every city is distinctive, it is all too easy to embrace the myth of a wholly exceptional New Orleans. This sort of thinking has a long history; as literary scholar Jennie Lightweis-Goff notes, the city has "unsettled discourses of national unity" since the nineteenth century.[9] Such a perspective comes, however, at great intellectual cost. In focusing solely on the city's unique and distinctive aspects, we risk marginalizing it. In the process, we blind ourselves to what the history of New Orleans has to teach us about the South and about the nation at large. In this case, New Orleans was more representative than unique. Black officers retained their positions longer in New Orleans than in most southern cities, but New Orleans was not alone in confronting the problem of black police in the Jim Crow era. According to Dulaney, white elites in Jacksonville, Florida, and Charleston, South Carolina, were unable to rid their police forces of black officers until 1889 and 1896, respectively. African American police served in Houston, Texas, and Knoxville, Tennessee, until at least 1910.[10]

For this reason, the trials of George Doyle must be understood as a part of a much larger story: the conscious (if protracted) whitening of southern police departments in the post-Reconstruction decades. Though this process is seldom discussed in connection with the birth of Jim Crow, its significance was readily apparent to turn-of-the-century white southerners. Indeed, a white police force was as indispensable to white supremacy as a white ballot or a white jury box. What is distinctive about George Doyle's case is not the mere fact of his dismissal from police duty but the spectacular manner in which it played itself out. As they grappled with Doyle's presence on (and later his removal from) the police force, commentators embarked on a widespread discussion of the vexed relationship between race and policing in the early twentieth-century South. George Doyle's culpability in the Allman killing remains open for debate. What is clear is that his dismissal from the New Orleans Police Department had as much to do with the work of white supremacy as it did with the fate of John Allman.

George Doyle was born in the late 1860s. The NOPD's rosters and the 1900 New Orleans city directory both place Doyle on St. Philip Street, in the heart of the Tremé neighborhood.[11] This was a historically French section of the city, suggesting that Doyle had ties to the city's Creoles of Color. Doyle joined the NOPD in 1893 as a supernumerary patrolman and was quickly promoted to patrolman. During his twelve years on the force, Doyle served in the First, Second, Fourth, Fifth, and Sixth Precincts, encompassing most of the central portion of New Orleans.[12] Doyle seems to have been a competent and well-respected officer. On at least one occasion, his actions earned praise in the city's white newspapers.[13] In 1893 Doyle was seriously injured when he stopped an ax-wielding assailant from killing another officer. It was this act that earned him his promotion to patrolman.[14] In 1897 he earned an official commendation from the city's Police Board for the arrest of an armed burglar.[15]

On at least two occasions, however, Doyle ran into disciplinary trouble. These incidents are instructive, given the nature of the 1906 murder case against Doyle. In 1894 Doyle pleaded guilty to an assault charge after striking a black suspect on the head with a club during an arrest.[16] The charges stemmed from Doyle's arrest of a man named Jim Cummings on the evening of June 10, 1894. During the court case, several white witnesses reported that Cummings refused to accompany Doyle to the police station and began to struggle with the officer. This "scuffle" lasted several minutes. Eventually, "Officer Doyle grabbed him and held him and threw him down and fell on top of him and clubbed him." One witness testified that Doyle struck Cummings "ten or twelve times" while he was on the ground. Doyle pleaded guilty to a charge of assault and battery and was ordered to pay a small fine.[17] Significantly, the assault charge does not seem to have prompted any disciplinary action against Doyle on the part of the NOPD.

In early August 1900 George Doyle was once again in court, this time facing a false imprisonment charge. In the immediate aftermath of the 1900 riot, when racial tensions ran extraordinarily high in New Orleans, Doyle arrested a white grocer named Leonce Duplantier for insulting and abusing a police officer. Doyle charged that Duplantier had made a derisive comment when the officer passed on patrol. Duplantier, however, insisted that he had simply said good night. After his own case was dismissed, Leonce Duplantier swore an affidavit against Doyle for false imprisonment. This case was continued several times and never came to trial.[18] Significantly, the NOPD responded much more forcefully to the false arrest accusation than it had to the earlier assault charge. In the wake of the Duplantier incident, Doyle was fined ten days' pay and relegated to levee patrol.[19] The obvious, if unspoken, difference between the two events was race. Jim Cummings, the 1894 assault victim, was black. Leonce Duplantier, the grocer who charged false arrest, was white. Doyle was able to plead guilty to an assault on a black man without disciplinary repercussions. His arrest of a white man, however, had more serious consequences. Together, these incidents hint at the complex interplay of racial tension and legal authority that structured the lives and work of New Orleans's black police officers.

By 1905 Doyle's reputation in the department seems to have recovered from the Duplantier controversy. In 1904 or 1905 Inspector Edward Whitaker appointed Doyle a special officer. Though not technically a promotion

(Doyle retained the rank of patrolman), the appointment was widely recognized as an honor and accomplishment.[20] The exact nature of Doyle's task as special officer is difficult to discern. After receiving this commission, Doyle began to work as a plainclothes officer, tasked with policing violations of the city's gambling and alcohol statutes, especially the so-called Sunday Law, which outlawed the sale of alcoholic beverages on that day. He also may have been charged with locating out-of-town fugitives hiding in New Orleans.[21] Inspector Whitaker would later claim that he specifically instructed Doyle to limit his investigations to *black* fugitives and violators of the Sunday Law.[22] If this was the case, however, Doyle seems to have misunderstood his charge.

Though commentators would spend a great deal of time debating exactly what happened on Sunday, September 17, 1905, it is easy enough to recreate the general sequence of events.[23] Around 4:00 p.m., George Doyle was on patrol in a sparsely settled area of the city. As usual, he was dressed in civilian clothes rather than in his uniform. A black man named Albert Potter accompanied him on his rounds. Potter was not a police officer, but he had a history of close cooperation with both the NOPD and the Sheriff's Department of Tangipahoa Parish, located on the other side of Lake Pontchartrain. Loud noises emanating from a barroom at the corner of Philip and Liberty Streets drew their attention. The pair entered the barroom through an open door. Doyle reported that he saw "several negro men and one or two white men" scattered around the room. Doyle walked up to the bar and asked John Allman, the white bartender, for two beers. Allman served them, in violation of the Sunday Law. After paying for the drinks, Doyle pulled his police badge from his pocket and informed Allman that he was under arrest. Allman reached into a drawer under the bar, pulled out a pistol, and muttered, "I ain't going to jail a damn bit."[24] Doyle and Potter drew their own weapons. Doyle quickly retreated toward the door and left the bar, but Potter was unable to make it to the exit. Believing that he was acting in self-defense, Potter fired several shots, mortally wounding Allman. From the street, Doyle heard "three or four" shots.[25] Potter soon emerged from the barroom and headed to the Twelfth Precinct to turn himself in. Doyle stayed at Philip and Liberty until the police arrived, at which point he was taken into custody.

Two witnesses, Bertha and Maud Stark, offered a much different version of events. The Starks—mother and daughter—owned and operated the barroom at Philip and Liberty Streets. When Doyle and Potter entered the establishment, Maud Stark was sitting on a pool table near the bar. Bertha Stark, Maud's mother, was asleep in a back room. Maud Stark's version of events conflicted with Potter's and Doyle's stories in several key respects. She insisted, first of all, that John Allman had refused to serve the beer that Doyle ordered. This would have put him in compliance with the Sunday Law, meaning that there would have been no legal basis for the attempted arrest. Second, Maud Stark insisted that Allman had done nothing to prompt the shooting. In her first interviews with police, Stark denied that Allman had even had a weapon. Allman "came from behind the bar with his old black pipe in his hand. That was a pipe," Stark insisted, "not a pistol."[26] When officers found Allman's pistol—which Stark herself had picked up and placed in the sink—she changed her tune, now admitting that Allman had a weapon in his hand but insisting that he did not threaten Doyle or Potter with it. Third, and arguably most significant, Maud Stark stated that it was George Doyle, not Albert Potter, who fired the first shot at John Allman. On this point, Potter's and Doyle's testimonies were in perfect accord—both said that Doyle had left the barroom and that Potter had been the only one to fire. The physical evidence also bore out the Doyle/Potter version of affairs. When the police seized Doyle's service revolver, it was fully loaded and clear of powder residue, indicating that it had not been fired recently. The only bullets they found on the scene were .38 caliber, matching Potter's gun but not Doyle's, which was .41 caliber.[27] In spite of all this, Stark was emphatic, repeatedly stating that "Doyle fired the first shot when he had absolutely no occasion to do so."[28] For the most part, Bertha Stark's statements echoed her daughter's, though the elder Stark also claimed that George Doyle had coldheartedly prevented her from wiping the blood from the dying Allman's face.[29]

The Starks were far from perfect witnesses. Maud Stark's initial insistence that Allman did not have a gun raised serious questions about her credibility. Bertha Stark's testimony was often confused, rambling, and evasive. Even so, they formed the heart of the prosecution's case. Largely on the basis of the Starks' testimony, Potter and Doyle were charged with murder. Though the prosecution could not prove that Doyle had fired a shot, he was considered an "accessory before and after the killing," justifying the murder charge.[30] The Starks testified at the preliminary hearing, where a judge denied bail. In mid-October 1905 the case went before the grand jury. Here too the Starks offered their version of the events at Philip and Liberty. Their story proved compelling enough for the grand jury to indict both Potter and Doyle.[31] The criminal trial—State of Louisiana v. Albert Potter and George Doyle—would take place in May 1906. In the meantime, the New Orleans Police Department suspended Doyle from service. His trial before the Police Board was put on hold, pending the verdict in the criminal case.

The Allman murder immediately became a sensation. New Orleans had four daily newspapers in this era: the *Daily Picayune*, the *Times-Democrat*, the *New Orleans Item*, and the *Daily States*. All four regularly devoted front-page coverage to the case. The papers uniformly sided with John Allman, in spite of the fact that he had broken the Sunday Law, resisted arrest, and drawn a gun on a police officer. Though Doyle was an officer and a public servant, the lines of race proved more enduring than respect for the authority of the police. In an editorial on the shooting, the *Daily Picayune*—probably the most temperate and evenhanded of the four dailies—seethed that "a negro policeman, one of the few on the force," had shot an innocent man to death, with "no resistance, so far as was shown, having been made by the man who was killed."[32] This reading of events was a selective, idiosyncratic one, to say the least, but it accurately captured the prevailing sentiments among white New Orleanians. The *Times-Democrat* urged the "fair-minded public" to give Allman—not Doyle and Potter—the "benefit of the doubt." The paper wrote: "If the negro policeman has a good and sufficient defense he should be given every opportunity to make it, but sight should not be lost of the rights of the slain man."[33]

Under most circumstances, refined white New Orleanians would have wanted little to do with John Allman or with Maud and Bertha Stark. Allman was an out-of-towner with no real ties to New Orleans. His line of work—tending bar in an establishment that regularly and willfully broke the color line in serving both black and white patrons—was one that white public opinion would have found distasteful in the extreme. As the white female owners and operators of such a bar, the Starks were even more problematic. The *Daily Picayune* admitted as much the month after the murder: "The barroom, owned and operated by whites, was one of those pernicious places frequented by both whites and negroes, who meet and drink together."[34] In her testimony at the preliminary hearing, Bertha Stark likewise acknowledged that her barroom served an interracial clientele.[35] For the prosecution and the city's white supremacist press, however, such considerations mattered little in the context of a black-on-white shooting. Indeed, the success of the prosecution would hinge on the jury's willingness to elevate race and gender over class and occupation. In the retelling, therefore, John Allman became an unlikely martyr for white supremacy, while the Starks were packaged as symbols of an embattled and defiant white womanhood.

The Allman killing quickly became a referendum on black policing in Jim Crow New Orleans. Though the presence of black police officers was neither a surprise nor a new development by 1905, the barroom shooting focused the city's attention on this question to an unprecedented degree. The *Times-Democrat* wondered "why it was necessary that the arrest of this white man should have fallen to the lot of negroes, when the greater part of the police force is composed of white men."[36] In an attempt to defend Allman's actions, the *Daily Picayune* appeared to condone (and even encourage) white resistance to arrest at the hands of black officers. "That he resisted arrest by the negroes was, perhaps, natural," the paper claimed. "No white man would willingly submit to arrest at the hands of a negro if he could possibly get out of it."[37] Such articles reminded readers that African American officers were a holdover from an earlier era, a remnant of Reconstruction. In the turn-of-the-century city, their authority would no longer be respected and their presence no longer tolerated.

The *Daily States*, the most unabashedly white supremacist of New Orleans's four daily papers, was particularly outspoken regarding the problem of black police officers. "There can be no doubt of the fact that the practically universal sentiment in New Orleans has crystallized into a demand that negroes shall not be permitted to serve in this city as policemen," the paper editorialized. "In a Southern city and under a Democratic administration, the employment of negro policemen is both an anachronism and a scandal." The *Daily States* rejoiced when two black police officers resigned in the aftermath of the Allman shooting. "The agitation started against negro policemen on the New Orleans force by the murder of John Allman is having a salutary effect on the black minions of the law who still are wearing the brass buttons," the paper gloated. It looked forward to "a force free of the colored gentry that was garbed in the policeman's uniform by the old regime."[38] In fact, it is not at all clear what caused these resignations, nor is it certain that they were related to the Doyle case in any way. Regardless, the *Daily States* spearheaded a campaign of propaganda and harassment designed to bring about a lily-white NOPD.

Though Albert Potter had done the shooting, the popular narrative advanced in the white press placed the blame for the violence directly on Officer George Doyle. The presence of a black police officer, the papers argued, exacerbated racial tension and made incidents like the Allman shooting unavoidable. "It will not do in New Orleans to send a negro officer to arrest a white man," the *New Orleans Item* explained the day after the shooting. "Arm a negro or a thug of any color and clothe him with police powers and tragedies will result."[39] The *Item* took particular umbrage at the fact that Doyle had been rewarded with a special officer commission. "Had he not been clothed with that authority, especially in civilian clothes," the paper reflected after the first day of the jury trial, "John Allman would [now] be alive and enjoying the happiness his youth would have allowed him, instead of filling an untimely grave at the hands of unscrupulous negro special officers."[40] From the perspective of New Orleans's white dailies, George Doyle's attempt to arrest a white man was, in and of itself, an act of racial aggression and violence. This viewpoint transformed John Allman's resistance to arrest into a righteous defense of personal and racial integrity. As usual, the *Daily States* was outspoken on these matters. "A tragedy is invited when a negro attempts to arrest a white man," the *States* wrote. "It makes no difference how discreet and law-abiding a negro may be, his attempt to arrest a white man is likely at any time to lead to violent infractions of the law."[41]

As if to emphasize the deeply unnatural and problematic character of black police officers, newspaper coverage occasionally denied Doyle the courtesy of his title. Though headlines invariably referred to Potter and Doyle as "negroes," journalists sometimes relegated reference to Doyle's position as a police officer to the body of the article. A reader unfamiliar with the case might have to read several paragraphs into such articles before learning that George Doyle was a member of the New Orleans Police Department.[42] Some reports even managed to ignore this essential fact completely. In their coverage of the first day of the jury trial, neither the *Daily Picayune* nor the *Times-Democrat* bothered to mention that Doyle was an officer of the law. Though the articles necessarily described Doyle's attempt to arrest Allman (thereby implicitly referencing his purpose in the barroom), they never explicitly mentioned his connection to the New Orleans Police Department.[43] George Doyle was a police officer who entered the bar at Philip and Liberty on official police business. To fail to mention this fact was to fundamentally misrepresent the nature of the case. Such treatments, however, reflect a rising consensus among white New Orleanians that a black police officer was a logical impossibility and a contradiction in terms. Doyle could be black, or he could be a police officer. He could not be both. In neglecting to mention Doyle's association with the police department, the city's papers denied the authority of black officers and silenced their contributions to public safety.

Rhetorically stripping George Doyle of his title was one thing. Actually removing him from the force was a thornier problem for the advocates of white supremacy. Spurred on by the Young Men's Democratic Association, a reform organization that briefly challenged machine rule in New Orleans, an 1889 reorganization of the police department had introduced civil service reforms designed to foster professionalism, attack cronyism, and lessen political influence over the police force.[44] The goal of these reforms was never to protect African American police officers like George Doyle, but this was an unintended side effect. The city's police manual described the terms and circumstances under which officers could be removed from the force and guaranteed accused officers the right to a trial.[45] No matter how problematic the presence of black officers seemed by 1906, these civil service rules offered some measure of protection. Barring misbehavior, there was little that the forces of white supremacy could do about the African Americans who remained on the force. "The police force is under the civil service regulations and policemen cannot be removed summarily," the *Daily States* complained. "But a way must be found . . . to rid the establishment of this standing menace to the peace and order of the community."[46] The 1906 trial of George Doyle seemed to offer just such an opportunity.

Calls to remove black police officers overlooked another significant fact: the New Orleans Police Department was woefully undermanned and underfunded. The department's annual reports to the city government invariably opened with a plea for money and personnel.[47] In this context, George Doyle and his fellow black officers might be publicly despised, but they were essential to the daily function of the department. Perhaps the best evidence for this was George Doyle's much-criticized special officer commission. While commentators outside of the department cast African American officers as vestigial hangers-on, the leadership of the NOPD had no choice but to utilize all of the resources at their disposal. Inspector Edward Whitaker would do all that he could to distance himself from George Doyle in the wake of the Allman shooting, but his earlier decision to commission Doyle as a special officer should not be overlooked.[48] Black officers like Doyle might be politically problematic, but they were still police officers. The department employed them accordingly.

Doyle and Potter's jury trial, which began in May 1906, generated much excitement. "The trial, in its way, is one of the most remarkable in the history of the State," one newspaper reported.[49] The courtroom was filled to a "suffocating pitch," with some audience members forced to share seats in order to witness the spectacle.[50] Spectators packed lunches to eat in their seats during the court recesses rather than risk losing a prime spot. A plucky elevator operator conspired to sell admission to the courtroom but had his plans foiled. Those who were denied seats crowded the halls outside, waiting for an "opportunity to sneak or force their way into the courtroom."[51] As the carnival atmosphere suggests, this was no ordinary murder trial.

Significantly, many (perhaps most) of the people who packed the courtroom were African Americans. Black responses to the Doyle trial are extraordinarily difficult to pin down, since the only extant African American newspaper published in Louisiana at the turn of the century is a black Methodist paper that largely avoided local New Orleans issues. Even so, the presence of so many black people in the courtroom is striking. Given his history—specifically the 1894 assault charge—it is not at all clear that Doyle would have enjoyed a stellar reputation among black New Orleanians. Yet spectators packed the courtroom to lend their support. The *Daily Picayune* was probably not far off when it suggested that Doyle, "having been a special officer on the police force, was considered quite an important character from the standpoint of the negro."[52] In the face of the rising Jim Crow regime, Doyle's continued presence on the force served as a reminder of a more equitable past and, perhaps, a harbinger of a brighter future.

In spite of the excitement leading up to the trial, two days of testimony before the jury offered few surprises. When Albert Potter took the stand on the trial's second day, he accepted the blame for the killing of John Allman, citing self-defense and insisting that Doyle never fired his weapon. "Doyle is perfectly innocent of having fired a single shot," Potter claimed. "I alone fired the shots which ended Allman's life."[53] The prosecution argued, however, that Doyle's presence in the barroom made him an accessory to the murder. Once again, Bertha Stark and Maud Stark (now Maud Oliveri, after her marriage) testified for the prosecution. As usual, Maud Oliveri testified that Allman had not broken the Sunday Law and that both Potter and Doyle had fired their weapons. The high drama of the courtroom proved too much for Oliveri, who fainted as she left the witness stand.[54] George Doyle's testimony, which occurred near the end of the trial, was unremarkable. Doyle corroborated Potter's version of events and strayed little from the story as he had presented it since the day of the shooting.[55]

At around 9:30 p.m. on May 18, 1906, the all-white jury returned a verdict of not guilty. The *Daily Picayune* reported that the "verdict seemed to strike most of those in the courtroom dumb," while the *New Orleans Item* claimed that "no verdict has ever invited the condemnation of an indignant people as did the verdict of the jury."[56] A large part of the popular furor stemmed from the nature of the testimony. In effect, the jurors were presented with two versions of the events at Philip and Liberty: the Starks' perspective pointed toward murder, while the Potter/Doyle narrative suggested self-defense. "There was no evidence save the testimony of the negroes themselves going to show that the barkeeper drew a gun, while, on the other hand, a white woman who lived in the place declared that the negroes began the trouble and that the barkeeper was unarmed," the *Daily States* fumed. Though the jury did not explain itself, the decision was a repudiation of Maud Oliveri and Bertha Stark, on whose patently unreliable testimony the prosecution's case had rested from the beginning. The city's irate editorialists were appalled that a jury of white men had "accepted the testimony of two negroes who were on trial for their lives" over the testimony of two white women.[57] The acquittal is surprising for any number of reasons, not least of which is the fact that the Starks—the erstwhile emblems of white southern womanhood—so thoroughly failed to sway a jury of white men.

Once they had recovered from the shock of acquittal, the city's white editorialists quickly returned to the issue at the heart of the Allman case: the continued employment of African American police officers. Searching for meaning in the verdict, the *Times-Democrat* argued that "the first lesson it teaches, is the danger of negro policemen, of negro deputy sheriffs, and, indeed, of negro officials of any kind."[58] The *New Orleans Item* worried that unless immediate action were taken, the Allman killing might not be the last of its kind, as "the arbitrary power of police appointment and of arrest without warrant still remain to invite future tragedies." To illustrate the point, the paper offered a sexually charged hypothetical: "If a negro policeman should without warrant arrest a white woman upon an obscure street and drag her away from her escort, and if the escort should resist with violence, the negro policeman could lawfully shoot him down and make off with his prey."[59] Obviously, such a state of affairs could not be tolerated. The *Daily States* was characteristically direct regarding black officers and the NOPD. "As we understand it, only three remain upon the force—Doyle and two others," the *States* wrote. Though the civil service regulations presented a challenge, the city must find a way to remove the remaining African American officers. "Their very presence in the uniform of policemen is an incentive to turbulence and lawlessness, to crime and bloodshed. A negro policeman in a Southern city is an anachronism and cannot be justified upon any reasonable hypothesis."[60]

In the end, the forces of white supremacy got what they wanted, at least as far as George Doyle was concerned. Doyle did not go to jail, but he did lose his position on the police force. A month after the acquittal, Doyle was called before the Police Board. He faced two charges relating to the Allman killing. The first, neglect of duty, was tied to his failure to arrest Albert Potter immediately after the shooting. Doyle was also charged with conduct unbecoming an officer. This charge, unbelievably, was for drinking beer while on police business—the beer in question being the one that John Allman had served him. Once again, Maud Oliveri was called to testify. She made the most of her final moments in the spotlight. When Doyle, arguing in his own defense, attempted a cross-examination, Oliveri refused to answer questions posed by "a nigger." Inspector Whitaker, presiding over the trial, informed Oliveri that she must answer Doyle's questions. "I simply will not do it," she said, collapsing into sobs on the desk. Doyle declined to press the examination any further.[61]

The trial was a mere technicality, as Doyle's dismissal was foreordained. Several weeks before the Police Board met to decide Doyle's fate, Inspector Whitaker made his intentions crystal clear. Whitaker assured a reporter that "no one in this city could accuse him of partiality towards negroes, for he had long since deemed the usefulness of the negro as a police officer had ceased." Whitaker also noted that "the deep prejudice" against Doyle "materially militated against his usefulness as a police officer" and promised that he would "not strain a point to save" a black officer "as he might do in the case of a white officer."[62] Whitaker's candor is striking, but he correctly judged the mood of the city. Given the torrent of bad publicity heaped upon the NOPD during the trial, the Police Board had little choice but to dismiss Doyle. On June 22, 1906, Whitaker and the other members of the Police Board found Doyle guilty on both counts and dismissed him from service. "Your mistake cost a man his life," Whitaker told Doyle, "and it will cost you your job."[63]

There is a footnote to this story. By 1913 the last of the Jim Crow era African American officers had left the force.[64] However, the memory of their service remained a raw wound for Louisiana white supremacists. In 1919 political opponents of future governor John M. Parker charged that several African Americans had served as police officers during the mid-1890s while Parker was a member of the New Orleans Board of Police Commissioners. Parker's supporters could not deny the charge, but they staunchly insisted that Parker had nothing to do with the appointments. The *New Orleans Item*'s coverage of this minor partisan squabble described (in unflattering terms) the careers of several black officers—including George Doyle. As might be expected, the article referred only to Doyle's most infamous moment as a police officer: "Doyle and another negro killed a white man named Allman on September 17, 1905."[65]

George Doyle, still living in New Orleans, had his own perspective on these issues. In response to the back-and-forth over Parker and the black officers, Doyle wrote a letter to the *New Orleans Item* defending himself. The *Item* summarized the contents of the letter: "Doyle writes that he had always borne a good record; that he saved several lives on different occasions, which he specifies; that he had done other meritorious pieces of police work; and that he was not at fault in the case in which he was tried."[66] Thirteen years after he was dismissed from the New Orleans Police Department, Doyle remained proud of his accomplishments. The Allman killing tarnished his record and led to his dismissal, but Doyle refused to allow a single act of violence to eclipse a dozen years of service. Doyle's response also points to something deeper. African American officers were little more than a memory by the late 1910s, but memory can possess extraordinarily political significance. There was a great deal at stake in remembering the contributions of the New Orleans Police Department's black officers. George Doyle's letter was a humble gesture but a significant one nonetheless. To refuse to contest the misrepresentations of white supremacy in the field of memory was to admit that Doyle's detractors had been right all along: African American police officers had been an aberration, an implausibility, a misplaced remnant in an age of white supremacy. For reasons both personal and political, George Doyle could not concede this point.

To study the trials of George Doyle—and, more generally, the experience of African American police officers in the Jim Crow South—is to expand our understanding of the relationship between race and policing at a transformative moment in southern history. The presence of African American officers in the New Orleans Police Department well into the first decade of the twentieth century forces us to recognize the legal, political, and social challenges associated with the institutionalization of white supremacy. With the benefit of hindsight, the rise of Jim Crow can appear foreordained and automatic. On the ground in the South, however, this was never the case. As historian Stephen Kantrowitz memorably puts it, "White supremacy was hard work."[67] Thanks to the civil service reforms put in place in 1889, creating a Jim Crow police department was no easy feat. Long after black New Orleanians lost the vote and the right to travel on the city's streetcars, black men walked the streets dressed in NOPD blue. The presence of these officers posed serious challenges for supporters of white supremacy. Through persecution, attrition, and selective disciplinary action, the Police Board would eventually achieve the lily-white force it desired. This result, however, required patience, commitment, and the sacrifice of otherwise qualified officers like George Doyle.

Doyle's story also speaks to the burgeoning historical literature on policing and the carceral state. As the editors of a recent special issue of the *Journal of American History* note, "Mass policing and incarceration began their staggering booms during the 1970s," but "the roots of the carceral state run much deeper in U.S. history."[68] The trial and dismissal of George Doyle played a role in the systematic rewhitening of the New Orleans Police Department in the decades after Reconstruction. These events, in turn, reflect a larger process by which the ideological and institutional links between blackness and criminality (and, by extension, between whiteness and police power) were reaffirmed in the early twentieth-century United States.[69] The police would become an essential disciplinary tool of white supremacy, but before this could happen, the last vestiges of an old order needed to be destroyed. The NOPD itself must be made white before it could effectively serve white supremacy. This, tragically, would be George Doyle's lasting legacy.

NOTES

1. Jeffrey S. Adler, "'The Killer behind the Badge': Race and Police Homicide in New Orleans, 1925–1945," *Law and History Review* 30, no. 2 (2012): 495–531.

2. Dennis Rousey, *Policing the Southern City: New Orleans, 1805–1889* (Baton Rouge: Louisiana State University Press, 1996), 194.

3. W. Marvin Dulaney, *Black Police in America* (Bloomington: Indiana University Press, 1996), 16–17.

4. Leonard N. Moore, *Black Rage in New Orleans: Police Brutality and African American Activism from World War II to Hurricane Katrina* (Baton Rouge: Louisiana State University Press, 2010), 30.

5. Vanessa Flores-Robert, "Black Policemen in Jim Crow New Orleans" (MA thesis, University of New Orleans, 2011).

6. C. Vann Woodward, *The Strange Career of Jim Crow* (New York: Oxford, 1955).

7. W. Fitzhugh Brundage, introduction to *The Folly of Jim Crow: Rethinking the Segregated South*, ed. Stephanie Cole and Natalie J. Ring (College Station: Texas A&M University Press, 2012), 7.

8. See also Jane Dailey, Glenda Elizabeth Gilmore, and Bryant Simon, eds., *Jumpin' Jim Crow: Southern Politics from Civil War to Civil Rights* (Princeton, NJ: Princeton University Press, 2000), esp. 3–6; Stephen Berrey, *The Jim Crow Routine: Everyday Performances of Race, Civil Rights, and Segregation in Mississippi* (Chapel Hill: University of North Carolina Press, 2015).

9. Jennie Lightweis-Goff, "'Peculiar and Characteristic': New Orleans Exceptionalism from Olmsted to the Deluge," *American Literature* 86, no. 1 (2014): 149. See also Rien Fertel, *Imagining the Creole City: The Rise of Literary Culture in Nineteenth-Century New Orleans* (Baton Rouge: Louisiana State University Press, 2014).

10. Dulaney, *Black Police in America*, 15–18.

11. *New Orleans City Directory* (New Orleans: Soards, 1900), 279; New Orleans Police Department Rosters, vol. 2 (microfilm), Louisiana Division, New Orleans Public Library.

12. New Orleans Police Department Rosters, vol. 2.

13. *New Orleans Item*, August 15, 1905, 1.

14. *Times-Democrat*, August 2, 1900, 2.

15. *Daily Picayune*, January 6, 1897, 9.

16. *New Orleans Item*, November 19, 1894, 1; *Daily Picayune*, November 20, 1894, 8.

17. Parish of Orleans Criminal District Court, Section A, Case 22238, Louisiana Division, New Orleans Public Library.

18. *Times-Democrat*, August 2, 1900, 2. The court record for this trial (*State of Louisiana v. George Doyle*, Parish of Orleans Criminal District Court, Case 30072) is missing. The entry in the Orleans Parish Criminal District Court docket book for this case contains a telling (if unintentional) commentary on the plight of black

police officers like George Doyle in turn-of-the-century New Orleans. The clerk charged with logging the trial seems to have begun to write "Officer George Doyle" before changing his mind. The word "officer" remains incomplete, with a thick line drawn through it. Criminal District Court, Parish of New Orleans, Docket Book F, Louisiana Division, New Orleans Public Library.

19. *New Orleans Item*, May 22, 1906, 1.

20. See, for example, *New Orleans Item*, May 18, 1906, 1.

21. Ibid.

22. *Daily Picayune*, May 20, 1906, 4.

23. This narrative is based on court transcripts, the New Orleans Police Department's homicide report, and contemporary newspaper coverage. See Parish of Orleans Criminal District Court, Section B, Case 34418, Louisiana Division, New Orleans Public Library; New Orleans Police Department Homicide Reports 1905 (microfilm), Louisiana Division, New Orleans Public Library; *New Orleans Item*, September 18, 1905, 1; *Daily Picayune*, September 18, 1905, 11; *Times-Democrat*, September 18, 1905, 5, 7.

24. Preliminary trial testimony, Parish of Orleans Criminal District Court, Section B, Case 34418.

25. Ibid.

26. *Daily Picayune*, September 18, 1905, 11.

27. *Daily Picayune*, September 20, 1905, 11, September 22, 1905, 8.

28. *New Orleans Item*, September 20, 1905, 1.

29. Preliminary trial testimony, Parish of Orleans Criminal District Court, Section B, Case 34418.

30. *Daily Picayune*, October 7, 1905, 11.

31. *Daily States*, October 18, 1905, 1; *New Orleans Item*, October 18, 1905, 5.

32. *Daily Picayune*, September 20, 1905, 6.

33. *Times-Democrat*, September 30, 1905, 6.

34. *Daily Picayune*, September 20, 1905, 6.

35. Preliminary trial testimony, Parish of Orleans Criminal District Court, Section B, Case 34418.

36. *Times-Democrat*, September 19, 1905, 6.

37. *Daily Picayune*, September 20, 1905, 11.

38. *Daily States*, September 22, 1905, 4, 1.

39. *New Orleans Item*, September 19, 1905, 4.

40. *New Orleans Item*, May 18, 1906, 1.

41. *Daily States*, September 19, 1905, 4.

42. For examples, see *Times-Democrat*, September 30, 1905, 6; *New Orleans Item*, May 19, 1906, 1; *Daily Picayune*, May 19, 1906, 5. These articles do not mention that Doyle was a police officer until their fifth, third, and thirteenth paragraphs, respectively.

43. *Daily Picayune*, May 17, 1906, 4; *Times-Democrat*, May 17, 1906, 3.

44. Rousey, *Policing the Southern City*, 189–92.

45. *Manual of the City Police, Adopted by the Board of Police Commissioners, January 1st, 1890* (New Orleans: Hunter & Genslinger, 1889), 15, 25.

46. *Daily States*, September 19, 1905, 4.

47. The 1900 annual report, for instance, claimed that it was "absolutely necessary" that the NOPD secure a 17 percent budget increase in order to appoint fifty new patrolmen. *Annual Report of the Board of Police Commissioners and the Superintendent of Police of the City of New Orleans for the Year 1900* (New Orleans: Mauberret's Printing House, 1901), 3.

48. *Daily Picayune*, May 20, 1906, 4.

49. *Daily States*, May 18, 1906, 1.

50. *New Orleans Item*, May 18, 1906, 1; *Daily States*, May 16, 1906, 1.

51. *Daily Picayune*, May 19, 1906, 5.

52. *Daily Picayune*, May 18, 1906, 5.

53. *New Orleans Item*, May 18, 1906, 7.

54. *Times-Democrat*, May 17, 1906, 3.

55. *Daily States*, May 18, 1906, 1.

56. *Daily Picayune*, May 19, 1906, 5; *New Orleans Item*, May 19, 1906, 1.

57. *Daily States*, May 19, 1906, 4.

58. *Times-Democrat*, May 20, 1906, 6.

59. *New Orleans Item*, May 19, 1906, 4.

60. *Daily States*, May 19, 1906, 4.

61. *Times-Democrat*, June 23, 1906, 11.

62. *Daily Picayune* May 20, 1906, 4.

63. *Times-Democrat*, June 23, 1906, 11. See also *Daily Picayune*, June 23, 1906, 4.

64. Flores-Robert, "Black Policemen."

65. *New Orleans Item*, December 9, 1919, 1.

66. *New Orleans Item*, December 17, 1919, 14.

67. Stephen Kantrowitz, *Ben Tillman and the Reconstruction of White Supremacy* (Chapel Hill: University of North Carolina Press, 2000), 3.

68. Kelly Lytle Hernández, Khalil Gibran Muhammad, and Heather Ann Thompson, "Introduction: Constructing the Carceral State," *Journal of American History* 102, no. 1 (2015): 20.

69. See Khalil Gibran Muhammad, *The Condemnation of Blackness: Race, Crime, and the Making of Modern Urban America* (Cambridge, MA: Harvard University Press, 2010), esp. 35–87. See also Nikhil Pal Singh, "The Whiteness of Police," *American Quarterly* 66, no. 4 (2014): 1091–99.

CHAPTER 2

"MANY PEOPLE 'COLORED' HAVE COME TO THE HOMICIDE OFFICE"

Police Investigations of African American Homicides in Memphis, 1920–1945

Brandon T. Jett

At 2:30 P.M. on Saturday, January 15, 1938, William Glover, a fifty-six-year-old black porter working in Memphis, Tennessee, awoke to the sound of Memphis police officers banging on his door. One of the officers informed Glover that the chief of police needed to speak with him, and without further information he placed Glover in the police car and drove him to the police station. Once at the station, three officers put Glover in an interrogation room and berated him for allegedly having an affair with a white woman, Miss Duke. Glover roundly denied the accusations, but with each denial the officers only became more vehement. One officer declared, "You remember that nigger George Brooks that was killed, you may join him before the day is over." Police then moved Glover to a cell, where he stayed for several hours. Later in the evening, officers brought Glover to Chief Lee's office, and he interrogated Glover himself. Lee struck Glover several times with his fists; Lee then pulled out his blackjack, and as Glover attempted to protect himself from the blows, "Chief Lee said—'Take your God damn black hand down I want to beat your head.'" Lee beat Glover so ferociously that he knocked a hole in his forehead. Glover received no medical attention while in custody and was not allowed to contact his family for forty-eight hours. Police held him until Monday morning, when officers took him to the Pullman office, made him resign his job, and brought him back to the station, where they held him until his wife came and paid the police twenty-five dollars. Officers then took Glover to the train station, where he met his wife and relatives, and they boarded a train and left Memphis.[1]

Seven months earlier, on May 30, 1937, forty-eight-year-old George Gordon, a black porter, left his job at an auditorium just before midnight and walked down North Main Street in Memphis. He eventually crossed paths with forty-four-year-old black man Sherman Miles, and minutes later Gordon stabbed Miles in the stomach. By 12:45 A.M. witnesses had transported Miles to the John Gaston Hospital, where he spent the last hours of his life. Shortly after his arrival, hospital officials called and reported the stabbing to the Memphis Police Department (MPD). Officers Bauer and McReight proceeded to the scene and arrested Gordon at the auditorium, where he sat awaiting their arrival. Following the arrest, police interrogated Gordon, who claimed, "Miles came on him with a knife and that he knocked the knife from his hand and then picked it up and stabbed Miles in the stomach." In addition to Gordon's testimony, at least five other African American witnesses recorded statements with police. Abe Moore insisted that he "was talking with Gordon and that Miles came walking south on Main Street and walked up to them and without a word, Gordon stabbed Miles in the stomach." Other black witnesses, however, informed police that "Miles had been picking at Gordon at the corner of Market and Main just prior to the trouble" and suggested that Gordon stabbed Miles in response to these insults. To supplement the witness testimony, MPD detectives later consulted their own records and discovered that Miles had an extensive rap sheet and "had been arrested several times on charges ranging from assault to murder to vagrancy." Several black witnesses further corroborated this history, and MPD reported that "many people 'colored' have come to the homicide office and report[ed] that Miles never worked and made his living by strong arming both negro men and women of their earnings."[2]

Instances when African Americans such as William Glover were subjected to horrific police violence and brutality have commanded copious attention from historians, while cases of nonviolent interactions between police and African Americans, such as the Sherman Miles homicide investigation, have received scant treatment from scholars.[3] Without a doubt, African Americans received harsh treatment by police, and at times their relationship was antagonistic at best. Yet these issues did not represent the totality of experiences between them. As historian of criminal justice Eric Monkkonen has argued, "A hostile attitude toward the police does not preclude the same person from perceiving the right to have a life free of crime and disorder or from perceiving that the police exist as agents to make an abstract right actual."[4] Despite hostilities between African Americans and law enforcement, members of the black community attempted to use the police in a number of ways that worked in their own specific interests, whether to remove violently inclined neighbors or relatives from the community, receive a reduced penalty for their own involvement in a criminal activity, or limit the likelihood of abuse from police on the streets. African American manipulation of the police coincided with the larger "war on crime" of the 1920s, 1930s, and 1940s, when local, state, and federal law enforcement utilized new technologies to combat criminal activity aggressively and targeted members of the black community as part of this strategy.[5] The efforts of various law enforcement agencies to control urban black communities provided African Americans an important space in which they could, at times, shape when and how police officers and detectives did their jobs. Even though criminal justice institutions usually did not serve black interests, through processes of adaptation and negotiation with law enforcement, African Americans sought to use modern state institutions to mediate the worst abuses of Jim Crow policing and to use the institution in ways that ultimately benefited themselves.[6]

An examination of police investigations of black-on-black homicides in Memphis between 1920 and 1945 sheds light on these processes. Faced with high violent crime rates in their communities, many African Americans capitalized on the MPD's growing interest in policing urban blacks and used law enforcement officers in a number of ways in the wake of potential homicides. By calling the police, acting as witnesses, assisting officers in gathering evidence, and apprehending suspects, African Americans not only chose when the police came into black neighborhoods and how the police proceeded with an investigation but also worked in ways to ensure that violent individuals were removed from black neighborhoods.[7] Black murder suspects also managed their encounters with the police in interesting ways. At times, suspects dictated the nature of their arrest by choosing when and how to surrender themselves to law enforcement officers. The harsh realities of life on the run, especially potential violence during the process of arrest or by members of the black community, pushed some black murder suspects to turn themselves in to try and mitigate these dangers. Black Memphians accused of murder faced two unattractive options: life on the run or time in police custody. When surrendering, African American murder suspects, who seemed the most vulnerable in their interactions with the police, actually used the police to limit the violence they potentially faced while on the run. In sum, an examination of these types of interactions moves our understanding beyond the usual African American as victim narrative, which is not inaccurate as much as it is incomplete and denies African Americans the acumen they exhibited in finding ways to use, manage, and even exploit Jim Crow policing.

Throughout the first half of the twentieth century, the MPD worked to reduce the astoundingly high homicide rate that plagued the city. In

Memphis, homicide rates surged higher than any other city in the country. In 1923, for example, the homicide rate in Memphis reached 65 per 100,000 residents, whereas New York, Chicago, and New Orleans totaled 4.2, 13.6, and 29.9, respectively.[8] These rates prompted a prominent statistician to declare Memphis the "most murderous civilized city in the world."[9] A majority of these homicides involved black Memphians. From 1920 to 1945, for example, black-on-black homicides accounted for 1,215 of the 1,741 homicides in the city. While black-on-black homicides comprised 69 percent of all homicides over that twenty-five-year span, the total black population of Memphis remained around 37 percent.[10] In response, the MPD investigated black homicides to try and reduce the high homicide rate, which tarnished the city's reputation, and control the African American population. MPD homicide reports indicate that the police cleared or arrested a suspect in 76 percent of black-on-black homicide cases.[11] As Figure 2.1 illustrates, the worst year for the MPD in terms of clearing black-on-black homicides was 1920, when out of forty total black-on-black homicides, police arrested eighteen suspects. Just four years later, the MPD cleared 86 percent of these cases. Over the next fifteen years, from 1925 to 1939, the clearance rate ranged between 65 and 77 percent, and from 1940 to 1945, the MPD cleared more than ninety of these homicide cases.[12] Not only did the MPD consistently arrest suspects in black-on-black homicides, but as the total number of homicides declined and the MPD embraced technological advances and improved training techniques, officers and detectives became more effective.[13] The MPD's focus on black homicide cases grew out of a larger strategy embraced by many southern cities in which police, prosecutors, judges, and juries attempted to alleviate white fears of black criminality by pursuing black suspects and placing more African Americans under the control of the formal criminal justice system.[14]

Despite the potentially negative effects of increased policing in black communities, middle-class African Americans routinely championed the cause of greater policing to try and rid their communities of criminals and high rates of violence.[15] In response to a string of robbery-related murders in September 1932, one anonymous black writer bemoaned the high rates of violence in the city and declared, "Every law enforcement agency of the city and county has been challenged. It is a challenge which officials cannot afford to ignore." The editorial concluded, "The record of the past few days clearly indicates that there must be more rigorous law enforcement without delay."[16] Black critics believed the city was "woefully underpoliced" and called for more police officers and improved technology to better combat

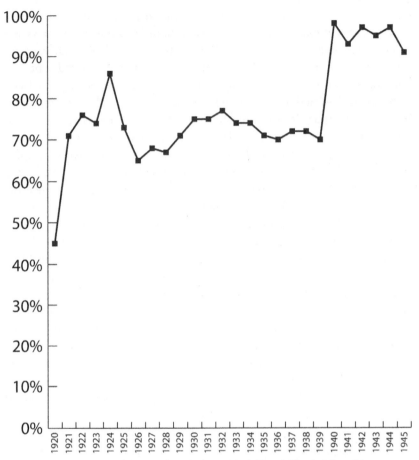

Figure 2.1. Percentages of Arrests for Black-on-Black Homicides in Memphis, 1920–1945

crime.[17] While middle-class African Americans suggested several remedies for high crime in their communities and critiqued the police for the abusive behavior toward black Memphians, they also supported the MPD's attack on crime and violence, hoping it would ultimately reduce violence in black neighborhoods.[18] While black Memphians undoubtedly viewed the police with skepticism and at times fear, faced with the reality of high crime and violence in their communities, middle-class African Americans believed the police offered a potential remedy. With regard to high homicide rates, the interests of the police and middle-class African Americans momentarily aligned.[19]

Working-class African Americans, the group most likely to be involved in or witness to a homicide, often demonstrated their dismay with widespread violence within their neighborhoods. They did so by reporting potential homicides, acting as witnesses, and assisting the police during investigations. Not only did black Memphians use the police to try and remove violent individuals from their neighborhoods, but because of their centrality to police investigations of black homicides, African Americans influenced the police in ways that they simply could not in other types of interactions.

The first step in the process of investigating homicides involved reporting the incident.[20] In many instances, police records noted who contacted police headquarters to report a potential homicide; unfortunately, the records are far from comprehensive or complete. Nonetheless, in dozens of cases, police reports indicated that African Americans reported homicides to the police.[21] By reporting these homicides, they essentially "invited" the police into their communities and urged them to investigate the deaths of their friends, neighbors, and relatives. The circumstances surrounding how and why each of these black Memphians decided to notify the police are not completely clear from the extant records. As formal institutions of criminal justice solidified themselves in the early twentieth century many black Memphians who witnessed homicides or who came across dead bodies turned to those state institutions to investigate these potential murders. High rates of violence troubled many black Memphians, and, faced with this fact, many African Americans decided to use the police to help remove violent individuals from their midst.[22] By reporting homicides to the police, black Memphians took advantage of law enforcement's growing concern with black criminality and called on the police to try and combat the high rates of violent crimes in African American neighborhoods.

Due to the lack of consistency in police reporting, it is impossible to say with any statistical precision how many times and in what ways African Americans reported homicides; nonetheless, it is possible to make some generalized conclusions about the ways African Americans notified the MPD of a homicide. When African Americans witnessed homicides or found bodies, they often called police headquarters themselves. Such was the case on April 25, 1923, when Genie May Whitfield walked up the steps to her residence and heard a gunshot. Seconds later, her husband, John Whitfield, ran past her on the stairway and out the door without saying a word. Genie then continued up the stairs and looked into the room, where she saw the body of John Henry Wooten, a twenty-five-year-old black man, lying on the floor and dying from a gunshot wound to the head. Upon seeing Wooten's body, "she then went to [the] phone and called police headquarters" and reported the incident.[23] In many instances there was not a phone near the scene, so African Americans asked other people to contact the police for them. On March 5, 1942, for example, "a negro man" witnessed Buster Jones stab Quintell Smith on the corner of Pioneer and West Trigg Streets. Shortly after the stabbing, the "negro man came back in [to a café near the scene] and told [Mr. Lashee, the white proprietor of the café] that Jones had cut Quintell Smith and he called the officers."[24] In some cases, African Americans could be very persistent in their efforts to call the police. In the early morning hours of April 14, 1929, Pauline Wade, a twenty-six-year-old black woman, stabbed Early Alexander, a twenty-two-year-old black woman, while she walked down Ayers Street. Following the stabbing, Alexander's friend Lena May Strickland "attempted to call the police but no one in the neighborhood would admit her in the house." According to the MPD, she then "remained [on the scene] until daylight and then got a phone and called in."[25]

African Americans also reported homicides to the police in person. On October 31, 1926, for instance, Gracie Robinson, who had just stabbed her husband, "came to police headquarters and reported the matter." Although she believed he was not seriously wounded, officers proceeded to the scene and found Jerry Robinson dead. Officers quickly arrested Gracie.[26] Other times, individuals not involved in the homicide came to MPD headquarters and filed reports. At 9:00 P.M. on December 29, 1934, Robert Duncan "came to police headquarters and reported that his brother George had been killed." He recounted to the officers that while walking along Commerce and Main Streets a black man named Jimmie Love stabbed his brother in the throat.[27] Although black southerners often viewed criminal justice institutions with fear and caution, these black Memphians overcame those fears in their efforts to report homicides to law enforcement officials.[28]

Once a crime was reported, two emergency patrolmen and two homicide detectives proceeded to the scene. When detectives arrived, ideally, they "made a minute examination and investigation."[29] The bulk of an officer's or a detective's work involved interviewing witnesses, determining what happened, and identifying suspects. Considering that most black-on-black homicides occurred in black neighborhoods, black homes, and establishments for blacks, it is not surprising that at this point in the investigative process African American witnesses played perhaps their most important role in MPD investigations.

When the police investigated black-on-black homicides they relied largely on the testimony of African American witnesses. From 1920 to 1945 MPD officers interviewed black witnesses in the vast majority of homicide cases: out of a total of 1,215 black intraracial homicides, MPD officers identified

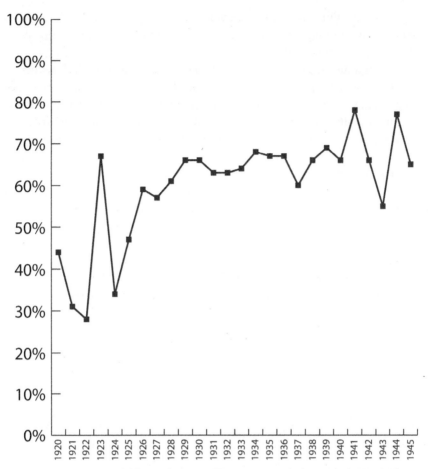

Figure 2.2. Percentage of African American Witnesses per Black-on-Black Homicide

at least one black witness on their report in 1,127 instances. Moreover, the majority of witnesses interviewed in black intraracial homicide cases were African American. Out of a total of 7,740 witnesses interviewed in African American intraracial homicides, MPD reports documented 4,871 black homicide witnesses who made statements between 1920 and 1945.[30] Over the course of twenty-five years, the percentage of black witnesses typically ranged between 55 and 78 percent (see Figure 2.2). The higher percentage of black witnesses is indicative of the separation between blacks and whites during the early twentieth century. Throughout the 1920s, 1930s, and 1940s, the social lives of black and white Memphians diverged, and instances of social interaction between the races became less common. As segregation solidified and black communities became more isolated from white communities, whites were less likely to witness a homicide involving African Americans.[31]

Throughout the 1920s, 1930s, and 1940s, the number of black witnesses listed on police reports of black intraracial homicides also increased (see Figure 2.3). The most detailed recordings of black witnesses began in 1925, when the police documented an average of 3.5 black witnesses/murders in their reports. Over the next twenty years that number steadily increased and peaked in 1941 at 7.25 black witnesses/murders. This increase coincided with a vast swell in Memphis's black population as the number of African American residents ballooned from 61,181 to 121,498 between 1920 and 1940.[32] While the population grew, black-on-black homicides comprised a larger number of the total homicides in the city. From a low of 47 percent in 1921, the percentage steadily increased and reached a peak of 85 percent in 1939. These killings also became more public. The number of black intraracial homicides occurring on the streets of Memphis rose from around 30 percent in the early 1920s to nearly 70 percent in the late 1930s.

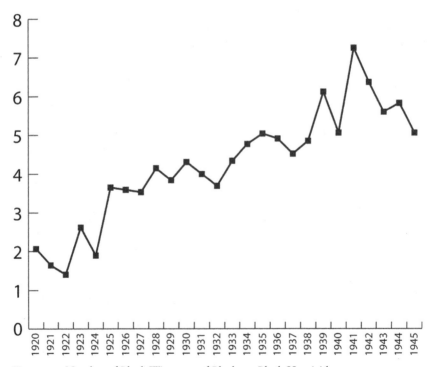

Figure 2.3. Number of Black Witnesses of Black-on-Black Homicides

As Memphis's black population grew, black intraracial homicides became more public, black-on-black homicides comprised a larger percentage of all homicides committed, and the number of black witnesses who made statements to MPD officers more than doubled.

The increased reporting of black witnesses per homicide is indicative of several potential trends. First, it is highly probable that MPD officers simply recorded more witnesses in their reports. This could be the result of the MPD's improved record keeping and better training for officers and detectives. Second, perhaps officers and detectives actually interviewed more witnesses during their investigations. More witnesses meant more evidence supporting the case, increased the chances of an indictment and eventual conviction, and allowed officers to bring more African Americans under the control of the criminal justice system.[33] Third, it could be the case that more black Memphians actually witnessed murders over time and that the officers had more witnesses to interview. The black population of the city nearly doubled between 1920 and 1940. As more African Americans migrated to Memphis, the more crowded black communities became, and there were more potential witnesses to black-on-black homicides. Finally, as black homicides became more public, African Americans became more forthcoming with their testimony over time and thus more likely to be listed as witnesses. While it is difficult to be completely sure, it is likely that a combination of all these factors contributed to the increase.

Black witnesses ensured that the police had the necessary information and evidence to make arrests of violent individuals in their neighborhood. By identifying the body, black Memphians helped begin the formal investigation process. When providing the police with statements regarding events leading up to murders, they pointed the officers in the direction of the suspect and only increased the likelihood of an arrest. African American witness testimony often countered the suspect's version of events, especially when suspects claimed self-defense. In so doing, they tried to make sure the killer would not be free to roam the streets. By providing the police with physical evidence, such as the murder weapon, black witnesses demonstrated their willingness to aid officers when doing so could potentially lead to the arrest of a suspected killer. In other words, black witnesses shaped police interpretations of events surrounding homicides and often provided critical testimony and evidence that increased the likelihood that violent members ' of the black community would be captured.

African American corpus delicti witnesses helped the police establish the fact that a criminal act had been committed, and in homicide cases they helped law enforcement establish the identity of the individual.[34] From 1925 to 1945, in 88 percent of cases, MPD reports listed black corpus delicti witnesses.[35] These witnesses identified the victim's body and, in conjunction with doctors, embalmers, and ambulance drivers, established for the record the identity of the victim. In homicide cases this usually meant summoning family members to identify the deceased and coroners to establish the cause of death. Corpus delicti witnesses contributed to the initiation of formal homicide investigations, and in homicides involving black victims, black witnesses proved vital in this early stage of the process.

Black southerners expressed the most influence over the police when they helped officers reconstruct the events leading up to the murder. They provided testimony to establish the cause of the murder, identified potential suspects, furnished descriptions of suspects who escaped, and informed the police of family members and friends who might know the whereabouts of suspects. When on August 22, 1926, for example, MPD officers arrived on the scene and found the body of Costie Louis Brown, they relied on the testimony of two black women, Dorothy Johnson and Mabel Simpson, to establish what had happened. Both women admitted that they did not see the actual shooting, but they claimed that the victim, Costie Brown, and her husband had an argument the night before and that they overheard Costie Brown's husband, James Brown, yell, "He was going to get his clothes and leave but that if he did the right thing he would kill her." A few minutes passed, and the witnesses heard five shots fired. Based on this testimony, detectives identified James Brown as their main suspect, and, using the description furnished by Johnson and Simpson, officers searched for and later arrested Brown near Horn Lake, Mississippi, on August 26, 1926. Two months later a jury sentenced Brown to life in the penitentiary for the murder.[36] In black-on-black homicides, detectives often relied solely on the information provided by black witnesses to determine what occurred, who was involved, and where to find suspects. By providing the police with this information, black witnesses shaped the way law enforcement officers interpreted the events and how they proceeded with their investigation; ultimately, these witnesses increased the likelihood that the police would arrest a violent offender.

At other times, witnesses supplied police officers with testimony that conflicted with the accused's version of events. On July 2, 1927, Virginia Bullock and Thomas Lee Tapping brought Rayfield Bullock to the General Hospital with a gunshot wound in his stomach. Hospital staff notified the MPD, and when officers arrived, Virginia Bullock, wife of Rayfield Bullock, claimed that she shot her husband by accident while trying to move their gun. She claimed that "she went to move [the] pistol from [the] mantel to

[the] chifforobe [*sic*] drawer and it went off accidentally." However, Thomas Lee Tapping relayed a different story to the police. When interviewed, he reported that Virginia "tried to kill Rayfield that morning and that at [the] time of [the] shooting she unlocked [the] chifforobe [*sic*] drawer and secured [the] pistol and shot and seriously wounded her husband." Other black witnesses corroborated Tapping's version of events. When interviewed by officers, they claimed that Virginia "made remarks recently that the law did not care anything about negro women killing men," suggesting that Virginia believed she could get away with killing her husband. Despite Virginia Bullock's initial self-defense claim, testimony from other African American witnesses brought her version of the murder into question. As a result, MPD officers arrested Virginia from the General Hospital, and she was tried for the murder of her husband.[37] Cases like this, in which black witnesses countered the narrative of events posed by black suspects, occurred throughout the period, and the police used the testimonies of black witnesses to reconstruct murders and determine their course of action.

In addition to interviewing witnesses, officers also needed to collect physical evidence. Similar to current homicide investigations, the murder weapon was one of the most important pieces of physical evidence.[38] On multiple occasions African Americans collected the murder weapon and delivered it to the police when they arrived.[39] Following the murder of Walter Woods by Conteller McFarland on September 11, 1926, for instance, officers appeared on the scene, surveyed the area, and interviewed witnesses. During the course of their investigation, detectives learned that the victim was shot as a result of an argument over a game of craps. The bullet that killed Woods "was recovered by Estelle Suggs [a black woman who lived in the residence where the killing occurred] who turned it over to Patrolman Kee."[40] In other cases, African Americans recovered the weapon used in a homicide and gave it to the officers. After Walter Meek, a forty-year-old black man, killed Will Ross on April 23, 1932, he fled the scene by running through back alleys and at some point dropped the shotgun used to kill Ross. Susie Clark, a black woman with no apparent association with either the victim or the assailant, found the weapon in the back alley and conveyed it to the police.[41] On a few rare occasions, black witnesses seized the murder weapon from the killers. After an argument over a crap game on October 9, 1933, Bill Looney shot and killed William Graham. Immediately following the shooting, "Walter Scott [a black man who witnessed the shooting] took the pistol away from Looney and kept it until officers arrived and turned it over to them."[42]

African American witnesses also helped apprehend potential suspects. Information provided by black witnesses such as descriptions of assailants and their relatives, as well as the location of their residences, helped detectives track down suspects. This is not to say that African Americans always went out of their way to assist the police, but it does suggest that at times working with law enforcement to apprehend suspects could potentially benefit black Memphians.[43] Some African Americans contributed to the MPD's investigation in order to receive a reduced criminal penalty for their role in a potential crime.[44] Following the murder of Moses Hart by several black men during a botched robbery, Walker I. Koen, a twenty-seven-year-old black man, surrendered to police officers. Koen, who took part in the robbery, "informed [officers] that he knew who killed the man Hart." Koen then agreed "to put Wright, and Carter [two suspects] on the spot for us, saying he would get them on a street car, or rather a trolley, which he did." Once on the trolley, the police rushed the car and arrested the two suspects. While police officers may have coerced Koen with threats of violence or promises of a lighter sentence, the fact that he surrendered to them suggests he was willing to work with the police in an effort to minimize his own role in the robbery. The MPD charged Koen and three other suspects with murder, robbery, and carrying a pistol, but Koen received a lighter sentence than the other individuals involved in the robbery/murder.[45]

Other African Americans seemed to have had little to gain materially from helping the police. Instead, their concern with potential murderers residing with and near their friends and family probably swayed them toward working with the police to apprehend a murder suspect. On September 17, 1922, John Coward and James Berry, two black men who witnessed the murder of Ike McKinney by Tommy Alston, chased the suspect for several blocks. Despite their effort, however, they failed to capture him. Nonetheless, when officers arrived, Coward and Berry revealed where Alston lived. MPD officers noted in their report that Coward and Berry "did good work in helping us locate Alston."[46]

In many cases, African American witnesses captured murder suspects and detained them until the police arrived on the scene.[47] Black Memphians who captured suspects and handed them to the police possessed the most influence over how officers understood homicides. Instead of relying on the police to investigate and make an arrest, these African Americans avoided any potential delay and simply used the police as a conduit through which to remove black murder suspects from the black community. On the evening of May 9, 1936, for instance, Cora Cole, Arcarrie Hudson, and Charlene Moss spent the night drinking at the Panama Café on Beale Avenue.[48] At some point, Hudson gave Moss a nickel to put in the jukebox. Cole resented this and said that "Charlene was her old lady and [she] did not want anybody messing with her." An argument ensued, and during the scuffle Cole stabbed Hudson in the heart, killing her immediately. According to the MPD, Howard Evans, a black man, "grabbed Cora and held her until Patrolman J. D. Benson arrived on the scene and she was turned over to him."[49] In other instances, groups of African Americans held suspects for the police. When Isaac Malone stabbed and killed Charlie Williams on March 10, 1934, in front of 379 North Dunlap Street, a crowd of at least seven people witnessed the event. After the stabbing, "Malone was held by some of the crowd until the police arrived and took him into custody."[50] Although the police only recorded these instances in a few cases, it is important to highlight these moments because they are indicative of a larger trend in which African Americans risked their own safety to ensure that police officers captured the suspect. On these occasions, black Memphians did not resort to extralegal retribution against the suspect and instead relied on formal criminal justice institutions.

In all, the roles of black witnesses throughout the police investigation of black homicides demonstrated their willingness to use law enforcement to diminish the threat of violence in black communities. Witnesses shaped officers' understanding of events, collected evidence, and provided the police with the information necessary to make arrests. In an era of incredibly high rates of violence in Memphis, black witnesses came forward in an effort to ensure that the police removed violent people from the African American community. Within black neighborhoods, the police represented a number of things. In some, if not most, cases, the police represented the white power structure that maintained black subordination for most of the twentieth century. In others, particularly the investigation of black homicides, the police represented an institution black Memphians could use to their own advantage. If the police made more arrests of suspected murderers, perhaps black witnesses believed crime and violence in their own community would decrease. As one black editorialist proclaimed in the *Memphis World*, "the certainty of punishment will lessen crime."[51] It appears that blacks who witnessed black homicides felt similarly and helped secure arrests of homicide suspects. In other words, black Memphians used the police as part of a larger strategy to improve black neighborhoods throughout the 1920s, 1930s, and 1940s.

While most killers fled following a murder, in 22 percent of cases black suspects surrendered themselves to police officers. From 1921 to 1945, 272 African Americans who committed, or the police suspected of committing, a murder surrendered themselves to MPD officers.[52] Over the twenty-five-year span, black suspects surrendering themselves to police officers became more common (see Figure 2.4). In the early 1920s less than 10 percent of all black homicide suspects surrendered, whereas in 1935 35 percent of homicide suspects surrendered. While the number of surrenders declined slightly by the 1940s, it remained above 20 percent. Although the numbers fluctuated, between the early 1920s and the early 1940s the number of black suspects who surrendered themselves increased. While it is impossible to know why each black murder suspect surrendered, evidence suggests that as the police became more aggressive in arresting homicide suspects and as black murder suspects better understood the potential dangers they faced while on the run, more of them decided surrendering proved the lesser of two evils.[53] When officers apprehended African Americans like William Glover and brought them to precinct houses or police headquarters, they were often held incommunicado and faced the threat of violence, abuse, and lack of representation.[54] By surrendering, African American homicide suspects tried to limit these possibilities and take control over when and how they were arrested.

Over the span of two and a half decades, when black suspects turned themselves in, 63 percent of the time they did so at police headquarters.

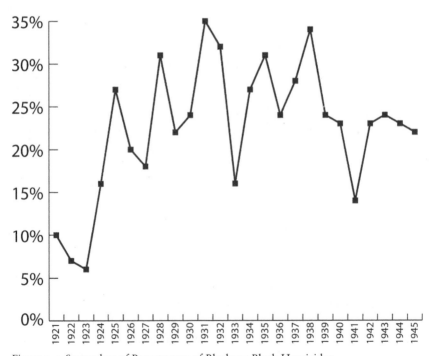

Figure 2.4. Surrenders of Perpetrators of Black-on-Black Homicides

In the early morning hours of June 29, 1937, for example, Henry Banks sneaked up on Charles Jackson as he walked to work and shot him once in the stomach. Banks, who according to the MPD had a long criminal record, "came to police headquarters and surrendered [on the] same day as the shooting."[55] In just over 18 percent of cases of surrender, black suspects called the police and awaited their arrival either at the scene, at home, or at another location. During a fight on the evening of May 26, 1934, forty-year-old Joe Ellis and forty-year-old Sylvester Harris got into a heated argument over Ellis's wife. As Harris attempted to walk away from the argument, Ellis followed him. Suddenly, Harris turned and shot Ellis five times. After the shooting, "Harris awaited the arrival of officers and surrendered to them, turning the pistol, a 38 calibre Colt pistol over to them."[56] In 11 percent of the cases, black suspects surrendered to police officers on the streets of Memphis. On the night of May 29, 1928, a group of black teenagers played a baseball game in a vacant lot on Beale Avenue. During the game, a fight broke out between two eighteen-year-olds, Walter Brown and Walter Hoyle. As they fought, Brown lunged at Hoyle with an ice pick, but Hoyle struck Brown with his baseball bat and then ran from the scene. Instead of fleeing the city or trying to hide from the police, Hoyle hurried several blocks and "went to Beale and Orleans and surrendered to Patrolmen Luttrell and W. F. Turner."[57] African American suspects in murder cases who surrendered exercised their own judgment and determined the nature of their own arrest.

Several suspects surrendered to support their claims of self-defense, accidental shootings, or defense of others. When Gracie Robinson came to police headquarters on October 31, 1926, to report her attack on her husband, she stated that "she and her husband had been having trouble for about four years and he often beat her and on the above date he came home and beat her up and then cut her on [the] leg with a knife and she got a knife and stabbed him several times." Robinson's claim of self-defense worked, and although police officers arrested her, a grand jury ignored the indictment, and Robinson was released.[58] Surrendering to the police provided black suspects with the ability to craft the narrative of events to their advantage and shape the way the police, prosecutors, and grand juries understood the homicides.

Equally important, however, surrendering mitigated the potential for violence these suspects encountered while they were fugitives from justice. In Memphis, rules and regulations provided officers much leeway in how they arrested fleeing suspects, especially in felony cases.[59] Southern police departments often relied on violence as part of a broader effort to control crime and preserve order.[60] Thus, when black suspects evaded arrest, the potential for violence remained ever present. According to MPD records, from 1920 to 1945 officers shot and killed ninety-three African Americans, and eighty-four of these cases (90 percent) occurred while officers were attempting to make an arrest. While discussions of police brutality undoubtedly occurred between black families and friends, it also made the pages of the local black press.[61] In a 1945 article in the *Memphis World* entitled "State of the City for Negroes," a black writer bemoaned the "fact about police brutality, police rapine and coercion of defenseless Negro women and girls, police intimidation of Negro soldiers and defense workers . . . police coercion of an entire segment of the local population."[62] Well aware of the potential for violence on the streets, black suspects who surrendered to the police limited the likelihood of abuse during the process of arrest.

Moreover, by surrendering themselves to law enforcement and then admitting to crimes, black suspects restricted the chances of police abuse during interrogations. Police departments across the nation employed harsh tactics during interrogations to elicit confessions, typically referred to as the "third degree."[63] Throughout the 1930s, the use of the third degree by southern police departments became more racialized, and officers routinely beat African American suspects to extract confessions.[64] In 9 percent of all surrender cases, black suspects surrendered themselves with attorneys present, which further limited the likelihood of police harassment, coercion, and abuse.[65] At times, attorneys advised their clients to avoid making statements, and in the case of abuse by officers, attorneys could act as witnesses on behalf of the African American suspects they represented. On the night of March 5, 1929, Annie B. Washington shot her husband, Mason Washington, during a fight. After the shooting, Annie immediately fled the scene before officers arrived. However, at 11:00 A.M. the next day, Annie Washington showed up at MPD headquarters to surrender with her attorney, Ed Bell. Once she surrendered, "she was instructed by Bell not to make any statement whatever and she would not admit the shooting."[66] Although a jury eventually sentenced Annie Washington to five years in the penitentiary, by surrendering with her attorney, she provided herself with both legal counsel and a bit of protection from the potential abuses and coercion that police departments in the 1920s and 1930s so infamously employed.[67]

While many African Americans surrendered because they feared potential violence during arrest, it is also possible that black suspects surrendered to the police because they feared extralegal retribution by other black Memphians. While instances of black-on-black lynching declined in the late nineteenth and early twentieth centuries, extralegal justice still permeated parts of the black community.[68] According to the *Memphis World*, on

August 8, 1944, "a group of Negro citizens" formed a posse in order to seek John Myers, a fifty-three-year-old black man who shot his estranged wife, Fredonia Myers. The day following the murder the posse located Myers and followed him several miles. "Just as he was about to enter some woods near where they found him, he told them again to stop following him and made a threatening move. It was then that Noel [a member of the posse] shot Myers in the leg," the paper reported.[69] Considering the potential for violence from within the black community, as the Myers case suggested, as well as the police when a murder suspect was on the run, it is likely that some black suspects surrendered to law enforcement to avoid such violence.

Similar to black witnesses, black suspects faced a dilemma. They could choose a life on the run and face the threat of violence at the hands of the police or other African Americans, or they could surrender to a criminal justice system that treated them unfairly.[70] Black suspects did not surrender themselves because they trusted the police but because they did not. By turning themselves in, they limited the potential for violence during the process of arrest. By surrendering with an attorney present, black suspects decreased the chances of abuse or manipulation by officers during interrogations. Finally, surrendering to the police lessened the chances of any type of extralegal revenge at the hands of black Memphians. Considering all the potential dangers faced by black fugitives, choosing the time, place, and way in which they were apprehended demonstrated African Americans' understanding of the complexities and dangers they faced both in the criminal justice system and in their own neighborhoods. While on the surface it might seem paradoxical to assume that black murder suspects would voluntarily turn themselves over to police officers, it actually revealed shrewdness and suggests how African Americans at times manipulated their encounters with the police for their own advantage.

On the whole, African Americans played vital roles throughout the entire process of police investigations of black-on-black homicides. By reporting crimes, acting as witnesses during investigations, securing evidence, or capturing suspects, black Memphians used the police to remove violent African Americans from their community. The efforts of black witnesses did more than just shape officers' interpretation of events; it was part of a broad strategy embraced by African Americans to use state institutions to their own advantage.[71] Throughout their involvement in police investigations of black homicides, African Americans demonstrated their willingness to use the police to remove violent people from their community. Moreover, because of their centrality to the investigative process, African Americans in Memphis exercised some influence over the way police worked in black neighborhoods. Equally important, African Americans suspected of murder could, at times, shape the way they were arrested by turning themselves in to police. By surrendering, black suspects exercised the greatest control over their arrests by police. They could choose the time and place of arrest, whether or not they surrendered alone or with an attorney, and could craft a self-defense narrative of the crime that improved their chances of release. Furthermore, black suspects who surrendered to police and admitted the crime, even if they claimed self-defense, reduced potentially violent encounters with police or other African Americans. In sum, whether aiding in police investigations or surrendering to law enforcement officers, African Americans proved to be more than just passive victims of police abuse. Instead, they used whatever influence they could to use, shape, and manage the police in ways that ultimately benefited themselves.

NOTES

1. William Glover on police brutality in Memphis, 1938, folder 39, carton 6, series II, Robert R. Church Family Papers, University of Memphis Special Collections, Memphis, Tennessee.

2. Homicide Report for Sherman Miles, June 1, 1937, Memphis Police Department Homicide Reports, 1917–46, Shelby County Archives, Memphis, Tennessee. Hereafter cited as Homicide Reports. The data utilized in this essay come from a database I compiled using the Homicide Reports from 1920 to 1945. When possible, the Homicide Reports were cross-checked with medical records, coroners' reports, and newspaper accounts. Moreover, since these records were compiled by the police, they are more accurate than other types of legal records, such as grand jury indictment records or arrest records, because the homicide records were not "filtered" by coroners, prosecutors, judges, or grand juries. The discovery of a dead body prompted the report, not an arrest, an indictment, or a conviction. The so-called dark figure, or the number of unreported crimes, is much lower with homicides than other types of crimes, and as a result these records prove to be a valuable resource through which the workings of the police can be understood.

3. See esp. Gunnar Myrdal, *An American Dilemma: The Negro Problem and Modern Democracy* (New York: Harper & Brothers Publishers, 1944), 535; Marilynn S. Johnson, *Street Justice: A History of Police Violence in New York City* (Boston: Beacon Press, 2003), 12–180; Khalil Gibran Muhammad, "Policing Racism: Jim Crow Justice in the Urban North," in *The Condemnation of Blackness: Race, Crime, and the Making of Modern Urban America* (Cambridge, MA: Harvard University Press, 2010), 226–68; Jeffrey S. Adler, "'The Killer behind the Badge': Race and Police Homicide in New Orleans, 1925–1945," *Law and History Review* 30, no 2 (2013): 495–531.

4. Eric H. Monkkonen, *Police in Urban America: 1860–1920* (Cambridge: Cambridge University Press, 1981), 150–51.

5. For more on the ways in which police and other criminal justice institutions targeted black Americans during this period, see Muhammad, "Policing Racism"; Jeffrey S. Adler, "Less Crime, More Punishment: Violence, Race, and Criminal Justice in Early Twentieth-Century America," *Journal of American History* 102, no. 1 (2015): 34–46.

6. This idea is loosely based on the theory of "interest convergence." According to Derrick A. Bell Jr., the "principle of 'interest convergence' provides: The interest of blacks in achieving racial equality will be accommodated only when it converges with the interests of whites" (*"Brown v. Board of Education* and the Interest-Convergence Dilemma," *Harvard Law Review* 93, no. 3 [1979–80]: 523). In the case of black southerners using law enforcement in homicide investigations, I am suggesting that African Americans' interest in removing violent individuals converged with white police officers' and city officials' efforts to impose greater control over the black population via the formal criminal justice system.

7. For more on the centrality of witnesses to police investigations, see Charles R. Swanson, Neil C. Chamelin, Leonard Territo, and Robert W. Taylor, *Criminal Investigation*, 10th ed. (New York: McGraw-Hill, 2009), 142–81.

8. Frederick L. Hoffman, *The Homicide Problem* (Newark, NJ: Prudential Press, 1924), 75–76.

9. Ibid., 80. Hoffman is a controversial figure; see Muhammad, *The Condemnation*, 35–87. However, his assertion that Memphis claimed the highest homicide rate in the United States for much of the early twentieth century is confirmed by the Division of Vital Statistics of the US Census Office.

10. Campbell Gibson and Kay Jung, US Bureau of the Census, *Historical Census Statistics on Population Total by Race, 1790–1990, and by Hispanic Origin, 1970–1990, for Large Cities and Other Urban Places in the United States* (Washington, DC: US Government Printing Office, 1996) table 43.

11. Police made arrests in 924 cases out of a total of 1,215 black-on-black homicides from 1920 to 1945.

12. Police typically arrested the assailant whom African American witnesses identified.

13. Despite the clearance rate, suspects routinely escaped punishment or received light sentences as their cases moved through the court system. See *Memphis Police Department Yearbook* (Memphis, TN: Memphis Police Relief Association, 1924), 62.

14. Adler, "Less Crime, More Punishment," 34–46; Muhammad, "Policing Racism."

15. The MPD had a well-known reputation for brutality in the black community. See Michael K. Honey, *Southern Labor and Black Civil Rights: Organizing Memphis Workers* (Urbana: University of Illinois Press, 1993), 1. For more on the abuses African Americans faced at the hands of the southern criminal justice system, see Silvan Niedermeier, "Torture and 'Modern Civilization': The NAACP's Fight against Forced Confessions in the American South (1935–1945)," in *Fractured Modernity: America Confronts Modern Times, 1890s to 1940s*, ed. Thomas Welskopp and

Alan Lessoff (Munich: Oldenbourg Verlag, 2013), 169–89; David M. Oshinsky, *Worse Than Slavery: Parchman Farm and the Ordeal of Jim Crow Justice* (New York: Free Press, 1997); Muhammad, "Policing Racism." For more on the divide between middle-class African Americans and their view of working-class African Americans who did not quite meet the "politics of respectability," see Jacqueline M. Moore, *Booker T. Washington, W. E. B. DuBois, and the Struggle for Racial Uplift* (Wilmington, DE: Scholarly Resources Inc., 2003); Robert J. Norrell, *Up from History: The Life of Booker T. Washington* (Cambridge, MA: Harvard University Press, 2009); Kevin K. Gaines, *Uplifting the Race: Black Leadership, Politics, and Culture in the Twentieth Century* (Chapel Hill: University of North Carolina Press, 1996); Evelyn Brooks Higginbotham, *Righteous Discontent: The Women's Movement in the Black Baptist Church, 1880–1920* (Cambridge, MA: Harvard University Press, 1993).

16. *Memphis World*, September 20, 1932, 8.

17. Ibid., and October 17, 1944, 1.

18. Michael Javen Fortner found similar support among middle-class African Americans for tougher crime policies in the 1970s and 1980s; see *Black Silent Majority: The Rockefeller Drug Laws and the Politics of Punishment* (Cambridge, MA: Harvard University Press, 2015). For a critique of Fortner's argument, see Donna Murch, "Who's to Blame for Mass Incarceration?," *Boston Review*, October 16, 2015. For examples of police shootings and abuse, see *Memphis World*, December 20, 1932, 1, and April 5, 1932, 1.

19. Sociologist Elijah Anderson argued that law-abiding African Americans in the 1980s, well aware of the potential for abuse and manipulation, turned to the police to help combat violence and drug-related crimes in their own communities. See *Street Wise: Race, Class, and Change in an Urban Community* (Chicago: University of Chicago Press, 1990), 203–4.

20. For a breakdown of how the ideal police investigation of a homicide played out in Memphis during this era, see Jack Carley, "Behind the Scenes at Headquarters," in *Memphis Police Department Yearbook*, 57–58.

21. The MPD recorded 1,215 black-on-black homicides. Police listed fifty-four total instances when African Americans reported potential homicides to police, which accounted for 4.43 percent of the cases. While this number is low, the actual number is probably much higher, as the reports were very inconsistent in their reporting. For more on inconsistencies in police reporting, especially in the 1920s and 1930s, see Marvin E. Wolfgang, "Uniform Crime Reports: A Critical Appraisal," *University of Pennsylvania Law Review* 111, no. 6 (1963): 713–17.

22. Elijah Anderson noted a similar dilemma faced by urban African Americans in the 1980s. See *Streetwise*, 204.

23. Homicide Report for John Henry Wooten, April 25, 1923.

24. Homicide Report for Quintell Smith, March 5, 1942.

25. Homicide Report for Early Alexander, April 14, 1929.

26. Homicide Report for Jerry Robinson, November 5, 1926.

27. Homicide Report for George Duncan, December 29, 1934.

28. Sherrilyn A. Ifill, *On the Courthouse Lawn: Confronting the Legacy of Lynching in the Twenty-First Century* (Boston: Beacon Press, 2007), 76–77, 125–26.

29. Carley, "Behind the Scenes," 57.

30. In black intraracial homicides, MPD homicide reports listed 7,740 total witnesses, and African Americans made up 63 percent of all witnesses interviewed in these cases. The number of white witnesses is somewhat higher due to the fact that the MPD usually listed coroners, undertakers, and ambulance drivers on the reports as witnesses. As a point of comparison, the MPD identified a total of 910 white witnesses for the 199 white intraracial homicides that occurred between 1920 and 1945 in Memphis. During the same years MPD homicide reports identified 1,215 black intraracial homicides and listed a total of 4,871 black witnesses. A straight comparison between the total number of black witnesses interviewed and the total number of white witnesses interviewed is difficult because of the vast disparity in the number of black intraracial homicides and white intraracial homicides. However, the average number of black witnesses interviewed per black-on-black homicide totaled 4, and the average of white witnesses interviewed per white-on-white homicide totaled 4.5.

31. Gloria Brown Melton, "Blacks in Memphis, Tennessee, 1920–1955: A Historical Study" (PhD diss., Washington State University, 1982), 1, 10–14.

32. Honey, *Southern Labor*, 16.

33. For a discussion of the importance of eyewitness testimony to criminal prosecutions, see Elizabeth F. Loftus, *Eye Witness Testimony* (Cambridge, MA: Harvard University Press, 1979); William Carrol and Michael Seng, *Eyewitness Testimony: Strategies and Tactics*, 2nd ed. (Eagan, MN: West Publishing, 2003), 1–5. For more on the criminal justice system's interest in controlling African Americans, see Adler, "Less Crime, More Punishment."

34. Rollin M. Perkins, "The Corpus Delicti of Murder," *Virginia Law Review* 48 (March 1962): 181.

35. This excludes 1941 because the MPD listed witnesses differently for that year, making it difficult to reliably identify the corpus delicti witness.

36. Homicide Report for Costie Louis Brown, August 22, 1926.

37. Homicide Report for Rayfield Bullock, July 2, 1927.

38. Robert L. Snow, *Murder 101: Homicide and Its Investigation* (Westport, CT: Praeger Publishers, 2005), 88.

39. Homicide Reports noted thirteen occasions when African Americans handed murder weapons over to police.

40. Homicide Report for Walter Woods, September 11, 1926.

41. Homicide Report for Will Ross, April 23, 1932.

42. Homicide Report for William "Peacie" Graham, October 9, 1933.

43. For more on African Americans' distrust of law enforcement, see John Dollard, *Caste and Class in a Southern Town*, 3rd ed. (Garden City, NY: Doubleday & Company, 1957), 71; Muhammad, *The Condemnation*, 251.

44. Sociologist Alice Goffman found similar trends occurring in Philadelphia in the twenty-first century. See *On the Run: Fugitive Life in an American City* (Chicago: University of Chicago Press, 2014), 47–52.

45. Homicide Report for Moses Hart, March 26, 1933.

46. Homicide Report for Ike McKinney, September 17, 1922.

47. Homicide Reports noted six occasions when this occurred.

48. While popularly known as Beale Street, it was actually named Beale Avenue until the city officially changed the name to Beale Street in May 1955.

49. Homicide Report for Arcarrie Hudson, May 9, 1936.

50. Homicide Report for Charlie Williams, March 10, 1934.

51. *Memphis World*, September 18, 1931, 8.

52. This number comprises all the instances when the homicide reports explicitly stated that someone surrendered to police. Occasions when someone was arrested at the scene were not included unless it was noted that he or she surrendered.

53. Adler, "'The Killer,'" 520.

54. William Glover, Church Family Papers.

55. Homicide Report for Charles Jackson, June 29, 1937.

56. Homicide Report for Joe Ellis, May 26, 1934.

57. Homicide Report for Walter Brown, May 29, 1928.

58. Homicide Report for Jerry Robinson, November 5, 1926.

59. Sections 334–35, "Rules and Regulations of the Police Department of the City of Memphis, Tennessee," 95–96, Memphis and Shelby County Room, Memphis Public Library, Memphis, Tennessee.

60. Adler, "'The Killer.'"

61. For an examination of the effect of African Americans discussing police abuses and negative experiences, see Rod K. Brunson, "'Police Don't Like Black People': African-American Young Men's Accumulated Police Experiences," *Criminology & Public Police* 6, no. 1 (2007): 71–101.

62. "State of the City for Negroes," *Memphis World*, August 10, 1945, 1.

63. Niedermeier, "Torture,"; Jeffrey S. Adler, "The Greatest Thrill I Get Is When I Hear a Criminal Say, 'Yes, I did it': Race and the Third Degree in New Orleans, 1920–1945," *Law and History Review* 34, no. 1 (2016): 1–44; Wickersham Commission, *Report on Lawlessness in Law Enforcement* (Washington, DC: US Government Printing Office, 1931).

64. Adler, "The Greatest Thrill."

65. Out of the 272 total surrender cases there were 25 cases in the homicide records that noted that a suspect surrendered with an attorney present.

66. Homicide Report for Mason Washington, March 5, 1929.

67. Wickersham Commission, *Report on Lawlessness*.

68. For more on extralegal violence within the black community, see Karlos Hill, "Black Vigilantism: The Rise and Decline of African American Lynch Mob Activity in the Mississippi and Arkansas Deltas, 1883–1923," *Journal of African American History* 95, no. 1 (2010): 26–43; Jeffrey S. Adler, "Black Violence in the New South:

Patterns of Conflict in Late-Nineteenth-Century Tampa," in *The African American Heritage of Florida*, ed. David R. Colburn and Jane L. Landers (Gainesville: University Press of Florida, 1995), 225–28; E. M. Beck and Stewart E. Tolnay, "When Race Didn't Matter: Black and White Mob Violence against Their Own Color," in *Under Sentence of Death: Lynching in the South*, ed. W. Fitzhugh Brundage (Chapel Hill: University of North Carolina Press, 1997), 137–43.

69. *Memphis World*, August 8, 1944, 1, 6.

70. For an examination of life as an African American fugitive in the twenty-first century, see Goffman, *On the Run*.

71. For more on African Americans attempting to use the state to improve their own communities, see Glenda Gilmore, *Gender and Jim Crow: Women and the Politics of White Supremacy in North Carolina, 1896–1920* (Chapel Hill: University of North Carolina Press, 1996).

CHAPTER 3

FORCED CONFESSIONS

Police Torture and the African American Struggle for Civil Rights in the 1930s and 1940s South

Silvan Niedermeier

On Monday, February 26, 1940, at 11:30 p.m., four officers of the Atlanta Police Department (APD) came to the home of Rosa South, an African American woman living in Southeast Atlanta, and took her sixteen-year-old son, Quintar South, for questioning on a suspected burglary. Ten days later, Quintar South's story hit the front pages of Atlanta's newspapers. According to the *Atlanta Constitution*, an APD detective named W. F. Sutherland had "burned" South with a "tacking iron" to force him to confess to the burglary. The instrument was described as an electric iron used for gluing photographs onto police records. According to the report, the case only came to light after Mrs. C. E. Harrison, the "wife of a Southern Bell Telephone company executive" who had employed South as a yard worker, had visited him in his cell at the juvenile detention home and had seen the "raw, unbandaged wounds." The newspaper also cited Judge Garland Watkins of the Atlanta Juvenile Court, who had ordered an internal investigation of the case: "If the boy's story is true, no more shameful thing has ever happened in Atlanta. If such an act of medieval torture had taken place, the officer guilty must be found out and punished to the fullest extent of the law."[1]

Judge Watkins was not alone in his outspoken indignation. Other prominent white citizens and institutions of Atlanta, including Atlanta's mayor, William B. Hartsfield, the Georgia Women's Democratic Club, the Georgia Association of Women Lawyers, the Child Welfare Association, and the Georgia Humane Association, joined his criticism and called for the legal punishment of the accused officer should the allegations prove to be true.[2] In an editorial with the headline "Justice for the Weak," the *Constitution* called the case "an atrocity" that "has been perpetrated upon every decent

Atlantan" should the accusation prove true. "There isn't a decent man or woman in Atlanta who doesn't feel shame," the newspaper claimed.[3]

Equally outraged, albeit less surprised, were the reactions of the local black press. Openly calling the South case an instance of "police torture," the editors of the *Atlanta Daily World* took the opportunity to report on another police brutality case that had been brought to the attention of the local grand jury. The case involved two Atlanta police officers who had allegedly beaten a local black taxicab driver on his face and head with "a short piece of rubber hose."[4] The newspaper also used the public attention on the South case to highlight the long-lasting and pervasive reality of abusive police practices against African Americans in Atlanta. In a comment published three weeks after the case became public, an editor of the *Daily World* called upon the members of Atlanta's black community to press charges against abusive police officers, notwithstanding "the fear of repetition of the brutalities, . . . injury of their business or occupation and so forth." Only by constant efforts to speak out against assaults and mistreatment by the police could black citizens hope to gain help "by law or any official," even though the "state" had done "little or nothing about brutalities" in the past, the paper asserted.[5]

Despite its seemingly univocal condemnation, the presumed torture of Quintar South yielded no legal sanctions. Two and a half months later, Detective Sutherland was put on trial in the Fulton County Criminal Court. After Quintar South testified against Sutherland, numerous city policemen took the stand and stated that they "did not see any signs of burns on the boy" while South was in police custody. After forty-five minutes of deliberation, the white jurors declared Sutherland not guilty.[6]

Quintar South's case points to three central features of the history of police torture against African Americans in the 1930s and 1940s South and beyond. First, southern juries refused to punish police officers accused of this form of racial violence. Second, African American newspaper editors, civil rights activists, witnesses, and victims themselves persistently and publicly challenged police torture. Third, members of the white southern elite occasionally critiqued police torture methods, albeit fruitlessly, while the larger southern white community reacted with indifference.

Following these observations, this chapter discusses individual and institutional forms of resistance against police torture and the use of forced confessions in trials against African Americans in the 1930s and 1940s South. These activities must be reconsidered as an integral element of the "long civil rights movement." Although this concept has been criticized for its tendency to override the multiplicity and historicity of black civil rights

/ freedom struggles between the 1930s and the 1980s and to overemphasize the organized Left's involvement in the movement's early phase, I argue that this concept retains its usefulness when used to highlight the gradual local formations of a mass-based movement for civil rights prior to the mid-1950s.[7] It is important to acknowledge that these developments were part of a much longer and continuing struggle for freedom and civil rights by African Americans in the American South and beyond. To support this argument, I analyze two court cases from Mississippi and Alabama that highlight both the sobering reality of abusive interrogation practices within the southern criminal justice system and the emancipatory significance of individual, collective, and institutional forms of resistance to it. The testimony of black defendants in courtrooms and the activities of lawyers, local citizens, and civil rights institutions in these cases reveal the rigid and, at the same time, contested nature of white supremacy in the Jim Crow South.

Police brutality against blacks has long been a central element of white supremacy in the South. After the end of slavery and the failure of Reconstruction, it became a crucial tool for white southerners to reinforce white supremacy and uphold the evolving system of racial segregation far into the twentieth century.[8] Reflecting on the central position of urban police officers for the perseverance of Jim Crow in segregated southern cities, W. E. B. Du Bois noted in 1940: "No one who does not know can realize what a tyranny a low-grade white policeman can exercise in a colored neighborhood."[9]

Police officers in southern cities and towns were usually recruited from the middle and lower ranks of the white community. While some police forces had educational requirements like a high school diploma or the equivalent, others had no requirements at all. The same applied to southern sheriffs, who gained their position through public election and most often hired uneducated white men as deputy sheriffs. In 1939 only six of the twenty-four members of the Athens, Georgia, police department had graduated from high school. Newly admitted officers had previous occupations as knitting mill operator, hosiery mill worker, mechanic, filling station operator, salesman, and farm worker. No formal training was given to the Athens policemen. Instead, they learned through an apprenticeship method, which meant walking the beat with older policemen for a period of six months. The salary for regular patrolmen in Augusta, Georgia, ranged from $100 to $125 per month; the chief of police earned $250 per month.[10] Policing was also a nearly exclusively white occupation in the South at the time, as the police were perceived as the key institution for the preservation of white supremacy and the established system of racial segregation. In 1939 not a single black police officer served in Mississippi, South Carolina, Louisiana,

Georgia, Alabama, Arkansas, and Virginia.[11] Only in the late 1940s did increasing agitation combined with the rising registration of black voters lead to the reluctant admission of black officers to southern urban police forces.[12]

Statistical data collected during the 1930s show that African Americans were not the only victims of police violence. An unpublished study conducted by sociologist Arthur Raper in the late 1930s found that between 1935 and 1940 the police in fourteen southern states killed 139 black and 32 white persons.[13] The study also presented the numbers for twenty-six nonsouthern cities where 76 blacks and 105 whites had been killed between 1935 and 1940. These numbers were highest in the so-called Middle states, including Michigan and Illinois, where 55 blacks and 70 whites had been killed by the police.[14] Projected on the total population, the rate of police violence against blacks and whites in the South and the Middle states was nearly identical. In both regions, blacks were about seven times more likely to be killed by the police than whites.[15] Pointing to the need to address the problem of police abuse on a national level, Raper concluded that "police brutality [against blacks], though concentrated in the South," was "by no means limited to that section."[16]

Raper's study also questioned the causes of the widespread police brutality against African Americans in the United States at the time. Perceiving the problem from a class- and race-centered approach, Raper concluded that police killings "occur most often in the larger Southern communities where competition between races is keenest." Police officials throughout the country had a different explanation for the frequent slayings of black suspects by white police officers, one that may sound all too familiar to today's readers. As several of Raper's interviewees declared, policemen pulled the trigger out of fear of the "strange 'bad nigger,'" who was vaguely described as an "energetic" and "dangerous" person with the "willingness to resort to violence both with [his] fellows or the police."[17] In other words, the familiar stereotype of the volatile and inherently aggressive black man served as the most important justification for police killings of blacks.[18]

African Americans' significantly higher likelihood of being killed by southern police officers indicates that police violence constituted a racist form of oppression that was tightly connected to the system of racial segregation. As Gunnar Myrdal observed in his 1944 seminal study on American race relations (which was in part based on Raper's findings), southern policemen commonly perceived physical violence as a necessary means to keep African Americans "in their place." He concluded that the southern police officers served as "upholder of the caste order." The torture of black prisoners and defendants, too, was an integral instrument for preserving the segregated order of the South. Myrdal observed that the use of force to gain confessions from black suspects was a "routine device" in many southern police stations.[19] Although no statistical data exist on the spread and use of police torture methods throughout the South, my own research suggests that blacks were more likely to become victims of police torture, although the evidence shows that whites too were beaten into confessions. Class seems to be the most important factor in the latter case, as white victims of police torture were often considered to have "bad reputation[s]." Moreover, archival sources indicate that police officers resorted to more extreme and degrading forms of violence to force confessions from black suspects.[20]

By the mid-1930s the issue of police brutality and torture against blacks in the South began to reach the attention of federal courts and the broader American public. One major reason for this was the campaign of the National Association for the Advancement of Colored People (NAACP) against prosecutors' use of forced confessions in trying black defendants in southern courts. Since its founding in 1909, the NAACP had been active in combating the discrimination of African Americans in the fields of education, work, voting rights, and criminal justice. One of its focal points was its antilynching campaign. By publicizing accounts and photographs of the lynching of black men by white mobs, the association lobbied the US Congress for the passage of antilynching legislation that would allow federal law enforcement agencies to prosecute the members of lynch mobs, as well as local officials who failed to prevent the violence. The NAACP's efforts, however, ran counter to the interests of southern members of Congress, who, in the Senate, were able to filibuster such legislation.[21]

In the 1930s the NAACP gradually changed its emphasis. Under the guidance of Charles Houston and his successor, Thurgood Marshall, the NAACP's Legal Department in New York City began to use litigation as a key instrument in the fight for civil rights. Its lawyers based their struggle on a slowly but steadily evolving network of NAACP branches that would become the base and backbone for civil rights activism in the South and beyond.[22] Believing that a legal approach was the only way to effect long-lasting change, the NAACP's Legal Department also began to challenge the widespread use of forced confessions in southern courts.

This NAACP campaign was closely interrelated to what Michael J. Klarman has called a "fundamental shift in race-relation jurisprudence" by the US Supreme Court during the New Deal era. Most important in this regard was the Court's reinterpretation of the Fourteenth Amendment as a safeguard against state governments' violation of criminal-procedure protections. In several major decisions during the 1920s and 1930s, the Court broadened the application of the amendment's due process clause by arguing that it allowed the Court to intervene in state criminal cases when they violated the right to a fair and impartial trial.[23] These precedents also led the Court to challenge the use of forced confessions in southern courts. Between 1935 and 1945 the Court reviewed eight trials involving black southern defendants whose confessions had been allegedly enforced by physical and/or psychological coercion. It reversed the sentences in all but one of these cases. In seven of them, the NAACP's Legal Department was directly involved.[24]

Notwithstanding the crucial role of the NAACP and the US Supreme Court, the fight against forced confessions depended first and primarily on the initiatives of individual actors "on the ground," including lawyers, local civil rights activists, sympathetic citizens, and, not least, the defendants themselves. A telling example is the 1936 case *Brown v. Mississippi*, the first case in which the US Supreme Court rejected the use of forced confessions in a state's trial.[25] On March 30, 1934, sixty-year-old planter Raymond Stuart was found in a state of unconsciousness in his house in Scooba, Mississippi, bleeding from severe wounds to his head and chest. Stuart, described in local newspapers as a prominent citizen of the local community, died on the way to the hospital. Soon after the news of his death had spread, a crowd of two hundred people gathered at Stuart's house to begin a search for the murderers, assisted by bloodhounds. The sheriff of Kemper County and several of his deputies took part in this search.[26] Shortly afterward, Ed Brown, a thirty-year-old black worker on Stuart's farm, was arrested and taken to the local jail. The next day, police officers arrested twenty-seven-year-old Henry Shields, a black farm worker living in Stuart's neighborhood. The police then transferred both prisoners to the jail in Meridian, thirty miles from Scooba, most likely to prevent a lynch mob from storming the local jail.[27] In fact, shortly afterward, local newspapers reported on rumors regarding the formation of a mob that was on its way to Meridian. In response, the local sheriff stationed police officers around the jail, armed with machine guns, shotguns, and tear gas grenades.[28]

On April 2 local newspapers announced that the two suspects had admitted to committing the crime and provided readers with the details of their confessions.[29] One day later, a third suspect, twenty-year-old Arthur Ellington, was arrested and reportedly confessed to the crime shortly afterward.[30] The next day, the local grand jury charged the three suspects with murder. As the defendants had no money to provide for their own legal assistance, the judge of the Kemper County court appointed four white lawyers as defense counsel. The trial started on the following day and lasted only one and a half days.[31] After only thirty minutes of deliberation, the jury declared the three defendants guilty, and the judge ordered the three to be executed by hanging.[32]

The local press praised the community's reaction to the case. Under the headline "Kemper Proves Itself," the *Meridian Star* commented: "The case has seemingly been handled expeditiously—[w]ith due justice to the accused and with due consideration for the social order. . . . Apparently, the negroes have enjoyed a fair, impartial trial."[33] What the newspaper did not mention, however, was that all three defendants had disclaimed their confession in open court, stating that local police officers had forced them to confess. Asked by his lawyers to describe his alleged "confession," Ed Brown identified a deputy sheriff named Cliff Dial as one of his tormentors: "They had me behind across chairs kind of like that. I said I didn't kill him, and they said put it on him again, and they hit so hard I had to say: 'Yes, sir.' Mr. Cliff [Dial] said: 'Give it to me, and I will get it.' He took it, and it had two buckles on the end. They stripped me naked and bent me over a chair and I just had to say it; I couldn't help it."[34] Brown also exhibited the bodily traces of the whipping in the courtroom:

> Q. They whipped you hard there?
> A. Yes, sir. I will show you. There are places all the way up.
> Q. Did you bleed any?
> A. Did I bleed? I sure did.[35]

Several officers testified that they had participated in the whipping of the defendants. Most direct was Deputy Sheriff Dial. Responding to the inquiry of one of the defense attorneys, he stated: "We warmed them up a little—not too much." Before the jurors declared the three defendants guilty, the presiding judge, J. I. Sturdivant, reminded them that they should not consider the confessions as evidence if they had been "solicited by threats or coercion or force or intimidation."[36]

The conviction of Brown, Ellington, and Shields exemplifies the precarious status of African American defendants within the southern criminal justice system at the time. It highlights an often neglected underside of the decline of lynching in the 1930s and 1940s South. While southern law enforcement officers took increasing measures to protect black defendants from lynch mobs, they often resorted to physical coercion against those defendants to secure their fast conviction in court and appease the local white community's desire for swift and harsh justice.[37] In addition, the fates of African American defendants in such trials depended on their support by local white lawyers and the feeble infrastructure of black civil rights activism in the South at that time. Since black defendants and their families often had no money to hire a lawyer, they usually depended on the legal assistance provided by court-appointed white lawyers. Due to their own reservations or pressure of the local white community, those lawyers often had little interest in defending their clients with full commitment. Sometimes, however, they defied those pressures and challenged the abuse of black defendants' legal rights in court, as they did in this case.

After the three men's conviction, one of their appointed lawyers decided to file an appeal in their case. John Clark's motion was all the more surprising because he and his wife were active politically in Mississippi and well connected to the state's conservative political establishment. Two of the three other lawyers refused to participate in the appeal, while the third allowed Clark to use his name in the appeal but did not want to take an active part in any future proceedings. Apparently, Clark's colleagues believed that their involvement in the appeal could potentially harm their legal careers. The meager financial outlook of the case might have played a role too. As his defendants were not able to finance the appeal, Clark wrote to the NAACP national office in New York City to ask for help. Facing a difficult financial situation, the NAACP sent Clark only a small check and decided to wait for the outcome of his appeal before taking further action.[38]

In January 1935 the Mississippi Supreme Court affirmed the judgment against the three defendants on the technical argument that the defense lawyers had made no motion during the trial to exclude the coerced confessions as evidence. One judge, however, wrote a sharp dissent from the majority's decision. Judge William D. Anderson, a longtime Mississippi attorney and former mayor of the city of Tupelo, concluded that the defendants had been "driven to confess their guilt by most brutal and unmerciful whippings." He argued that the proceedings in the trial should be invalidated under the Fourteenth Amendment due process clause. This verdict meant that the three defendants still faced their execution. After the decision, they were transferred to Hinds County jail in Jackson, Mississippi, to secure them from the possible attack of a lynch mob after a rumor circulated that, should the case be appealed to the US Supreme Court, their lives would be in danger.[39]

Following the decision of the Mississippi Supreme Court, attorney John Clark wrote to the NAACP, pressing the organization to take over the case. Clark stated that he could not take the case any further, even though he firmly believed that the three men had been tortured into their confessions. After a physical and nervous collapse, he entirely withdrew from the case. As his wife stated in a letter to Arthur Garfield Hays, the longtime general counsel of the American Civil Liberties Union, her husband had received "strong and unjust criticism" for his support of the defendants, adding that the "justice loving, law abiding people" in Mississippi had been in sympathy with Mr. Clark's work "but dare[d] not to express their opinions because of inflamed public sentiment." Her comment indicates that some members of the local white community disapproved of the police's strong-arm methods against the three defendants, yet they were not able, allowed, or willing to express their disapproval publicly. Another indicator of local whites' empathy toward Brown, Ellington, and Shield is that their case received the support of an even more prominent member of Mississippi's white political elite after John Clark resigned. Mississippi's former governor Earl Brewer, a widely respected criminal lawyer and a longtime political opponent of the notorious racist Theodore Bilbo, took over the case at the request of Clark's wife and prepared a second appeal to the Mississippi Supreme Court. Brewer appropriated the main argument in Judge Anderson's dissenting opinion to claim that the trial had violated the Fourteenth Amendment due process clause and Mississippi law.[40]

In March 1935 the NAACP announced it would financially support Brewer and a possible appeal to the US Supreme Court. In the same month, an article in the NAACP monthly, *The Crisis,* criticized the black community in Kemper County for having remained "silent" on the case.[41] This comment, as well as the obvious mistreatment of Brown, Ellington, and Shields, stirred up the local black community, and an NAACP chapter was organized in Meridian, with 126 members, by the end of the month. As in similar cases of civil rights litigation in the 1930s and 1940s, the egregious violation of black defendants' civil rights and the NAACP's initiative on their behalf strengthened black civil rights consciousness on the ground and led to the formation of a basic infrastructure of civil rights activism.

At the end of April 1935, the Mississippi Supreme Court again upheld the verdict against the three accused. This time, Judge Anderson and a second judge dissented from the decision, repeating the argument that the verdict had been in violation of the due process clause of the Fourteenth Amendment. Even though Brewer had agreed to work pro bono, the costs for the appeal to the US Supreme Court proved too high for the financially strained national office of the NAACP. As a consequence, the money was raised with much difficulty by an alliance of several donors and institutions. Of the overall costs of the proceedings of almost $2,000, the NAACP contributed $690. Another $574.67 was donated by the Commission on Interracial Cooperation (CIC), whose director, Will Alexander, notified the NAACP in May 1935 that his organization would add 50 percent to any funds collected by the NAACP or other sources. J. Morgan Steven, a member of the Association of Southern Women for the Prevention of Lynching (ASPWL), and Theodore D. Bratton, a bishop of the Episcopal Diocese of Mississippi, collected the remaining $650 needed for the appeal within local white and black communities in Mississippi.[42]

In February 1936 the US Supreme Court reversed the decision in *Brown v. Mississippi* and ordered a new trial against the three defendants. The Court's judgment made clear that the use of forced confessions in state court procedure constituted a violation of the Fourteenth Amendment due process clause. The leading national newspapers hailed the Court's decision as a significant step in the protection of "the human rights guaranteed to every citizen."[43]

For Brown, Ellington, and Shields, however, the Court's verdict at first meant little more than being spared from their imminent execution. All three remained in jail in Jackson, Mississippi, expecting their retrial. Eight months later, the three defendants agreed to a plea bargain with the local district attorney. Apparently, Brown, Shields, and Ellington were convinced that the local court would convict them again of murder, no matter how meager the evidence against them was. The three were sentenced to prison terms of ten, five, and three years, respectively. As their prior prison terms were taken into account, Ellington was finally discharged from prison in May 1937, Shields in February 1939, and Brown in December 1941.[44]

The Kemper case highlights both the severe limits and the emancipatory significance of the fight against the use of forced confessions in the 1930s South. On the one hand, it reveals the widespread acceptance of physical abuse and legal discrimination within Mississippi's criminal justice system. The brazen statements of the police officers during the trial indicate that they perceived the resort to torture as a self-evident and necessary method against African American suspects who were accused of serious offenses that put into question the racial order of the local community. Furthermore, the case shows that black defendants had little to expect from the local southern criminal justice system, as state attorneys, judges, and juries willfully ignored their basic legal rights. Moreover, the case documents that the men's fate hinged on their good fortune to be represented by well-meaning, supportive white lawyers and on gaining the support of the NAACP Legal Department and other supportive groups within the South.

On the other hand, the case indicates that extreme cases of civil rights abuse could function as a catalyst for civil rights activism. The founding of the Meridian chapter of the NAACP in reaction to the case institutionalized black civil rights activism on a local level. Furthermore, the financial assistance given by groups such as the CIC and the ASWPL highlights the support southern white liberal institutions and individuals offered the black civil rights struggle, even though they stopped short of attacking the structures of racial discrimination and oppression that supported the growth of this form of abuse.

A second court case from late 1930s Alabama further accentuates these findings. In addition, it directs our attention to another crucial dimension of the fight against forced confessions: the testimony of black defendants in southern courts. In March 1938 a forty-eight-year-old white nurse, Eunice Ward, and her sister Lillian Ward were assaulted and robbed in the outskirts of Alabama's capital, Montgomery. Eunice was killed in the attack, and Lillian was severely wounded. After Lillian claimed that their attacker was an unknown black man, police departments from several Alabama counties began the search, supported by bloodhounds. Six days after the attack, police officers arrested a twenty-six-year-old African American man, Dave Canty, in Mobile, Alabama, and transferred him to the state prison, Kilby Prison, in nearby Montgomery.[45] When the police brought Canty face-to-face with Ward, she could not say with certainty whether he was her attacker. One week later, the local newspapers reported on Canty's admission of guilt, accompanied by a word-for-word copy of his alleged confession.[46]

In the trial against him, which began two months later, Canty vocally repudiated his confession and declared himself not guilty of the crime. The local newspaper reported that, in a courtroom "packed with many spectators standing," he testified that he had been forced to confess to the crime after prolonged beatings.[47] To substantiate his allegations, Canty detailed the names and actions of several officers who had participated in his torture. In addition, he made use of nonverbal means to verify his claim. On request of his attorney, he walked to the jury bench and presented the scars on his body to the jury. The trial transcript notes that Canty "showed scars he said the officers put on him in beating him on both his legs and knees. Also scars on his hands." According to the transcript, Canty supported his gestures by saying: "All these scars there, and there." When state prosecutor W. T. Seibel sought to challenge Canty's claims by questioning the whereabouts of his scars, the defendant again presented his injuries to the jury. This action in turn provoked the anger of the prosecutor. Unnerved by the defendant's behavior, Seibel approached Canty aggressively: "Don't pull your pants up, I didn't want to see your ugly legs. Nobody wants to see your leg. Pull it down."[48]

These selected passages in the trial transcript reveal that Canty took an active part in his own defense. Canty's words and gestures must be read, following bell hooks and others who have conceptualized the implications of blacks' resistance to racial oppression, as a highly symbolic performance of opposition that comprised an integral element of the black freedom struggle. As hooks has argued, "Throughout African-American history, performance has been crucial in the struggle for liberation," since the "voice as instrument could be used by everyone, in any location."[49]

The concept of performativity directs our attention to the fact that meaning is constantly produced through public words and acts. While meaning can assume the notion of being fixed and stable through repetition of certain words and acts, it can also be challenged by adverse, unorthodox practices and speech acts.[50] The testimony of Dave Canty can be seen as such an adverse practice, as it broke with expectations on the appropriate behavior of black defendants in southern courts. The controversial nature of his speech acts and gestures became most evident in the angry reaction of the district attorney. By substantiating his torture allegations and asserting his innocence in front of the jury members, the judge, and the audience in the courtroom, Canty challenged his and other black defendants' subaltern positioning in southern criminal procedures. The report of the *Montgomery Advertiser* supports this interpretation, as it put special emphasis on Canty's performance in court. "Dave [Canty] described the alleged whippings with gesticulations which he said the officers went through in punishing him," the newspaper noted. "He frequently stood and on a few occasions walked to the rail in front of the jury box." The article also cited reactions to Canty's performance in court by several unnamed veteran police officers, who claimed that his "'tale about the beating he suffered' was 'the most fantastic account of the 'third degree' they had heard from the lips of any defendant or witness."[51]

These observations and findings are important because they broaden our understanding of the oppression endemic to the criminal justice system in the Jim Crow era. They show that trial procedures against black defendants were highly discriminatory yet at the same time contested events in which the accused questioned their inferior position in open court, even though their actions did not usually affect the initial outcome of their trials.[52]

The proceedings against Canty demonstrate this point. After the three-day trial, the jury in Montgomery declared him guilty of murder and sentenced him to death by electrocution.[53] The future development of Canty's case, however, also attests to the crucial legal implication of black defendants' courtroom testimony. Only when defendants and their lawyers repudiated their alleged confessions during the initial proceedings and challenged the legal admissibility of those confessions could verdicts be appealed to a higher court. This was especially true after the US Supreme Court's decision in

Brown v. Mississippi in 1936. Before this, the verdict of the Montgomery
Circuit Court would have most likely sealed Canty's fate. Now, however,
Canty's testimony and his support by two white local lawyers, the NAACP
Legal Department, and an emerging local NAACP branch eventually saved
him from the electric chair.

In April 1938, shortly after the police had released Canty's alleged confession to the local press, William G. Porter, assistant secretary of the NAACP
branch in Montgomery, Alabama, wrote a letter to New York to inform
Walter White, the longtime executive secretary of the NAACP, of the case.
His letter closed with the note: "They handled this man very roughly to get
his confessions."[54] In response, the NAACP Legal Department asked Porter
to send further information on the case.[55] A month later, after Porter did
not respond to this request, NAACP Special Counsel Thurgood Marshall
asked Dr. E. W. Taggart, president of the NAACP branch in Birmingham, to
conduct a "preliminary investigation" of the case. Marshall advised Taggart
to interview Canty's lawyer and seek permission to interview Canty himself.
He also cautioned that it might be "dangerous to make too searching an
investigation," as this was "the type of case which is being protected by the
authorities."[56] Two and a half weeks later, Taggart sent his report to Thurgood Marshall. Based on interviews taken in Montgomery, Taggart deemed
it most likely that Canty had been wrongly accused because of the "$1000
reward offered" and "the desire of the police to save their faces," adding,
"They have saddled the case upon Canty because it seems to fit him." Taggart
also reported on the findings of the Civic League, a local committee of black
citizens: "They beat Canty into confession. Dave is said by the committee
who talked to him that he 'just soon die one way as another' and signed
the confession the police had dictated."[57]

In his answer to the report, sent after Canty's conviction by the Montgomery Circuit Court in June 1938, Marshall asked Taggart to keep him
informed about the case and let him know if there were ways the Legal
Department could cooperate with the local effort on Canty's behalf. "I
personally believe this is a very important case which not only involved
the rights of Dave Canty, but will be of benefit to Negroes in the South in
general," Marshall wrote.[58] Taggart himself sent a letter to E. C. Jackson,
editor of the *Alabama Tribune*, Montgomery's black newspaper, urging him
to help revive the existing NAACP branch and foster within the local black
community the willingness to unite in the fight against racial injustice: "The
people of Montgomery ought [to] see, as a result of this apparent miscar-
riage of justice, that they need to form an organization that has the power
and moral courage to raise a voice of protest against that sort of thing."[59]

The archival records of the Montgomery NAACP branch indicate that "the people of Montgomery" did react to the case. Even before Canty's trial, Porter wrote to Walter White to ask for support in "reorganizing" the NAACP branch in Montgomery by supplying him with campaign literature and sending him the names and addresses of other NAACP activists in the South who might assist him in this undertaking.[60] Six weeks later, Porter reported that the Montgomery NAACP branch was "well organized" and had "taken over the Canty case," having paid $250 to have the briefs filed for the appeal of Canty's case to the Alabama Supreme Court. At the end of his letter, Porter wrote, "This is going to be a mean case and we are going through with it."[61] Maybe Porter felt assured by the rising membership numbers of the Montgomery branch, which gained fifty new members in July 1938 and thirty-six new members in August 1938.[62]

Through continuing efforts by local and national NAACP activists, the Montgomery branch collected $520, of which $270 were paid to Canty's lawyer, Edward W. Wadsworth, and $250 for the trial transcript, while Canty's family paid $500 to the lawyer. As many observers had expected, however, the Alabama Supreme Court affirmed the death sentence against Canty in June 1939.[63]

After the verdict, Marshall and Canty's new lawyer, Alex C. Birch, started to work on the appeal of the case to the US Supreme Court.[64] As Canty's execution drew closer, the NAACP branch membership numbers in Montgomery rose to about a thousand members.[65] In a letter of November 21, 1939, its new president, T. T. Allen, reported that "a Mrs. Rutledge who represents a group of liberal minded people here talked with me yesterday. . . . It appears that there is a great number of fairminded whites who believe that Canty is absolutely NOT GUILTY." Allen also noted that Rutledge had offered "to go before The [*sic*] Governor and the Pardon board and tell them what rumors are circulating in their circle."[66] As they did in the case of Brown, Ellington, and Shields, a well-meaning white lawyer and an unspecified number of well-meaning individuals within the local white community, some of whom became members of the local NAACP branch, supported Canty.[67]

Four months later, the US Supreme Court reversed the verdict against Canty and ordered a new trial. The Court based the decision on its verdict in *Chambers v. Florida* of the same year, in which it had annulled the death sentences against four black defendants from Florida on the grounds that police officers had applied "compulsion" to gain their confessions in another murder case.[68] As in the case of Brown, Ellington, and Shields, national newspapers hailed the decision as a further example of the Court's determination to secure equal justice for all Americans.[69] The NAACP itself celebrated the decision as a "reaffirmation of the fourteenth amendment of the Constitution" secured by the association.[70]

The enthusiasm proved to be largely unfounded, however. Although the Supreme Court's decision saved Canty from the electric chair, he was again tried for murder in Montgomery Circuit Court. To prevent a possible appeal, Montgomery state prosecutor Seibel refrained from introducing Canty's alleged confession as evidence. Canty was again convicted, now to life imprisonment. After the Alabama Supreme Court upheld the verdict, the US Supreme Court declined to review the decision. Canty died several years later in Kilby Prison, the same place where the police had allegedly tortured him into his purported confession.[71]

Different and ambiguous lessons can be drawn from the fight against forced confessions in the 1930s and 1940s South. By telling a story of extreme abuse and successful civil rights activism, the two cases presented here illuminate the transformation of the southern racial order at the time. While they show that white supremacy was still secured and defended by extreme and highly symbolic forms of physical abuse and an overtly discriminatory system of criminal justice, they also indicate that the racial order was contested. Those forces of contestation were located within and outside southern society. From outside the South, the use of forced confessions was challenged by a US Supreme Court, which, in accordance with the New Deal policy of the federal government, extended its oversight over state criminal procedure and challenged the racially discriminatory structures of the southern criminal justice system. The NAACP Legal Department's litigation campaign took up and strengthened this development by appealing controversial verdicts to the Court. The organization's legal victories established legal precedents that helped to appeal further decisions and erect legal barriers for the use of confessions in future trials both in the South and beyond.

The forces that contested the southern racial order from within are more difficult to discern. The two case studies presented, however, attest to the workings of those forces. In the case of Brown, Ellington, and Shields, the reckless beating and legal abuse of the three defendants initiated a quiet legal defense campaign by members of both the local white and black communities. Eventually, local resistance to the abuse of Brown, Ellington, and Shields led to the founding of a small but active NAACP chapter in one of the most racist places in the country at the time.

Similarly, the campaign for Dave Canty strengthened the civil rights consciousness of Montgomery's black community. It created the local organizational structures that five years later provided the base of actions on behalf of Recy Taylor, who was raped by six white men in Abbeville, Alabama. Eleven years later, the same NAACP chapter would buttress a further groundbreaking event in the African American fight for civil rights: the Montgomery Bus Boycott of 1955 and 1956.[72]

Moreover, both cases shed light on the emancipatory agency of black defendants in southern trial procedures. They highlight that black resistance to white forms of oppression was not limited to organized forms of protests but could also be located in individuals' words and gestures within the repressive context of southern courtrooms. At the same time, the cases indicate the complexities of this resistance and the severe limits placed on it. Both cases affirm that black civil rights struggles were highly contingent, as their outcomes depended on various factors, including defendants' initial support by local lawyers, their willingness to accuse the police of torture in court, and the successful mobilization of financial resources. It is safe to assume that many other black defendants at the time who were forced into confessions and afterward convicted failed to receive such support.

It is furthermore safe to say that the campaigns against forced confessions had no direct impact on the everyday use of police brutality and police torture against African Americans in the South. As police brutality was a matter of state criminal law, it had to be challenged from within by local initiatives. Southern state attorneys, however, hesitated to press charges against police officers accused of brutality against African Americans. When such cases came to court, southern juries regularly acquitted police officers. As a consequence, the NAACP national office called upon its local chapters to address the matter of police brutality through continuous protest and legal action. In a pamphlet published in June 1939, it advised its branches to record and investigate cases of police brutality in their respective communities and push criminal charges "in extreme cases of death or serious injury."[73] Despite these efforts, however, police brutality remained a widespread and largely unchallenged form of racial discrimination and oppression in the South well into the 1950s and beyond.

The systematic abuse of African Americans by southern police officers also continued largely unabated when the US Justice Department used the Federal Bureau of Investigation to prosecute selected cases of police brutality against African Americans in the South from the early 1940s on. The FBI's very first investigation was the case of Quintar South, discussed at the beginning of this chapter, which led to two mistrials in Atlanta's District Court. As I have shown elsewhere, the all-white juries of southern federal courts commonly acquitted southern police officers from civil rights violation charges throughout the 1940s and early 1950s. While the Department of Justice strove to enforce basic civil rights principles by prosecuting especially abusive police officers and sheriffs, southern white jurors perceived such prosecutions as unwarranted interferences into the southern racial order.[74] The history of police torture thus illustrates both the rigidity and the fragility of white supremacy in the Jim Crow South. While it attests to the slow and painful process of the African American struggle to assert basic civil rights against a profoundly racist social order, it also depicts a white southern community in a state of transition, when more whites began to consider the question of black humanity, and many others continued to refuse to.

NOTES

This chapter is adapted and translated from *Rassismus und Bürgerrechte: Polizeifolter im Süden der USA 1930–1955,* by Silvan Niedermeier. Copyright © 2014 by Hamburger Edition, Hamburg, Germany. Used by permission of the publisher. This chapter is also adapted from *Racism and Civil Rights: Police Torture in the American South, 1930–1955,* by Silvan Niedermeier. Translation by Paul Cohen. Copyright © 2019 by the University of North Carolina Press. Used by permission of the publisher. www.uncpress.org.

1. *Atlanta Constitution,* March 8, 1940, 1, 2.

2. *Atlanta Constitution,* March 9, 1940, 1, 2, March 10, 1940, 1; *Atlanta Journal,* March 9, 1940, 1, 2.

3. *Atlanta Constitution,* March 9, 1940, 4.

4. *Atlanta Daily World,* March 9, 1940, 1.

5. William A. Fowlkes, "Shall Brutalities Continue," *Atlanta Daily World,* March 31, 1940, 4.

6. *Atlanta Daily World,* June 21, 1940, 1, 6.

7. See Jacqueline Dowd Hall, "The Long Civil Rights Movement and the Political Uses of the Past," *Journal of American History* 91, no. 4 (2005): 1233–63. For critical perspectives on the "long movement" concept, see Sundiata Keita Cha-Jua and Clarence Lang, "The 'Long Movement' as Vampire: Temporal and Spatial Fallacies in Recent Black Freedom Studies," *Journal of African American History* 92, no. 2 (2007): 265–88; and Eric Arnesen, "Reconsidering the 'Long Civil Rights Movement,'" *Historically Speaking* 10, no. 2 (2009): 31–34.

8. See Silvan Niedermeier, "Police Brutality," in *The New Encyclopedia of Southern Culture,* vol. 19, *Violence,* ed. Amy Louise Wood (Chapel Hill: University of North Carolina Press, 2011), 130–32.

9. W. E. B. Du Bois, *Dusk of Dawn: An Essay toward an Autobiography of a Race Concept* (New York: Harcourt, Brace and Company, 1940), 182.

10. Arthur Franklin Raper, "Race and Class Pressures," Carnegie-Myrdal Study, "The Negro in America," June 1, 1940, manuscript, appendix A, 8–9, microfilm, New York Public Library.

11. Ibid., 24.

12. See Marvin W. Dulaney, *Black Police in America* (Bloomington: Indiana University Press, 1996).

13. Raper, "Race and Class Pressures," appendix D, table A-2, 11. Raper's numbers are based upon questionnaires filled out by the police chiefs of 228 towns and cities throughout the United States. The southern states included Alabama, Arkansas, Florida, Georgia, Louisiana, Mississippi, South Carolina, Kentucky, North Carolina, Tennessee, Virginia, Oklahoma, and Texas.

14. Ibid. The so-called Middle states included Indiana, Illinois, Michigan, Minnesota, Missouri, and Ohio.

15. Ibid., appendix D, tables A-1 and A-2, 10–11.

16. Ibid., 46.

17. Ibid., 55, 54.

18. See, for example, the recursion on the stereotype of the black aggressor by police officers and others in the debate on the police killing of Michael Brown in Ferguson, Missouri, in August 2014. Very instructive is Jake Halpern's "The Cop," *New Yorker*, August 10 and 17, 2015, www.newyorker.com/magazine/2015/08/10/the-cop (accessed May 5, 2017).

19. Gunnar Myrdal, *An American Dilemma: The Negro Problem and Modern Democracy* (New York: Harper, 1944), 536, 541.

20. See Silvan Niedermeier, *Rassismus und Bürgerrechte: Polizeifolter im Süden der USA 1930–1955* (Hamburg: Hamburger Edition, 2014), 212–31.

21. See Robert L. Zangrando, *The NAACP Crusade against Lynching, 1909–1950* (Philadelphia: Temple University Press, 1980); Amy Louise Wood, *Lynching and Spectacle: Witnessing Racial Violence in America, 1890–1940* (Chapel Hill: University of North Carolina Press, 2009), 179–221.

22. See Patricia Sullivan, *Lift Every Voice: The NAACP and the Making of the Civil Rights Movement* (New York: New Press, 2009), 216.

23. Michael J. Klarman, *From Jim Crow to Civil Rights: The Supreme Court and the Struggle for Racial Equality* (Oxford: Oxford University Press, 2004), 115, 117–35.

24. See Michael J. Klarman, "Is the Supreme Court Sometimes Irrelevant? Race and the Southern Criminal Justice System in the 1940s," *Journal of American History* 89, no. 1 (2002): 119–53; John F. Blevins, "*Lyons v. Oklahoma,* the NAACP, and Coerced Confessions under the Hughes, Stone, and Vinson Courts, 1936–1949," *Virginia Law Review* 90, no. 1 (2004): 387–464; Silvan Niedermeier, "Torture and 'Modern Civilization': The NAACP's Fight against Forced Confessions in the American South (1935–1945)," in *Fractured Modernity: America Confronts Modern Times, 1890s to 1940s,* ed. Thomas Welskopp and Alan Lessoff (Munich: Oldenbourg, 2012), 169–89.

25. The following analysis of *Brown v. Mississippi* is based in part on Richard Cortner's *A "Scottsboro" Case in Mississippi: The Supreme Court and "Brown v. Mississippi"* (Jackson: University Press of Mississippi, 1986).

26. *Daily Clarion-Ledger*, March 31, 1934, 1.

27. *Meridian Star*, April 1, 1934, 1.

28. *Meridian Star*, April 3, 1934, 1, 9.

29. *Meridian Star*, April 2, 1934, 1, 9.

30. *Meridian Star*, April 3, 1934, 1, 9.

31. *Meridian Star*, April 5, 1934, 1.

32. *Meridian Star*, April 7, 1934, 1.

33. "Kemper Proves Itself," *Meridian Star*, April 8, 1934, 4.

34. Brown v. Mississippi, 297 U.S. 278 (1936), Transcript of Record, 43, in *U.S. Supreme Court Records and Briefs, 1832–1978*, Gale, Cengage Learning, http://galenet.galegroup.com/servlet/SCRB?uid=0&srchtp=a&ste=14&rcn=DW3904120749 (accessed May 5, 2017).

35. Ibid.

36. Ibid., 113, 124.

37. See Niedermeier, *Rassimus und Bürgerrechte*, 76–110.

38. Cortner, *A "Scottsboro" Case*, 46, 49.

39. Ibid., 56, 57, 70.

40. Ibid., 59, 60, 64–77.

41. Cited in ibid., 72.

42. See ibid., 81, 89–108, 95 (table), 94.

43. *Washington Post*, February 19, 1936, 8; *New York Times*, February 21, 1936, 16.

44. Cortner, *A "Scottsboro" Case*, 153, 159.

45. *Montgomery Advertiser*, March 27, 1938, 1.

46. *Montgomery Advertiser*, April 4, 1938, 1, 3.

47. *Montgomery Advertiser*, June 4, 1938, 1, 3; Dave Canty v. State of Alabama, October Term 1939–40, 3rd Division 293–300, Trial Transcript, 147, Alabama Supreme Court, Record of Cases, 1824–1974, vol. 3, 697, Alabama Department of Archives and History.

48. *Dave Canty*, Trial Transcript, 149, 147, 156.

49. See bell hooks, "Performance Practice as a Site of Opposition," in *Let's Get It On: The Politics of Black Performance*, ed. Catherine Ugwu (Seattle, WA: Bay Press, 1995), 210–11.

50. See Judith Hamera, ed., *Opening Acts: Performance in/as Communication and Cultural Studies* (Thousand Oaks, CA: Sage Publications, 2006); Jürgen Martschukat and Steffen Patzold, "Geschichtswissenschaft und 'Performative Turn': Eine Einführung in Fragestellungen, Konzepte und Literatur," in *Geschichtswissenschaft und "Performative Turn": Ritual, Inszenierung und Performanz; Vom Mittelalter bis zur Neuzeit*, ed. Jürgen Martschukat and Steffen Patzold (Cologne: Böhlau, 2003), 1–32.

51. *Montgomery Advertiser*, June 4, 1938, 1, 3.

52. For a similar perspective on African American testimony, see Kidada E. Williams's study *They Left Great Marks on Me: African American Testimonies of Racial Violence from Emancipation to World War I* (New York: New York University

Press, 2012). See also Lisa Lindquist Dorr's analysis of black defendants' testimony in rape trials in Virginia: *White Women, Rape, and the Power of Race in Virginia, 1900–1960* (Chapel Hill: University of North Carolina Press, 2004), 169–204.

53. *Montgomery Advertiser*, June 5, 1938, 1, 2.

54. William G. Porter to Walter White, Montgomery, AL, April 4, 1938, NAACP Papers, Group II, box B-27, Library of Congress (LOC).

55. Charles Houston to W. G. Porter, New York, NY, April 14, 1938, NAACP Papers, Group II, box B-27, LOC.

56. Thurgood Marshall to Dr. E. W. Taggart, New York, NY, May 12, 1938, NAACP Papers, Group II, box B-27, LOC.

57. Dr. E. W. Taggart, "Facts in the Case of Dave Canty," Birmingham, AL, March 31, 1938, NAACP Papers, Group II, box B-27, LOC.

58. Thurgood Marshall to E. W. Taggart, New York, NY, June 16, 1938, NAACP Papers, Group II, box B-27, LOC.

59. E. W. Taggert to E. C. Jackson, Birmingham, AL, June 8, 1938, NAACP Papers, Group II, box B-27, LOC.

60. W. G. Porter to Walter White, Montgomery, AL, May 31, 1938, NAACP Branch Files, Montgomery Branch, NAACP Papers, Group I, box G-7, LOC.

61. W. G Porter to Walter White, Montgomery, AL, July 9, 1938, NAACP Papers, Group II, box B-27, LOC.

62. See the membership lists of July 18, August 1, and August 4, 1938, in NAACP Branch Files, Montgomery Branch, NAACP Papers, Group I, box G-7, LOC.

63. T. M. Blair to Walter White, Montgomery, AL, June 24, 1939, NAACP Papers, Group II, box B-27, LOC.

64. Thurgood Marshall to Alex C. Birch, New York, NY, August 3, 1939; Alex C. Birch to Thurgood Marshall, Montgomery, AL, October 14, 1939, NAACP Papers, Group II, box B-27, LOC.

65. This number is given in a letter of W. G. Porter to Walter White, Montgomery, October 29, 1939, NAACP Papers, Group I, box G-7, NAACP Branch Files, Montgomery Branch, LOC. In March, April, and September 1939 the Montgomery branch gained about 350 new members. See NAACP Branch Files, Montgomery Branch, NAACP Papers, Group I, box G-7, LOC.

66. T. T. Allen to Walter White, Montgomery, AL, November 11, 1939, NAACP Papers, Group II, box B-27, LOC.

67. The local membership reports do not indicate the race or skin color. They show, however, that the above-mentioned Mrs. T. B. Rutledge became a member in September 1939. See NAACP Branch Files, Montgomery Branch, NAACP Papers, Group I, box G-7, LOC.

68. Justice Hugo L. Black quoted in *Washington Post*, March 12, 1940, 4.

69. See, for example, *Chicago Defender*, March 23, 1940, 8; *New York Times*, March 12, 1940, 22.

70. "U.S. Supreme Court Stops Execution of Dave Canty, Alabama Torture Victim," March 15, 1940, NAACP Press Release, NAACP Papers, Group II, box B-27, LOC.

71. See Rawn James Jr., *Root and Branch: Charles Hamilton Houston, Thurgood Marshall, and the Struggle to End Segregation* (New York: Bloomsbury Press, 2010), 121.

72. See Danielle L. McGuire, *At the Dark End of the Street: Black Women, Rape, and Resistance—a New History of the Civil Rights Movement from Rosa Parks to the Rise of Black Power* (New York: Alfred A. Knopf, 2010).

73. NAACP National Office, "Legal Defense Materials: Part IV, Methods of Combating Police Brutality," New York, June 1939, NAACP Papers, Group I, Series B, box 16, LOC. I thank Brandon Jett for bringing this pamphlet to my attention.

74. See Silvan Niedermeier, "Violence, Visibility, and the Investigation of Police Torture in the American South, 1940–1955," in *Violence and Visibility in Modern History*, ed. Jürgen Martschukat and Silvan Niedermeier (New York: Palgrave Macmillan, 2013), 91–111.

CHAPTER 4

THE SOUTH'S SIN CITY

White Crime and the Limits of Law and Order in Phenix City, Alabama

Tammy Ingram

A stranger passing through Phenix City, Alabama, around 1950 would have found a sleepy-looking town nestled in the bluffs along the Chattahoochee River. A string of storefronts with names like Yarbrough's Café and Davis Sporting Goods lined the streets, and a steady flow of cars and pedestrians crossed the two bridges linking Phenix City to Columbus, Georgia, just across the river. Residents bragged that one of the last battles of the Civil War—sometimes they claimed *the* last battle—occurred there on April 16, 1865, a week after the Confederate surrender at Appomattox. Phenix City had been called Girard for nearly a century before merging with a neighboring town in 1923. It became the county seat of Russell County in 1932.[1] By 1950 Phenix City was one of the ten largest cities in Alabama, still less than a quarter of the size of the state capital, Montgomery, eighty miles to the west, and not even a third of the size of Columbus, just one hundred yards to the east, but prosperous enough to have a modern courthouse, a brand new hospital, a movie theater, and fifty churches, thirty-seven white and thirteen black, one for every 450 residents.[2]

Yet, Phenix City was no ordinary Bible Belt town. During the first half of the twentieth century, it was the headquarters of a powerful organized crime syndicate. Downtown turned into the mob's central business district after dark, when the neon lights of bars, brothels, and gambling dens lit up the night sky along Fourteenth Street. Yarbrough's Café and Davis Sporting Goods were mob fronts, as were other innocuous-sounding businesses like the Bridge Grocery and Cliff's Fish Camp, which doubled as a brothel. Soldiers from nearby Fort Benning made up most of the clientele in the cheap clip joints, but serious gamblers traveled from as far away as New York and Chicago to play at elite casinos like the Bama Club. Fats Domino even played in Phenix City, though only at black clubs. Crime lords did not respect the law, but in Jim Crow Alabama not even the mob dared to cross the color line.[3]

Any semblance of law and order in Alabama ended at the Russell County line, where local officials made sure the mob could work unimpeded. The number of cops and city officials on the syndicate's payroll made it hard to tell where the rackets ended and local government began. The mob cultivated political connections outside Russell County as well. They mingled with Democratic Party officials at fund-raisers in Washington, DC, and campaigned for candidates in state elections. In return, state officials turned a blind eye to what went on in Russell County.[4] The mob's connections shielded it from prosecution but also from public scrutiny. It seemed as if everyone and no one knew the truth about Phenix City.

All of that changed on the night of June 18, 1954, when someone assassinated a local crime-fighting lawyer named Albert Patterson outside his downtown law office. Eight days earlier Patterson had won the Democratic primary—the only election that mattered in Alabama in 1954—in the attorney general's race by vowing to use his authority as the state's chief law enforcement officer to shut down the Phenix City mob. The high-profile murder stunned Alabamians and captured the attention of the nation. *Look* magazine profiled the dark history of "America's Wickedest City," and *Life* published a photo editorial about the investigation into the nation's "most sinful" small town.[5] Once Alabama's dirty secret, Phenix City became synonymous with crime and corruption nationwide.

The publicity embarrassed locals, but it fulfilled Albert Patterson's goal of cleaning up Phenix City faster than a crime-fighting crusade could have. Outside scrutiny shattered the impunity of the racketeering conspiracy by exposing its ties to corrupt government officials and forcing the state to respond. Pulitzer Prize–winning newspaper coverage by the *Columbus Ledger-Enquirer* and a Hollywood feature film called *The Phenix City Story* kept the city in the headlines while state investigators pursued Patterson's killers and shut down the illegal businesses. By the end of the year, most county and city officials had been fired, and 144 people had been indicted.[6]

Within a year of Albert Patterson's death, the national fascination with the Phenix City organized crime scandal had faded. The swift completion of what locals called "the cleanup" transformed the tragedy of the Patterson assassination into a story of the city's triumph over the mob. Like the mythical bird for which the city was said to be named, Phenix City rose from the ashes of crime and corruption and was reborn a clean, quiet town. Newspapers praised state investigators for their diligence and portrayed Patterson as a martyred hero. Grateful citizens erected a historical marker on the spot where he died and memorialized him with a statue on the grounds of the state capitol in Montgomery. Just a year after the murder, the National Civic League named Phenix City an "All-America City" for eradicating crime and corruption. Townspeople and political luminaries celebrated with a parade and a televised ceremony in front of a freshly painted city hall, and Governor James Folsom used the occasion to announce state funding for new highways and bridges in Phenix City.[7] Soon the city's transformation became more memorable than its old reputation. Three years after Patterson's murder, a reporter who had seen Phenix City at its worst returned and found it "as quiet and respectable as a prayer meeting." By the fiftieth anniversary of the Patterson murder in 2004, nothing was left of the city's sordid past. Even the historical marker was gone. Alabama's Sin City was "just a memory," a quirky anecdote about a town that had long since moved on.[8]

This refolding of Phenix City back into a familiar narrative of post–civil rights era progress in the South has all but erased it from popular and scholarly memory. It has obscured the scope and seriousness of organized crime in the Jim Crow South and precluded important questions about why organized crime thrived there in the first place. And it has cost historians the opportunity to examine more fully the ways in which race and politics shaped official responses to criminality. Although scholars of southern politics have written volumes about antidemocratic, segregationist regimes, few focus on crime and corruption in those administrations, and none address organized crime.[9] Outstanding scholarship on crime and punishment has illuminated the deep historical roots of black criminalization and the brutal carceral systems that disproportionately imprisoned African Americans, but this work, too, has overlooked the rise of white criminal enterprises under those same Jim Crow governments.[10] Similarly, the timely new work on policing and mass incarceration has deepened our understanding of law-and-order politics but locates the origins of law-and-order campaigns in the late 1960s and early 1970s, when urban black communities were targeted almost exclusively, and overlooks the campaigns of the late 1940s and early 1950s that exposed white crime and government corruption.[11] While organized crime syndicates in New York, Chicago, and Los Angeles have been written into historiographies spanning the entire first half of the twentieth century, the native-born Phenix City mob has attracted only a handful of true crime writers and novelists, none of whom explore it in its full historical context.[12]

White criminal syndicates were not as pervasive as the mechanisms that criminalized African Americans in the Jim Crow South, but the failure to prosecute even the most egregious cases of white crime under Jim Crow governments suggests that the decriminalization of whites was as important a function of those governments as the criminalization of African Americans. While the Phenix City rackets were not representative of white crime in the South more generally, the fact that such a visible and violent operation could flourish there underscores just how consciously white citizens and especially public officials tolerated, minimized, and even enabled white criminal enterprises. Immunity from prosecution was one of the rewards of white supremacy. Safeguarding that immunity in a place like Phenix City, however, also required the same fierce reverence for local control that had enabled Jim Crow regimes for decades.

This chapter uses the Phenix City mob to explore how state-sanctioned crime shaped politics and justice in Jim Crow Alabama. It briefly establishes the mob's origins in the nineteenth and early twentieth centuries in order to show how the institutionalization of white supremacy and local political control allowed organized crime to expand. The rest of the chapter focuses on the mob in the 1940s and early 1950s, at the height of its power, in order to show that the relationships between racketeers and public officials were critical to consolidating the power of the mob and shielding it from prosecution. By midcentury, government and organized crime in Phenix City were interdependent. From this perspective, Albert Patterson's law-and-order campaign looks like a direct challenge to an entrenched criminal regime, not just a simple moral crusade against vice and corruption. Patterson's murder was the mob's downfall, but his crusade and martyrdom did not represent the triumph of law and order. Instead, they were testaments to the difficulty of targeting white criminal enterprises in the Jim Crow South.

While this chapter does not explore the differences between southern syndicates and their more famous counterparts in the urban North, it does challenge the stereotypes that dominate histories of northern crime syndicates. Rather than trivialize the Phenix City mob or make gangster caricatures out of racketeers and corrupt politicians, this chapter argues that the region's unique economic and political challenges allowed organized crime to grow unfettered. The mob thrived especially well in Phenix City, a town not actually named for a mythical bird that regenerated itself but for an imposing cotton mill just over the river in Georgia, the name a nagging reminder that the only real industry in Phenix City for over half a century was vice.[13]

When Irish stage actor Tyrone Power visited Georgia on his tour of America in 1833, he stopped in Columbus and marveled at the differences between that city and the "wild looking village" populated by "gamblers, and other desperate men" just over the river. Although Alabama had become a state in 1819, Russell County was still mostly Creek territory and a safe haven for fugitives and outlaws from Georgia. In Columbus, residents talked about "the condition of this near community, and the crimes perpetrated by its members . . . with a mingled sentiment of detestation and fear." Criminals regularly crossed back and forth between the two cities, but the US marshal in Columbus did not have the manpower to stop them. Although the lawless town was named Girard, Power adopted the local custom of calling it Sodom.[14]

Power's description of the wild village that became Phenix City echoes other accounts of the "Old Southwest" of present-day Alabama and Mississippi, where drunkenness, violent brawls, and murders were testaments to the lawlessness of frontier life, but his observations about the town's strained relationship with Columbus foreshadowed the geographic and economic circumstances that allowed illegal enterprises to thrive in Alabama well into the next century.[15] Two decades after Power's visit, a dispute between mill owners in Girard and Columbus ended in a US Supreme Court decision affirming that most of the Chattahoochee River belonged to Georgia.[16] The ruling crippled Girard's fledgling industry by restricting access to waterpower but helped Columbus become the South's second largest cotton manufacturing city by the Civil War and home to its largest mill by 1900.[17] The city expanded further after the construction of the Fort Benning army base in 1918. As Columbus grew ever larger in the 1920s, the newly renamed Phenix City became a commercial backwater, literally on the margins of the industrial South. But it was also within shouting distance of mill villages and an army camp, both teeming with thousands of customers for the dingy taverns and gambling dens clustered around the bridges at Fourteenth Street and Dillingham Street that linked the city to Columbus.[18]

While Phenix City's location facilitated the growth of illegal industries, Jim Crow state making helped to shield them from scrutiny. In 1901 Alabama joined other Deep South states by disfranchising black voters through a new state constitution. In addition to a labyrinthine system of poll taxes and literacy tests designed to disfranchise African Americans while providing loopholes for poor or illiterate whites, delegates to the constitutional convention also disfranchised citizens for a broad range of felony and misdemeanor convictions. Criminal disfranchisement was a common feature of new southern state constitutions, but it was more pronounced in Alabama, where the range of crimes for which a citizen could lose voting rights was much broader. Although this provision served as an extra safeguard against black suffrage, it also reinforced ideas about black criminality and increased the incentive for law enforcement and judicial officials to exercise discretion in applying the law equally to whites.[19]

The new state constitution facilitated that process primarily at the local level. While shoring up white supremacy was the convention's top priority, delegates also crafted what historian Sheldon Hackney characterized as "a small passive referee state" that preserved local control over day-to-day governance. One provision cut the legislative session in half, while another curtailed the power of the executive branch by prohibiting officials such as governors, secretaries of state, treasurers, and attorneys general from serving consecutive terms in office.[20] This created a fractious and disordered state government in which political contests were, as V. O. Key observed in his landmark study of southern politics, "free-for-all[s], with every man looking out for himself," and contributed to an atmosphere of "frontier independence" in which local citizens were unafraid to defy state leaders.[21] These restrictions on state power also insulated local officials from close oversight by state leaders in the first place. A rare instance of state intervention in Russell County proved the rule in 1916, when Attorney General Logan Martin impeached Sheriff Pal M. Daniel for refusing to enforce the state's new prohibition law. Angry citizens and local officials obstructed the investigation, and Governor Charles Henderson condemned Martin's display of "unlimited authority" and refused to pay his expenses. Saloons remained open, and citizens voted Daniel back into office in 1923.[22]

By the time Key published his analysis of Alabama politics in 1949, however, frontier metaphors underestimated the regime in control of Phenix City. The outlaws and simple saloonkeepers of the city's early years had been replaced by more organized and dangerous professionals by the 1940s. Some had criminal records dating back to the 1920s that included charges for murder, manslaughter, and theft and, in the case of Metropolitan Lottery owner Clarence Revel, a felony conviction for smuggling Chinese immigrants into the United States through Cuba. Most were from Phenix City originally, all were from the South, and all were white. Phenix City served as both a safe haven and a business opportunity for them. By 1940 the undisputed kingpin of the rackets was Hoyt Shepherd, a transplant from the cotton mills of nearby LaGrange, Georgia, who partnered with Phenix City native Jimmy Matthews to form the S&M Amusement Company. Their Old Reliable Lottery, known as "the Bug," was Phenix City's largest lottery by the 1940s. Shepherd and Matthews also installed slot machines in regular businesses around town, including the local drugstore. There was even one in the Phenix City post office. By the 1950s slots alone earned the S&M syndicate between $30,000 and $50,000 a week.

Gambling was the biggest business in town, but racketeers were also involved in narcotics and prostitution. The best-known brothel in town was run out of Beachie's Swing Club, named for "Ma" Beachie Howard, a tiny woman in her fifties whose white dresses, wire-framed glasses, and hair bun belied her role as a madam. Fewer than twenty people owned the various rackets in Phenix City, but they employed hundreds of local residents as bartenders, bouncers, dancers, prostitutes, lottery ticket writers, janitors, and runners. By the 1950s the county had no fewer than fifty-one bars, brothels, lottery headquarters, and casinos. Most were segregated, and all were white-owned; only three served black patrons exclusively. Only the lotteries, which sold tickets on the streets for as little as a penny, did not discriminate on the basis of race. Around town the lottery was known as a black trade, even though whites were the only ones who profited from it.[23]

What transformed Phenix City from an outlaw town into a headquarters for organized crime, however, was not the business acumen of a new generation of racketeers but their unique partnership with the city government, one born of economic necessity and nurtured by laissez-faire state government. Saloonkeepers and gaming house operators profited from the expansion of textile mills and the growth of Fort Benning in the 1920s, but the rest of the local economy remained stagnant. By the start of the Depression the city was close to defaulting on more than a million dollars in debt. In 1933, with no other industries to turn to, city commissioners voted to tax illegal businesses by issuing licenses and instituting a system of fines and fees that generated money for the city treasury but no serious legal consequences for the guilty party. The arrangement kept both the city and the rackets afloat. It made city officials appear vigilant in enforcing the law but enabled racketeers to expand their operations without fear of being shut down.[24] It was the first formal alliance between local government and the rackets, and it would be the foundation of two decades of unprecedented growth, prosperity, and corruption in Phenix City.

Hoyt Shepherd and Jimmy Matthews tested the limits of this fledgling financial and legal partnership for the first time in 1938, when they defied city inspectors who had warned them about structural problems in the "Bug House," their lottery headquarters. On April 20 a section of the floor gave way, injuring ten patrons, but Shepherd and Matthews refused to close the doors. The following afternoon, while as many as 250 ticket holders waited on the top floor for the winning numbers to be announced, the entire building collapsed. The crowd that gathered outside could hear the cries of injured people trapped in the rubble.[25] A photographer captured grisly images of bodies trapped between the pancaked floors of the building, and reporters described a "ghastly" scene littered with "lottery tickets tinged scarlet with the blood of the players." The governor sent National Guardsmen to help with the rescue and recovery efforts, which continued overnight. By morning two dozen people were dead and eighty-three others seriously injured, all but four of them African Americans. Shepherd and Matthews, two of the wealthiest white men in the city, escaped the disaster unscathed. Newspaper accounts did not even mention the two men, despite noting that the number of casualties made this one of the deadliest accidents in state history. Police dodged questions about possible charges. Survivors were afraid to testify, so the city commission dropped its half-hearted inquiry. The lottery never missed a beat. One reporter observed that the very next day "lottery slips were available to workers digging into the debris still seeking bodies."[26]

The Bug House disaster affirmed the immunity of the all-white Phenix City mob even as black residents faced grossly disproportionate rates of arrest and imprisonment. Between 1920 and 1940 70 percent of the people jailed in Russell County were African American, outstripping even the state average. In 1934, the year after the city went into business with the mob, the county did not record a single white arrest.[27] As historian Khalil Muhammad has argued, branding African Americans as criminals was central to the enforcement of white supremacy. What Muhammad calls the "condemnation of blackness" absolved whites of the responsibility to apply the rule of law with fairness and consistency in Alabama as it did elsewhere.[28] In Phenix City it also validated an unlawful and dangerous alliance between white violators of the law and the local government officials in charge of enforcing it.

That alliance took shape just in time for business to surge during World War II. Despite the city's reputation among big-time gamblers, the rackets depended primarily on traffic from Fort Benning. The base's population swelled to nearly one hundred thousand when the war began, and six times that many soldiers trained there during the war. A total of 1.3 million passed through the infantry school between 1941 and 1954. Payrolls averaged $53 million a year during that same period. Much of that money ended up in the dives and brothels across the river. Army officials worried about the dangers Phenix City posed to soldiers, who were cheated, robbed, or beaten if they complained or got out of line. Rates of venereal disease at Fort Benning exceeded the army's average as well. Base officials occasionally declared Phenix City off-limits, but realistically the army could not stop what one observer called "the khaki colored torrent" that poured over the Chattahoochee when the sun went down.[29]

Although Fort Benning had one of the highest concentrations of black soldiers of any base in the country, most of the dives in Phenix City were open to whites only. A handful of white-owned black clubs were located a couple of miles south of downtown, but they catered to a local clientele. Racketeers profited from black clubs, but only within the limits of a deeply segregated community in the Alabama Black Belt. Some of them were reported to be members of the local Klan chapter, alongside city officials and ordinary businessmen. Regular Klan parades through downtown Phenix City served as a reminder to black soldiers that the mob was not the only powerful white organization in town.[30]

So did the way Fort Benning officials treated black soldiers. In 1941 a nineteen-year-old black soldier named Felix Hall disappeared on his way to the post exchange, but there is no record of base officials either notifying his family or mounting a search for him. Instead, they declared him a deserter. When his body was found a month later, hanging from a rope in the woods between the barracks and the Chattahoochee River, a base physician ruled it a suicide. The FBI concluded that Hall had been murdered and zeroed in on two white soldiers as suspects, but Fort Benning officials continued to tell the public that Hall had taken his own life. Investigators also seemed fixated on Hall's reputation. Though he had no criminal record and a spotless military record, agents repeatedly questioned witnesses about his alleged transgressions, which included drinking with white men at a bar in Montgomery months before his death and associating with a white woman on base. And among the leading theories about motives for his murder was that Hall had refused to address his white bosses at the sawmill where he worked as "sir." (Like most black soldiers at Fort Benning, Hall was assigned to a labor crew on base.) The FBI file on Hall's murder does not mention Fort Benning's relationship to Phenix City or contain any references whatsoever to either white or black soldiers engaging in illegal activities there. After a lackluster investigation the case stalled and was never solved. His family never even found out where he had been buried.[31]

If Felix Hall's case served as a grim reminder that Jim Crow justice subjected black men, even soldiers murdered on federal property, to unjust scrutiny, the wartime boom proved its utility to white violators of the law. By the time the FBI concluded the investigation into Hall's death, his infantry unit had been sent to the Pacific. More soldiers poured into Fort Benning and more money into the pockets of white racketeers in Phenix City. While the mob's earnings are impossible to verify, estimates ranged between $50 million and $100 million annually during the war years.[32] Such staggering profits multiplied the incentives for Phenix City officials to cooperate with the mob. Mayor Homer Cobb admitted publicly that the city depended on organized crime to stay afloat. In 1946, he told a reporter, fines alone generated $83,000 and liquor taxes another $46,000. Cobb estimated that income from the rackets covered at least 60 percent of the city's expenses. This arrangement also paid dividends to residents through lower property taxes, a perk that city officials used more like a threat to forestall complaints. As Mayor Cobb warned, "Citizens must either be tolerant and depend on fines, forfeitures and license fees from the rackets or they must face a tax increase."[33]

By making illegal businesses part of Phenix City's normal revenue stream, even under the pretense of policing them with fines and penalties, city commissioners effectively decriminalized them. But they relied on the coordinated efforts of other city and county officials as well. Racketeers derived most of their power and virtually all their freedom to operate openly from law enforcement and the county courts, which shielded them from prosecution for violating state laws governing alcohol sales, gambling, and prostitution. Occasional arrests and minor penalties gave the impression of vigilance without posing any real threat to the mob's operations, especially since the most powerful racketeers were never targeted directly. Hoyt Shepherd's partner, Jimmy Matthews, was so confident in his own immunity that he enjoyed making the weekly rounds to empty the syndicate's slot machines. Shepherd bragged to associates that he never had to worry about any trouble from the law. He was close to Russell County sheriff Ralph Mathews and treated the sheriff's office in the courthouse as his own, using it to make phone calls and conduct business.[34] Mathews did not involve himself in the mob's business affairs, but he ran interference when they needed it, usually by pretending not to notice that anything was wrong. When a group of ministers confronted the sheriff about having failed to respond to a string of complaints about the rackets, he simply ignored them too.[35]

The mob's most important ally in local law enforcement was Mathews's chief deputy, Albert Fuller. Fuller was an omnipresent figure around Phenix City, known for his big western hats and ever-present sidearm. He joined the Sheriff's Department soon after graduating from high school in Phenix City in 1937 and became Mathews's second-in-command and the mob's chief enforcer after Mathews was elected sheriff in 1946. Fuller had a reputation as a bully. He used his badge as a license to beat, harass, and arrest competitors or troublesome patrons, and in 1949 it saved him from a murder charge. In March of that year Fuller killed Guy Hargrett during what the sheriff and Fuller claimed was a liquor raid, but was probably retribution for Hargrett's side business: an unauthorized lottery that cut into the syndicate's profits. Fuller made as much as $6,000 a week working for the mob, most of it from his partnership in Cliff Entrekin's Fish Camp, a restaurant on Highway 80 that doubled as the county's largest brothel.[36]

Albert Fuller's direct involvement with the mob had a profound impact on the size and scope of the rackets, especially the prostitution business. After World War II at least six brothels operated openly in Russell County—Beachie's Swing Club, the Social Club, the Hilltop House, the Circle Motel, Cliff's Fish Camp, and the Uchee Fish Camp—but some bars and casinos sold sex as well. With Fuller's help the owners of some of these businesses also established a prostitution ring that trafficked young women throughout the South. State investigators later estimated that approximately five hundred prostitutes were employed in Phenix City at any given time, but many more worked the sex circuit in cities such as Miami, Jacksonville, Savannah, and New Orleans. Although some women were pressed into service by their husbands or male guardians, Fuller and his business partners used the threat of arrest and the specter of debt to draw young poor white women into the business. Potential recruits were sometimes bailed out of the county jail and made to work off the debt. Once ensnared by the rackets, they were coerced into staying. Physical violence and drugs were methods of control, and any infractions of syndicate rules incurred fines that effectively forced women into debt bondage. During the cleanup in 1954, state investigators discovered that some sex workers had been tattooed with the initials of their employers inside their bottom lip to prevent competitors from poaching them.[37]

Fuller's involvement in the prostitution ring was arguably the most damaging of all the links between public officials and the rackets. Not only did it endanger hundreds, probably thousands, of women, but it also helped to block the only possible avenue for federal intervention in Phenix City before 1954. While gambling and alcohol sales were governed by state and local laws, and fornication was illegal under Alabama law, the interstate sex ring violated the federal Mann Act of 1910, which forbade the transportation of women across state lines for any "immoral purpose."[38] Phenix City's proximity to the Georgia border, especially to Fort Benning, made violations of the Mann Act all the more likely.[39] Fuller's involvement shielded sex traffickers from local or state charges, but so did the federalism that shored up his authority. Two Alabama congressmen had led the southern opposition to the Mann Act in 1910 on the grounds that it "invaded" the "police rights" of the state "under the pretense of aiding and improving morality," and opposition to federal intervention had only intensified in the years since. The Mann Act was difficult to enforce without local and state cooperation because the FBI deferred to local law enforcement and prosecutors during investigations. Nationwide the FBI's conviction rate for violations was only 13 percent, and the vast majority of cases never made it to court at all.[40] With no possibility of cooperation from corrupt law enforcement officials in Phenix City, then, one of the few instruments that might have curtailed the growth of organized crime there was rendered useless.

By the 1940s a corrupt political regime had turned Phenix City into a refuge for white criminals. But the mob's immunity was never fixed. Maintaining it demanded constant effort and adaptation, because as racketeers expanded their operations they also pushed the limits of the local government's protection. In September 1946 Hoyt Shepherd killed a rival gambler named Fayette Leeburn at the Southern Manor, a downtown gambling den, after a months-long dispute over the slot machine business. The murder scandal might have been easier for local officials to contain had it not occurred in the middle of a party celebrating the election of Shepherd's friend Elmer Reese to the Phenix City council. Witnesses implicated Shepherd, but Shepherd and his brother Grady claimed that Grady shot Leeburn in self-defense. A grand jury indicted both for murder. Shepherd hired all four lawyers in Phenix City, including Albert Patterson, a middle-aged family law practitioner whom Shepherd put in charge of his defense. Patterson's inexperience proved to be of little consequence during the trial. The Phenix City Police Department failed to record the names of most eyewitnesses at the party and did not preserve evidence at the murder scene. Under questioning from the prosecutor, Circuit Solicitor A. S. Borders, one police officer testified that he had inadvertently destroyed fingerprint evidence by handling the murder weapon. A parade of defense witnesses backed up Shepherd's version of events and attacked the credibility of the state's key witness, a former "dice girl" named Jeanette Mercer. Clyde Yarbrough did so even while admitting under oath that he was Shepherd's partner in an illegal gambling operation. After deliberating for just four hours, the jury acquitted Hoyt Shepherd in October 1946, scarcely a month after the murder. Grady Shepherd was acquitted in a separate trial a few months later.[41]

While the verdicts surprised no one, the trial put the crime ring on the defensive. Solicitor Borders went to the press with allegations of jury tampering following the first trial, claiming that thousands of Russell County residents were being systematically excluded from jury duty to prevent convictions. A week after Hoyt Shepherd's acquittal, *Columbus Ledger* reporters looking into Russell County court records found evidence of routine failures to prosecute racketeers. The paper ran a front-page story detailing how, in one eighteen-month period between mid-1945 and late 1946, fifty-six people were arrested for violating the state gambling laws, but none went to trial. All were allowed to forfeit bonds instead. The city moved quickly to control the damage, but not by cracking down on the rackets. Just four days after the *Ledger* story, the city commission voted to ban reporters from accessing court and police records. Shortly thereafter the city passed a resolution imposing steep business taxes on any newspapers with local circulations of one thousand or more, an obvious effort to target the *Ledger*, technically an out-of-state publication but the largest of the "local" papers in Phenix City. Meanwhile, the racketeers used patronage, not punishments, to counter the negative press. A few weeks after the trial, Hoyt Shepherd, Jimmy Matthews, and Clyde Yarbrough donated $80,000 toward the construction of a new city hospital. The Cobb Memorial Hospital, named for the mayor, opened the following year.[42]

It would take more than vengeance or charity, however, to shield the mob from outside scrutiny, as it grew more powerful, more visible, and more violent after the war. During closing arguments in the Shepherd trial, A. S. Borders warned that Phenix City was at a crossroads. "One road leads to hoodlumism and anarchy," he said, "and the other road to peace and law and order."[43] For Borders the trial was a referendum on the city's future and a guilty verdict the first step toward dissolving the criminal alliance between racketeers and city officials. Borders lost the case, but his strategy convinced the racketeers that they were at a crossroads as well. The mob's political power did not extend beyond the county line in 1946. For years the mob had depended upon the tacit cooperation of conservative state officials who did not want to intervene in local affairs, but it had little influence at the state level. The election of the mob's preferred candidate for governor, James Folsom, a few days after Hoyt Shepherd's acquittal buoyed its hopes but did not solve its problems.[44] The trial proved the necessity of extending the mob's influence over state officials a little closer to home. As the state prosecutor assigned to Russell County, Borders would have been the person to target. But unlike state's attorneys or district attorneys in larger urban areas, the Russell County circuit solicitor's jurisdiction covered three other counties in the Third Judicial District, distancing him, geographically but also politically, from local officials.[45] Borders's challenge to the Phenix City machine during the trial had made that all too clear. Turning the solicitor into an ally of the mob required more than just a new face. It demanded remaking the job altogether.

No one proved more instrumental in that process than Albert Patterson. Patterson had moved his young family to Phenix City from nearby Alexander City in 1933, hoping it might jumpstart his struggling law practice. For years, though, he steered clear of the mob. While Shepherd was consolidating his illegal empire, Patterson built a reputation as a good lawyer and devoted citizen. He joined every community organization in town and served on the city school board and the local draft board.[46] But Patterson's political ambition was bigger than Russell County. He was in the middle of a campaign for the state senate when he agreed to join Hoyt Shepherd's defense team in September 1946. Patterson insisted to a friend that the kingpin had only "hired his services, not bought his soul," but after he defended Shepherd and Shepherd helped Patterson win the senate race, he continued working to give Shepherd exactly what he wanted. Along with Jabe Brassell, the other state representative from Russell County, Patterson cowrote legislation in the spring and summer of 1947 that made Russell County its own judicial circuit, and immediately afterward he helped to engineer Governor Folsom's appointment of another of Shepherd's attorneys, thirty-year-old Arch Ferrell Jr., as the new circuit solicitor. The maneuver got rid of A. S. Borders and made Ferrell the most powerful state official directly under the mob's control. Ferrell's grand juries rarely returned indictments against anyone associated with the rackets. He intimidated witnesses on the stand and declined to prosecute whenever he could.[47] If Patterson regretted his decision, he did not show it right away. Two years after Shepherd's trial Patterson defended gambler Clarence Revel against charges of murdering a federal witness in Georgia. Though he failed to prevent Revel from being extradited to Georgia to stand trial, Patterson leaned on his and the mob's ties to Governor Folsom to try to stop it.[48]

Albert Patterson's actions put him in the company of both the corrupt local officials who enabled the mob and the ordinary, law-abiding citizens who tolerated it. Whatever their personal feelings about gambling or prostitution, many locals depended on the mob. The traffic from Fort Benning and beyond not only created jobs and paid the city's bills but also subsidized the diners, gas stations, and taxi companies, which shared the same customers. Although the rackets exploited poor whites, African Americans, and itinerant soldiers, they sustained and even empowered the middle-class and elite whites who voted and paid taxes in Russell County. Racketeers cultivated good relationships with their neighbors, whose children went to school with theirs and who attended the same churches.[49]

The understanding forged between racketeers and their white neighbors reflected the pernicious entitlements of white supremacy, but law enforcement's partnership with the mob was entangled with more violent and widespread abuses of power in the southern judicial system, including debt peonage. Sheriff Mathews forced black inmates in Russell County to work on his personal farm. He also coerced a woman named Annie Mae, who may not have been an inmate, to work as his family's cook and maid and to sleep at the jail every night.[50] Mathews and Albert Fuller protected white racketeers but meted out brutal punishment to African Americans charged with petty crimes. When a black youth named Otis Lamb was arrested for burglary, Fuller, two other deputies, and Ben Scroggins, the Alabama Beverage Control (ABC) agent assigned to Russell County, beat Lamb so badly that the doctor had to be called to the jail to attend to him. Scroggins was later implicated in the beating of another African American man and his young son, whom Scroggins tried to bribe to keep quiet.[51] The mob and local officials employed other familiar strategies of white supremacy to conceal and rationalize white crime and corruption as well. Election fraud and jury tampering were as critical to the mob's control over Phenix City as they were to segregationists' control over the South. Racketeers paid prostitutes and other employees to vote, sometimes more than once. They even turned African American disfranchisement to their advantage by registering black voters without their knowledge and marking ballots in their names. And between 1944 and 1954, only 1,966 male voters out of a total county population of 43,000 were called for jury duty, and 1,151 of those were called at least five times during that decade. One resident from Georgia was even called and served.[52]

Individuals cooperated with and tolerated the mob, but segregationist methods empowered it. Like Jim Crow, organized crime in Phenix City operated under the supervision of local and state governments. In this context, it was easy for an ambitious man like Albert Patterson or any other ordinary citizen to collaborate with criminals without sacrificing his reputation. Respectable white men lived and worked and thrived on the margins of the law in the Jim Crow South.

What proved more difficult for Patterson was maintaining an alliance with men who needed him less than he needed them. The first breach occurred between Patterson and Governor Folsom. The two men had been friends and political allies since being elected on the same mob-backed ticket in 1946. Three years later, however, Folsom's fondness for patronage backfired on Patterson when the governor rejected Patterson's recommendation for a probate judgeship in his home district in order to appoint Folsom's own candidate. Patterson learned about it from the press. The snub embarrassed him and led to a public spat.[53] When Patterson stopped supporting the governor's agenda in the state legislature, his fate was sealed. His campaign for lieutenant governor in 1950 foundered when the racketeers opposed him, but the final break occurred a year later, when Arch Ferrell used his influence to have Patterson, a decorated veteran of the First World War, removed from the Russell County Draft Board, where he had served for more than a decade.[54]

Patterson's break with the Phenix City machine coincided with the rise of a new citizen watchdog group that would soon replace the mob as his political benefactor. While periodic antivice campaigns had been launched before, the Phenix City Citizens Committee initiated a more aggressive and public crusade that focused on corruption in local government. The group's activism was not prompted by any single event but was a response to the mob's expansion during the postwar years. And while the group reflected growing concerns among many locals, membership remained slim for the first couple of years. Formed around 1950, it was comprised of only a handful of local ministers and businessmen who had been around Phenix City long enough to know that trying to fight the mob through local channels would be futile. When Folsom's term as governor ended in 1950, the Citizens Committee was hopeful that his successor, Gordon Persons, would be more receptive to intervening with local officials. Throughout the spring of 1951, they petitioned him to launch a state investigation into graft and corruption in Phenix City. In letters to the committee, Persons promised very little, but privately he discussed the possibility of a state investigation.[55] When committee members circulated this news, Persons began receiving letters from Phenix City residents contradicting the committee's complaints. The letters were almost certainly part of a coordinated campaign by the mob. The short appeals were all from women and were written on identical postcards with nearly identical dates, and they bore variations of the same three messages: "I am satisfied with our city," wrote one. "We do not desire any changes," said another. "Please let us continue to enjoy local self-government in Phenix City," wrote a third.[56] A few days after the notes arrived, Persons sent a long and defensive letter to the editor of the *Columbus Ledger* in which he insisted that committee members had exaggerated his promise to investigate Phenix City. Calling himself a firm believer in states' rights, the governor wrote, "I do not want the Federal government policing Alabama and I feel equally certain that no elected city or county official would want the State interfering in local affairs." Soon thereafter Persons sent a perfunctory letter to Sheriff Mathews, asking him to look into the Citizens Committee's complaints and refusing to do anything more. When the committee persisted, Persons told the group's leader, Hugh Bentley, to move if he thought Phenix City was such a bad place to live.[57]

The governor had reason to be worried about federal intervention in the spring of 1951. The Citizens Committee's campaign drew Phenix City into a national conversation about organized crime that had become serious enough by May 1950 that the US Senate authorized the creation of a special subcommittee to investigate organized crime under the direction of Tennessee senator Estes Kefauver.[58] Over the next year and a half the Kefauver Committee conducted televised hearings in major cities around the country. Except for stops in Miami and New Orleans, the committee ignored the South, but not for lack of evidence that organized crime thrived there.[59] Hundreds of people from small towns like Colbert, Georgia, and Seneca, South Carolina, wrote to Senator Kefauver asking him to investigate local rackets and corrupt local officials. Dozens of Alabamians wrote to him about Phenix City. Many of the letters conflated concerns about crime and corruption with fears about communism, but some also indicted the very power structure that had kept the Phenix City syndicate in power for so long. Calling himself "formerly a rock-ribbed Democrat" who "believes in law and order," one war veteran told senators that he had joined the Republican Party.[60]

Collectively, the letters revealed two important things: white crime and government corruption were pervasive in the Jim Crow South, and US senators knew this and declined to act. Kefauver perceived organized crime in big cities to be a greater threat, and targeting famous mob bosses in New York and Chicago also generated more attention for the committee's work. An estimated twenty million Americans nationwide watched as Kefauver and his associates questioned famous underworld figures like Frank Costello and Virginia Hill. Some of the individual hearings drew the largest television audiences up to that time.[61] The only outcome of the hearings that affected Alabama was a new federal gambling tax. In Phenix City, racketeers gladly bought "gambling stamps" to protect themselves against federal indictments, even though possession of a stamp was proof that they were violating state gambling laws.[62] Racketeers had little to fear from the state, however. The law went into effect in November 1951, and in the first year 223 of the 238 stamps issued in Alabama were in Phenix City. A year later there were 350.[63] Rather than bolster the Citizens Committee's war on organized crime, the Kefauver Committee's work ultimately safeguarded racketeers against federal inquiry.

By the end of 1951, after state and federal authorities had declined to intervene in Phenix City, violence was escalating in response to the Citizens Committee's crusade. After renaming their organization the Russell Betterment Association (RBA) and recruiting Albert Patterson as their attorney, the local crime fighters went public with a new campaign to impeach Sheriff Mathews for dereliction of duty. The impeachment crusade prompted a vicious backlash from the mob. In January 1952 someone bombed Hugh Bentley's home while his family was inside. They escaped unharmed, but during an election later that year a group of roughnecks beat Bentley, his teenage son, and another RBA member who were working as poll watchers. Someone set fire to Patterson's law office that year as well. These violent retaliatory attacks won new supporters over to the RBA's side, but they did not compel local or state officials to intervene. Neither Sheriff Mathews nor Police Chief Pal Daniel made arrests in any of the cases. Silas Garrett, the state's new attorney general and a close friend of Arch Ferrell, told the press that he did not believe there to be any connection between the bombing and Hugh Bentley's involvement in the RBA. State ABC officers continued to side with the mob. Under state law they were supposed to revoke liquor licenses from businesses that violated state gambling laws, but they never did. Similarly, even when Fort Benning put those same businesses off-limits for breaking the law, ABC agents did not write up the owners, and Mathews backed them up. The sheriff's failure to act on such obvious violations of the law was the focal point of his impeachment trial in June 1953, but testimony from ABC agents, the attorney general, and other powerful state law enforcement officials convinced the state supreme court to rule unanimously in favor of Mathews.[64] Despite the RBA's best efforts, the alliance between the Sheriff's Department, the circuit solicitor's office, and now the attorney general made the mob seem untouchable.

Unable to fight the mob from the outside, the RBA and Albert Patterson devised one final plan: Patterson would run for attorney general at the end of Garrett's term in 1954 and take down the Phenix City machine from the inside. As the state's chief law enforcement officer, the attorney general could investigate violations of state laws and bring indictments against the racketeers without the aid of local law enforcement or the circuit solicitor. The problem until then had not been that every attorney general had been corrupt—only Silas Garrett had direct ties to the mob—but that no one had been willing to use the full power of the office to police local officials.[65] Patterson described himself as "a strong believer in the principles and practices of local self government and home rule," but his message during the campaign was clear and consistent: the Phenix City mob was a state problem, not a local one. Drawing on RBA promotional literature, Patterson likened the mob to an octopus whose reach threatened law and order in every corner of the state. He pledged to use his authority to stop it once and for all.[66]

To stop Patterson, the mob poured tens of thousands of dollars into the campaign of Lee Porter, an attorney from Gadsden and an old friend of

Arch Ferrell. But when Patterson forced Porter into a runoff on May 4, they panicked. Over the next month Hoyt Shepherd, Jimmy Matthews, and Godwin Davis worked alongside Arch Ferrell and Silas Garrett to devise a strategy to put Porter in office. Davis called a meeting of fifteen to twenty racketeers at the Bama Club to raise money, and Garrett summoned all circuit solicitors to the state capitol, where he urged them to back Porter. During the meeting Arch Ferrell reportedly snapped, "That goddamned son of a bitch Albert Patterson is not going to take the attorney general's office." When it looked like he might, Garrett and Ferrell conspired to alter the election returns in Jefferson County. Patterson won anyway, but the press and Patterson's own campaign staff caught wind of the vote-stealing scheme and immediately exposed it. Not only had the mob failed to stop Patterson, they had handed him his next crusade.[67] Patterson's margin of victory, however, was telling. After the altered returns were accounted for, he won by only 854 votes out of a total of 382,678 cast.[68] Patterson's challenge to the Phenix City machine resonated with voters who resented the mob's influence in local and state government, but it also ran up against blind reverence for local control and indifference to white "vice."

Although Alabama voters were divided over Patterson's crusade, his win shook the Phenix City machine to its core. On June 15, just five days after state election officials confirmed Patterson's victory, James Folsom, who had just won the primary to become governor again, called Patterson and offered to help him clean up Phenix City if Patterson would help stop the grand jury investigation into the vote theft. Patterson agreed, but apparently only to placate Folsom: by that time he had already agreed to testify before the grand jury on June 21. The news unnerved Ferrell and Garrett. Patterson went to his downtown office on the night of June 18, 1954, to sign thank-you notes to campaign supporters. As he left around 9:00 to go home, Albert Fuller and Arch Ferrell confronted him. Patterson got into his car and tried to drive away, but Fuller stopped him by firing three bullets into his face at point-blank range.[69]

Albert Patterson's murder is the primary focus of the small body of published work on the Phenix City mob, but it is not the starting point for understanding white crime in Alabama. Patterson received death threats for promising to shut down the rackets, but he was murdered for targeting the political machine that had kept the rackets in business for decades. Understanding this distinction makes the links between crime and government corruption clearer. Patterson's willingness to testify against Ferrell and Garrett in the election fraud investigation proved his commitment to collapsing the political infrastructure that supported organized crime. With

Ferrell out of the way, Patterson would have had a free hand as attorney general to shut down the rackets and dismantle the local political machine.

The machine's desperation to stop Albert Patterson prompted the very intervention that they had always feared. Just days after the murder, Patterson's son told the press what many people already knew: the very local officials investigating his father's murder were probably the ones responsible for it. Under tremendous pressure, Governor Persons declared martial law and appointed Bernard Sykes as acting attorney general to take over the Patterson murder investigation. Investigators believed that Silas Garrett had engineered the whole thing, but shortly after the murder he checked into a mental hospital in Galveston, Texas, and remained there, out of reach of investigators. Two eyewitnesses placed Fuller and Ferrell at the scene, and they were tried separately in early 1955. Both professed their innocence. Ferrell was acquitted, but a single palm print on Albert Patterson's car window sealed Fuller's conviction for murder. He was sentenced to life in prison. By then the National Guard had emptied the casinos and made bonfires of slot machines and card tables, and the state had overseen the city's first clean elections in decades.[70]

The murder investigation and the trials of Fuller and Ferrell collectively became known as "the cleanup," but they did not lead to any serious investigation of crime and corruption. A grand jury returned 741 indictments against 144 different people, but only Fuller and Ferrell faced serious charges. Ferrell was acquitted, and Fuller served just ten years of his life sentence before being paroled. Although many racketeers were arrested, most never served any time at all, and those who did received light sentences. Hoyt Shepherd, Jimmy Matthews, and the Davis family all served a few weeks or months in prison for gambling violations. Others, like Clarence Revel, fled the state and later paid fines and received probation for their roles in the crime ring.[71]

The most far-reaching consequence of the Patterson case was the political career of his son, John M. Patterson, who ran first for his slain father's seat as attorney general and then for governor in 1958. John Patterson's legacy is forever associated with his defense of segregation and his condemnation of the Freedom Riders in 1961, and he also played a role in reorienting the focus of law-and-order rhetoric to African Americans. During his campaign for governor, Patterson adapted his father's law-and-order message and explicitly linked it to the dangers of the burgeoning civil rights movement. He warned that crime and corruption were invading the state again, only in a new form. "Huge sums of money from outside sources," he charged, "are being used in this governor's race to reestablish such crime capitals as existed in Phenix City. Gangsters and the NAACP have sent in large sums of money in an attempt to defeat me."[72] As attorney general and then governor, Patterson also oversaw the state's five-year battle to declare the NAACP an illegal organization in Alabama.[73]

Any serious concerns about white crime and corruption in Alabama ended with Albert Patterson's death. His campaign had threatened the very basis of mob rule, which depended upon a noninterventionist state that let local officials run amok. Even as he inadvertently challenged a justice system that was designed to protect powerful whites, he also helped to lay the rhetorical foundation for tough-on-crime, law-and-order politicking that would further criminalize African Americans in the years to come. But as the Phenix City story suggests, the legacy of local and state government corruption in the Jim Crow South has much to teach us about the scope and consequences of white criminal regimes in the decades between the criminalization of African Americans and the rise of mass incarceration.

NOTES

1. Russell County Heritage Committee, *The Heritage of Russell County, Alabama* (Clanton, AL: Heritage Publishing Consultants, 2003), 17; Anna Kendrick Walker, *Russell County in Retrospect: An Epic of the Far Southeast* (Richmond, VA: Dietz Press, 1950), 275–78.

2. *Census of Population: 1950, Vol. I, Number of Inhabitants* (Washington, DC: US Government Printing Office, 1952), table 8; Edwin Strickland and Gene Wortsman, *Phenix City: The Wickedest City in America* (Birmingham, AL: Vulcan Press, 1955), 181. Strickland and Wortsman were Birmingham newspaper reporters who compiled their articles on Phenix City into what remains the only account of crime and corruption that does not focus exclusively on the murder of Albert Patterson in 1954.

3. Strickland and Wortsman, *Phenix City*, 94–97, 5; Alan Grady, *When Good Men Do Nothing: The Assassination of Albert Patterson* (Tuscaloosa: University of Alabama Press, 2003), 8; Gene Howard, *Patterson for Alabama: The Life and Career of John Patterson* (Tuscaloosa: University of Alabama Press, 2008), 15.

4. Warren Trest, *Nobody but the People: The Life and Times of Alabama's Youngest Governor* (Montgomery, AL: NewSouth Books, 2008), 54.

5. "America's Wickedest City," *Look*, October 5, 1954; "Here Were Bad Old Days in 'Most Sinful City,'" *Life*, October 4, 1954, 47–49.

6. Trest, *Nobody but the People*, 156–59.

7. Ibid., 187. Newsreel footage of the ceremony is available at www.youtube.com/watch?v=wgc1cVjXoM4 (accessed August 17, 2017).

8. "To Sinful Phenix City, Cleanup Was a Godsend," *Des Moines Register*, July 14, 1957, 1, clipping in LPR 54, Series A: Correspondence, folder 10, John Patterson

Papers, Alabama Department of Archives and History (hereafter cited as ADAH); "Alabama's 'Sin City' Just a Memory 50 Years after High Profile Assassination," *Florida Times-Union*, June 13, 2004; "Slaying Led to Sin City's Deliverance," *Washington Post*, June 20, 2004. The historical marker has since been replaced.

9. Political histories that address antidemocratic regimes and systemic corruption are usually biographies of firebrands and demagogues. See, for example, T. Harry Williams, *Huey Long* (New York: Vintage Books, 1981); and William Anderson, *The Wild Man from Sugar Creek: The Political Career of Eugene Talmadge* (Baton Rouge: Louisiana State University Press, 1976).

10. See especially David Oshinsky, *Worse Than Slavery: Parchman Farm and the Ordeal of Jim Crow Justice* (New York: Free Press, 1996); Alex Lichtenstein, *Twice the Work of Free Labor: The Political Economy of Convict Labor in the New South* (New York: Verso, 1996); Kali Gross, *Colored Amazons: Crime, Violence, and Black Women in the City of Brotherly Love, 1880–1910* (Durham, NC: Duke University Press, 2006); and Khalil Muhammad, *The Condemnation of Blackness: Race, Crime, and the Making of Modern Urban America* (Cambridge, MA: Harvard University Press, 2010). Muhammad does analyze the different treatment of white crime, but only for ethnic whites in the urban North.

11. For the most recent overviews of the postwar origins of law and order politics, see Elizabeth Kai Hinton, *From the War on Poverty to the War on Crime: The Making of Mass Incarceration in America* (Cambridge, MA: Harvard University Press, 2016); and Heather Ann Thompson, *Blood in the Water: The Attica Prison Uprising of 1971 and Its Legacy* (New York: Pantheon, 2016).

12. See Strickland and Wortsman, *Phenix City*; Grady, *When Good Men Do Nothing*; and Margaret Anne Barnes, *The Tragedy and the Triumph of Phenix City, Alabama* (Macon, GA: Mercer University Press, 1998). Grady's book is rigorously researched, but his analysis focuses primarily on the outcome of the Patterson murder investigation. See also Ace Atkins's novel, *Wicked City* (New York: G. P. Putnam's Sons, 2008).

13. *Heritage of Russell County*, 161–62.

14. Tyrone Power, *Impressions of America during the Years 1833, 1834, and 1835, in Two Volumes* (Philadelphia: Carey, Lea, and Blanchard, 1836), 2:86–87.

15. Oshinsky, *Worse Than Slavery*, 2–3.

16. Farris W. Cadle, *Georgia Land Surveying History and Law* (Athens: University of Georgia Press, 1991), 477–78n13.

17. *The New Georgia Guide* (Athens: University of Georgia Press, 1996), 367–75; Peggy A. Stelpflug and Richard Hyatt, *Home of the Infantry: The History of Fort Benning* (Macon, GA: Mercer University Press, 2007), 16.

18. Grady, *When Good Men Do Nothing*, 3. On links between mill villages and vice, see Harold S. Coulter, *A People Courageous: A History of Phenix City, Alabama* (Columbus, GA: Howard Printing Company, 1976), 188–91.

19. Sheldon Hackney, *Populism to Progressivism in Alabama* (Princeton, NJ: Princeton University Press, 1969), 191–94; Pippa Holloway, *Living in Infamy: Felon*

Disfranchisement and the History of American Citizenship (New York: Oxford University Press, 2013), 98–101. Holloway argues that Alabama delegates were less concerned than white leaders in other states about the possibility of disfranchising whites convicted of crimes. However, this must be considered alongside the fact that criminal disfranchisement did not threaten the voting rights of the vast majority of whites, since they made up a much smaller percentage of those arrested or convicted of crimes. Crimes are outlined in Article VIII, Section 182 of the Alabama Constitution of 1901, Government Records Collection, ADAH.

20. Hackney, *Populism to Progressivism*, 209–22, quote on 213. Term limits are outlined in Article V, Section 116 of the Alabama Constitution of 1901. Local rule is a complex topic in Alabama political history. The 1901 Constitution, which is still in effect, has weakened home rule overall by giving no general grant of power to county authorities, forcing them to appeal to the state legislature for the authority to perform duties that local governments in most other states already have. More than one-third of Alabama's more than eight hundred constitutional amendments—making it the longest state constitution in the United States—are a consequence of this law and apply to only one county or city. This arrangement has done more to weaken state power than to weaken counties, however, because it forces the state to expend resources handling what should have been routine local matters. Moreover, it has had no real impact on local law enforcement or the courts, and it has not restricted the authority of city officials to levy most forms of taxes. These powers enabled the local government in Phenix City to do as it pleased. Alabama's laws on home rule certainly have not compelled local regimes to follow the law. Rather, these laws have made it more difficult even for lawful governments to function efficiently. See Wayne Flynt, *Alabama in the Twentieth Century* (Tuscaloosa: University of Alabama Press, 2004), 22–24; and David L. Martin, *Alabama's State and Local Governments* (Tuscaloosa: University of Alabama Press, 1994), 27–31.

21. V. O. Key, *Southern Politics in State and Nation* (Knoxville: University of Tennessee Press, 1949), 36–37; Flynt, *Alabama in the Twentieth Century*, 24.

22. Charles Henderson to Logan Martin, August 24, 1916, Alabama Attorney General's Office Correspondence, 1878–1996, container SG010760, folder 22, Government Records Collections, ADAH. For an overview of the Martin raids, see Steve Suitts, *Hugo Black of Alabama: How His Roots and Early Career Shaped the Great Champion of the Constitution* (Montgomery, AL: NewSouth Books, 2005), 190–224; and Trest, *Nobody but the People*, 48–49.

23. Strickland and Wortsman, *Phenix City*, provide the most detailed overview of Phenix City rackets and racketeers in the 1940s and 1950s. For a list of businesses, see 94–97. A more comprehensive list is in a memo from Lt. M. J. Wiman to Gen. Walter J. Hanna, September 16, 1954, in the private collection of Jim Cannon in Phenix City, Alabama. Slot estimates are from *Birmingham News*, June 27, 1954, D1.

24. Trest, *Nobody but the People*, 49; Grady, *When Good Men Do Nothing*, 5.

25. John M. Patterson, interview by the author, May 14, 2015, Goldville, Alabama. Patterson was sixteen and rode his bike to the scene to watch the rescue efforts.

26. Quotes are from Trest, *Nobody but the People*, 59–60; and Strickland and Wortsman, *Phenix City*, 68–69. See also *Phenix-Girard (AL) Journal*, April 22, 1938, 1; *Birmingham News*, April 22, 1938, 1. The papers went to press before all of the casualties had been counted.

27. Annual and Biennial Reports of the State Prison Inspector of Alabama, Alabama Department of Corrections State Publications, 1920–40, Government Records Collections, ADAH.

28. Muhammad, *Condemnation of Blackness*. Muhammad examines the decriminalization of white immigrants more carefully in "Where Did All the White Criminals Go? Reconfiguring Race and Crime on the Road to Mass Incarceration," *Souls* 13, no. 1 (2011): 72–90.

29. Strickland and Wortsman, *Phenix City*, 195–99; Peggy A. Stelpflug and Richard Hyatt, *Home of the Infantry: The History of Fort Benning* (Macon, GA: Mercer University Press, 2007), 120–21.

30. Trest, *Nobody but the People*, 54–55; interview with John Patterson.

31. "A Lynching Kept out of Sight," *Washington Post*, September 2, 2016; Federal Bureau of Investigation, Felix Hall Investigation Report, Part I, Washington, DC.

32. "A Lynching Kept out of Sight"; Strickland and Wortsman, *Phenix City*, 197.

33. *National Police Gazette*, May 1947, 7. Cobb is quoted in Howard, *Patterson for Alabama*, 23.

34. *Birmingham News*, June 27, 1954, D1–3; Strickland and Wortsman, *Phenix City*, 1.

35. R. K. Jones et al. to Sheriff Ralph Mathews, September 6, 1951, Alabama Governor (1951–55: Persons) Administrative Files, 1950–55, container SG12760, folder 6, Government Records Collections, ADAH.

36. Strickland and Wortsman, *Phenix City*, 136–38; Grady, *When Good Men Do Nothing*, 155–56.

37. Memo from Wiman to Hanna; Strickland and Wortsman, *Phenix City*, 23–36.

38. Jessica Pliley, *Policing Sexuality: The Mann Act and the Making of the FBI* (Cambridge, MA: Harvard University Press, 2014), 1.

39. *Birmingham News*, June 27, 1954, 1.

40. Pliley, *Policing Sexuality*, 71, 215–16.

41. "Gunmen Blaze, Gangland Style, at Kingpin Hoyt Shepherd," *Columbus Ledger*, July 8, 1954, 1; "America's Wickedest City"; Grady, *When Good Men Do Nothing*, 10–12; Trest, *Nobody but the People*, 101.

42. "America's Wickedest City."

43. Ibid.

44. Trest, *Nobody but the People*, 61–62; "America's Wickedest City."

45. Trest, *Nobody but the People*, 101.

46. Ibid., 50–51. Patterson remained active in those organizations until his death. See membership cards, LPR 254, Series A: Correspondence, folder 15, Patterson Papers, ADAH.

47. Quoted in Trest, *Nobody but the People*, 101; Grady, *When Good Men Do Nothing*, 11–13; S. 141, *General Laws and Joint Resolutions of the Legislature of*

Alabama Passed at the Regular Session of 1947 (Birmingham, AL: State Printers, 1948), 269–70. The bill was introduced by state senator Rankin Fite. A few years later, as Speaker of the House of Representatives, Fite tried to help Governor Folsom talk Albert Patterson into stopping the grand jury investigation into voter fraud that would eventually get Patterson killed. See Strickland and Wortsman, *Phenix City*, 160–61. On Ferrell's tactics, see *Birmingham News,* June 25, 1954, 1.

48. Albert Patterson to James Folsom, June 10, 1948; Patterson to Folsom, telegram, July 1, 1948, container SG013726, folder 7, Albert Patterson Case Files, ADAH; interview with John M. Patterson.

49. Trest, *Nobody but the People,* 54; interview with John Patterson.

50. Memo by John Patterson, n.d., Series A: Correspondence, box 7, folder 20, Patterson Papers, ADAH. On the broader history of debt peonage, see Douglas A. Blackmon, *Slavery by Another Name: The Re-enslavement of Black Americans from the Civil War to World War II* (New York: Doubleday, 2008); and Pete Daniel, *The Shadow of Slavery: Peonage in the South, 1901–1969* (Urbana: University of Illinois Press, 1972).

51. Strickland and Wortsman, *Phenix City*, 2–3.

52. Ibid., 172–79. On registering black voters, see container 013721, folder 2, Patterson Case Files, ADAH.

53. *Opeleika (AL) Daily News,* February 3, 1949, February 14, 1949. Both clippings in Alabama Governor (1947–51: Folsom) Administrative Files, container 013479, folder 36, Government Records Collection, ADAH.

54. Trest, *Nobody but the People,* 102–4; Grady, *When Good Men Do Nothing,* 14.

55. Open letter from Hugh Bentley and John Luttrell to Governor Gordon Persons, April 21, 1951; Jack Gunter to Gordon Persons, April 30, 1951; Persons to Gunter, May 3, 1951; John Luttrell to Gordon Persons, May 21, 1951; Persons to Luttrell, May 23, 1951, container SG012760, folder 6, Persons Correspondence, ADAH.

56. Evelyn Ratliff to Gordon Persons, May 6, 1951; Mrs. W. E. Smith to Gordon Persons, May 5, 1951; Mrs. J. M. Ratliff to Gordon Persons, May 5, 1951, container SG012760, folder 6, Persons Correspondence, ADAH.

57. Gordon Persons to L. P. Patterson, editor of the *Columbus Ledger* (the letter is undated but references a recent news article dated May 9, 1951); Gordon Persons to H. Ralph Mathews, June 18, 1951; speech by Hugh Bentley (this document is undated but is probably from the early 1950s), container SG012760, folder 6, Persons Correspondence, ADAH.

58. For an overview of the origins of the committee, see William Howard Moore, *The Kefauver Committee and the Politics of Crime, 1950–1952* (Columbia: University of Missouri Press, 1974), chap. 2.

59. Finding Aid, 2–3, Records of the Senate Special Committee to Investigate Organized Crime in Interstate Commerce, 1950–51, RG 46, National Archives and Records Administration, Washington, DC.

60. Daniel C. Davidson to Senate Crime Investigation Committee, January 25, 1952, Records of the Senate Special Committee to Investigate Organized Crime

in Interstate Commerce, 1950–51, box 52, CR 15: Complaints, RG 46, National Archives and Records Administration.

61. Finding Aid, 3, Records of the Senate Special Committee; Howard, *The Kefauver Committee*, 182–83.

62. Strickland and Wortsman, *Phenix City,* 77.

63. Ibid., 2; Trest, *Nobody but the People*, 123.

64. Trest, *Nobody but the People*, 119–23; Strickland and Wortsman, *Phenix City*, 164–71. In Alabama citizens can bring impeachment suits against local officials. The state's constitution does not provide for recall elections in most counties, so impeachment is the only way to remove local officials. Trials of constitutional officers (including county sheriffs) are heard by the state supreme court. See *Decatur (AL) Daily*, November 11, 2007.

65. Grady, *When Good Men Do Nothing*, 20–21. The only exception was Logan Martin in 1916, referenced earlier in this essay.

66. Albert Patterson to Alabama Bar Association, n.d., and Albert Patterson campaign speech, n.d., both in Series A: Correspondence, box 7, folder 1 ("Head Revel"), Patterson Papers, ADAH.

67. Grady, *When Good Men Do Nothing*, 20–33.

68. Trest, *Nobody but the People*, 130.

69. Grady, *When Good Men Do Nothing*, 31; Trest, *Nobody but the People*, 130–33.

70. Grady, *When Good Men Do Nothing*, chaps. 3–4. John Patterson made the accusation to the local papers. See "Son Charges Investigators Top Suspect," *Columbus Ledger,* June 24, 1954, clipping in Governor (1951–55: Persons) Alabama Governor (1951–55: Persons) Administrative Files, 1950–55, container SG12760, folder 9, Government Records Collections, ADAH.

71. "Phenix Crime Lords Find It Pays to Flee from Justice," *Birmingham News,* October 25, 1956, clipping in Series A: Correspondence, box 6, folder 9, Patterson Papers, ADAH; Grady, *When Good Men Do Nothing,* 227.

72. Quoted in Anne Permaloff and Carl Grafton, *Political Power in Alabama: The More Things Change* (Athens: University of Georgia Press, 2008), 72.

73. Trest, *Nobody but the People*, 202–6.

PART II
PUNISHMENT

CHAPTER 5

TESTIMONIAL INCAPACITY AND CRIMINAL DEFENDANTS IN THE SOUTH

Pippa Holloway

In the spring of 1940 in Briceville, Tennessee, a white coal miner named George Teaster fell while boarding a rail car that was to transport him down the mountain at the end of the workday. The car had stopped several feet from the boarding platform, and as the miners rushed to climb into it Teaster was knocked down, falling onto a railroad tie and injuring his hip. Based on an assessment by the company doctor, Cambria Coal authorized $2.81 in workers' compensation for the injury. Teaster challenged this meager payment, filing a claim in court for full, permanent disability. He could no longer work in the mine, he asserted, and could only do a couple of hours of farm work per day. He sought $5 per week (half his weekly salary) for the rest of his life. As the case dragged on, Teaster secured representation by John Grady O'Hara, an attorney for the United Mine Workers. In late 1941 Judge H. H. Brown ruled that Teaster had been undercompensated but was not permanently disabled. The court awarded Teaster four weeks of temporary disability, a total benefit of $20.[1]

Four weeks of compensation rather than a lifetime benefit must have been a disappointment to Teaster, but he would never even receive that assistance. Lawyers for Cambria Coal returned to court a few weeks later with a motion to set aside the judgment. George Teaster, they pointed out, should never have been allowed to testify in court because five years earlier he had been convicted of misdemeanor larceny. Since Tennessee law disqualified individuals with larceny convictions from testifying in court, Teaster should not have been allowed to present evidence of his injury. The judge agreed. Without evidence, Teaster had no claim, and Cambria Coal had no liability. The case was dismissed. A year later the Tennessee Supreme Court upheld the decision.[2]

The Tennessee law that prevented Teaster from testifying in court was far from unique. In the nineteenth century, many US states had limitations on court testimony by individuals convicted of serious crimes. Many states also prohibited testimony by criminal defendants. The rationale for the two restrictions was similar. Prohibitions on testimony by people with prior convictions were rooted in English common law and stemmed from the belief that individuals with criminal convictions were unreliable witnesses. Just as individuals with prior criminal convictions were seen under common law to be untrustworthy witnesses, so too were those who stood accused, because such individuals might commit perjury in order to spare themselves punishment.

From Teaster's perspective, being a Tennessee resident was unlucky, because most states had eliminated these restrictions on testimony by the 1880s.[3] But the expansion of the ability to testify had a regional pattern. Southern states were more likely than nonsouthern states to continue prohibitions on testimony by defendants and/or those with former convictions into the late nineteenth century and, in some cases, the twentieth century. This chapter documents and offers an explanation for this instance of southern exceptionalism, arguing that it was rooted in the desire to deny legal and civil equality to African Americans that characterized the Jim Crow era. Accounting for this regional difference requires examining the broad social and political context in which these prohibitions operated and considering the social and political implications of their perpetuation. Specifically, understanding this history involves recognizing that during the 1870s and 1880s—a key period in which restrictions on court testimony were lifted in much of the nation—southern states constructed and enhanced exclusions from citizenship with the intent of undermining Reconstruction. Like laws disfranchising for crime, which were expanded in this period across the South, restricting the rights of criminal defendants and individuals with prior convictions to testify offered a way to resist the federal mandates for equality of citizenship and maintain white political and social dominance. White southern political leaders recognized the utility of a racially unjust criminal justice system in limiting the ability of African Americans to achieve equality, and they had little motivation to enact reforms that would make court processes fairer for defendants.

Bans on court testimony by individuals charged with or convicted of crimes no longer exist in the United States and have been all but forgotten today, but such prohibitions had a tremendous impact on individual lives in the past, as George Teaster's case demonstrates. Today all adults can be witnesses if either of the parties in court desires their testimony. Prior convictions, like many other characteristics, may affect the credibility of the witness, but they cannot affect one's ability to testify. Pending convictions—being accused of a crime—can be weighed by a jury, which might choose not to believe a defendant's version of events, but criminal defendants can testify in their own cases if they choose.[4] In legal terms today, prior convictions affect the credibility of testimony, whereas in the nineteenth century and in some cases into the twentieth, prior or pending convictions affected one's competence to testify.

While there have been historical and legal examinations of other collateral consequences of criminal conviction, limitations on the ability of ex-convicts to testify in the United States have received little scrutiny, perhaps because these limitations are no longer operative. Legal scholars have considered the historical trajectory of rules of evidence with regard to the ability of the accused to testify but have paid less attention to restrictions on the ability of individuals with prior convictions to serve as witnesses.[5] One systematic study of the prohibitions on defendant testimony in US courts observes and evaluates the regional divergence outlined here. Legal scholar George Fisher looks at prohibitions on testimony by parties to civil suits that dated back to common law and tracks regional differences in their elimination. Southern states kept limitations on civil party testimony longer than northern states did, and Fisher compares this with the South's similar reluctance to allow sworn testimony by criminal defendants. He concludes, "In both cases the North acted first because of the distorting influence of a related but quite different issue—the right of non-whites to give evidence in Southern courts."[6] This chapter takes a similar approach, foregrounding the racial implications of these seemingly racially neutral rules of evidence in order to explain the longevity of these restrictions in the South.

Using appellate court rulings and legislation as sources, this chapter considers efforts at the state level to influence the process in lower courts. This approach reveals how appellate judges and legislators thought lower courts should work. However, examining appellate cases and statutory rules of evidence does not necessarily offer an accurate picture of the day-to-day evidentiary practices in lower courts, particularly in this era.[7] Judicial discretion could permit incompetent witnesses to testify. If neither party objected, for example, the testimony of individuals with prior convictions could stand, even if they were statutorily barred from testifying. In other instances, judges might overrule objections to testimony. While appellate rulings offer insights into how these cases proceeded at the lower level, they lack many details about what happened in these courtrooms. The exclusion of testimony is reported in these cases only if it was challenged on appeal, so exclusion may have been more common than such records indicate. Nonetheless, the value of appellate cases in establishing precedent makes them important to examine because their impact could be far-reaching. Further research on lower courts, the day-to-day function of these exclusions of testimony, and the exercise of judicial discretion is necessary to fully understand these cases' scope and impact.

The lack of scholarly attention to the ability to testify in court belies the significance of court testimony as a component of citizenship. Suffrage, in contrast, has been the focus of much historical study because it is recognized as a critical expression of one's rights as a citizen. However, the ability to present evidence in court—either in one's own defense or on behalf of another party—has far more immediate and personal implications than voting. Indeed, the ability to speak in one's own defense in a criminal case could be a matter of life or death. Being able to testify in defense of one's interests in a civil suit could affect one's property, livelihood, and in some cases survival. On a symbolic and practical level, a court acts as a place where an individual can assert his or her status as a member of a community with a voice in personal or community matters.

Although restrictions on those with prior convictions testifying as witnesses first appeared in ancient Greece and Rome, these practices in the United States derived directly from English common law.[8] Under common law, not all crimes necessarily brought civil incapacity, only certain serious crimes. The law labeled such crimes and the people who committed them "infamous." Infamous crimes evidenced deficiencies of character, usually involving falsehood or sexual immorality. A person labeled infamous faced limitations on civil capacity, including the loss of the right to vote and the ability to testify in court. Nineteenth-century American legal commenter Simon Greenleaf explained that conviction of these crimes made one's testimony untrustworthy: "Infamy has been defined as a state of incompetency implying such a dereliction of moral principle as carries with it a conclusion of a total disregard to the obligation of an oath."[9]

Limitations on the ability of accused individuals to testify in their own criminal cases followed a different historical path. Common law barred testimony by witnesses with "interest" in civil and criminal cases in order to prevent perjury. Anyone with a personal interest in the outcome was considered untrustworthy. This was the rationale, for example, for excluding spouses of parties to a case from testifying. A spouse was considered to have an interest because if one spouse had a stake in the outcome, the other spouse was presumed to have one also. Disqualification for interest affected business partners, tenants, parents, and legatees, but it also affected defendants, who, obviously, had a stake in the outcome of a case.[10]

Barriers to defendant testimony under common law existed not only in service of truth but also to protect those on trial. One concern was that defendants, anxious to avoid punishment, might commit perjury to avoid being found guilty.[11] Furthermore, if a defendant had the option to testify and chose not to, juries might presume that reluctance was due to guilt.[12] Finally, some feared that individuals on trial might be intimidated into confessing. Defendants could be threatened with perjury if they denied their crime under sworn testimony and were subsequently convicted.[13]

The common law rules for testimony that operated in Britain crossed the Atlantic with the settlers and heavily influenced court procedure in the new republic.[14] Common law formed the basis of the American legal system, but as states statutorily enacted common law they sometimes modified it. For example, in 1829 Tennessee's General Assembly barred the testimony of witnesses who had been convicted of infamous crimes from ever testifying in court again, but it also defined "infamy" by listing which crimes would be considered infamous under state law.[15] While some states followed the infamy standard, others drew the line at felonies. New York's 1836 code required, "No person sentenced upon a conviction for felony shall be competent to testify in any cause, matter or proceeding civil or criminal unless he be pardoned by the governor or by the legislature."[16] A few states avoided using terms like "infamous" and "felony" but simply listed the crimes that brought a loss of competency. In 1845 Florida's legislature passed a law barring testimony from those convicted of "murder, perjury, piracy, forgery, larceny, robbery, arson, sodomy, or buggery."[17]

A variety of restrictions on court testimony existed in the nineteenth-century United States. Children and people judged to be "insane," "lunatics," or mentally deficient were barred in most states. In states that permitted slavery, enslaved African Americans could not testify against white people. Other states, particularly in the South but also in the Midwest and West, prohibited African Americans, Native Americans, and Asian immigrants from serving as witnesses against defendants or civil parties who were white. In this era, in which citizenship was defined by the privileges one could incur as a citizen, the law prohibited many individuals from obtaining this status.[18]

Efforts to bring clarity to evidentiary standards sometimes seemed to make them even more complicated. In North Carolina a handbook for justices of the peace published in 1816 suggests how challenging the enforcement of these standards must have been: "If a witness is convicted of perjury or of forgery or felony and not pardoned nor burnt in the hand or if he hath by judgment lost his ears or stood in the pillory or hath been stigmatized or branded or whipped for any infamous crime he ought not to be received as a witness." In contrast, some punishments, once suffered, could restore one's rights: "A person convicted of felony who has his clergy and is burnt in the hand is a competent witness."[19]

In the mid-nineteenth century many states moved to end prohibitions on the ability of those with prior convictions to testify as a witness.[20] Legislators and citizens in Britain and the United States had become increasingly concerned that limitations on testimony had become barriers to finding truth and dispensing justice.[21] Indiana's 1852 criminal practice act was a typical example of how rules for testimony were revised. The law allowed individuals with infamous crimes to testify, but the conviction could be used to undermine their credibility.[22] Legislators in Connecticut approved a similar statute in 1848: "No person shall be disqualified as a witness in any suit or proceeding at law or in equity . . . by reason of his conviction of a crime but such interest or conviction may be shown for the purpose of affecting his credit."[23] Michigan (1846), Iowa (1851), and other states adopted similar practices around this time.[24]

Commenters celebrated the expansion of such testimony for deterring wrongful convictions and promoting justice. A report from Massachusetts in the 1867 *American Law Review* proclaimed, "We have always been of opinion that the law permitting criminals to testify would aid in the detection of guilt; we are now disposed to think that it will be equally serviceable for the protection of innocence."[25] In 1907 a federal court put it more simply: "It is the good order of society which is at stake, and the right that the 'whole truth and nothing but the truth' shall be presented before the court."[26]

These changes brought more pressure on states that still had limitations on the competency of witnesses with prior convictions to end them. In 1852 the Louisiana Supreme Court heard a case in which an appellant challenged his conviction because one of the prosecution's witnesses had been convicted of swindling a decade earlier. The court upheld the conviction, saying that laws of evidence were changing and there was growing support for allowing testimony by individuals with prior convictions. According to the court, the common law exclusion of testimony perhaps had a place in earlier eras when jurors were "ignorant and illiterate," but in the current era juries have "greatly improved in their composition, by learning and intelligence, and therefore there is much reason for the relaxation of the rules themselves."[27] The court concluded with a moving defense of civil rights for convicted individuals who have completed their sentence:

> The humane principle must prevail in our criminal code. Our statutes prescribe penalties, which, being suffered, no other can be inflicted. And yet it would be

the greatest possible additional punishment to subject a man, who had committed an offence and suffered the penalty, to the still further and great and cruel punishment of not being able, effectually, to complain when robbed of his property, deprived of his liberty, or his life in danger, because neither his oath or testimony would be taken to secure protection or redress. He should be permitted to say, "I have expiated my offence by suffering all the law imposed upon me for my correction and an example to others; I should not be subjected to still greater punishment."[28]

Despite this plea, change took several more decades in Louisiana, which was one of the later states to end common law exclusions of witnesses. Finally, in 1886 the state legislature declared, "The competent witness in all criminal matters shall be a person of proper understanding," meaning that no other characteristics produced incompetency.[29]

Beyond the "humane principle" were more practical considerations relevant to the daily operation of courts. Excluding witnesses from testifying due to a prior conviction was complicated. Courts debated which convictions resulted in this disability; what evidence constituted proof of conviction; whether convictions from courts in other states also brought these restrictions; whether infamy was produced by the judgment of the court, the conviction, or the sentence; and more. Mistakes in applying such standards could result in reversals on appeal. Prosecutors became frustrated when witnesses necessary for conviction were barred from testifying. They pressed for the expansion of the right to testify in order to secure convictions and reduce the possibility of such convictions being overturned on appeal. Rather than barring testimony, it was easier and clearer to allow all to testify and let judges and juries evaluate the credibility of the testimony.[30]

A move was also afoot across the nation to permit defendant testimony. In 1864 Maine was the first to allow all accused individuals to testify in their own criminal trial. In the next fifteen years, thirty other states passed "general competency statutes."[31] Federal courts gave all defendants the option to testify after 1878, when Congress passed a law allowing defendants to serve as witnesses in their own behalf.[32] Though many referred to the expansion of such testimony as liberalization, because allowing such testimony might protect defendants against wrongful convictions, some were concerned that changes might bring the opposite effect. Criminal defendants who exercised their Fifth Amendment right and refused to testify might be presumed guilty.[33] In response to this concern, federal courts and most states clarified that a refusal to testify could not be weighed against a defendant.[34]

By the 1880s the national consensus was well established with regard to the testimony of the accused. Every state outside the South permitted criminal defendants to testify in their own defense, and most specified that failure to testify should create no presumption of guilt.[35] But many southern states hung on to laws prohibiting testimony by defendants in their own trials and maintained bans on testimony as witnesses by those with prior convictions.

The case of Alabama is a good illustration of the regionally specific historical trajectory of these practices in the South. Rather than following the lead of other states and federal courts in eliminating these restrictions, Alabama's political leaders wrestled with the issue over a thirty-year period, equivocating and vacillating. Statutory interventions in common law rules for testimony by the Alabama legislature began with the Code of 1852, which allowed individuals to testify as witnesses in court, even if they had been convicted of a crime. Exceptions were made to maintain bans on those convicted of perjury or subordination of perjury.[36] This appeared to be the practice and precedent in the state until 1878. That year, in *Taylor v. State,* the Alabama Supreme Court found that when the state revised its code in 1867, section 2302 of the 1852 Code—the section that allowed individuals with criminal convictions to testify—was omitted. As a result, the court decided, common law was restored, and witnesses with infamous convictions could not testify.[37]

As the nation moved in one direction by expanding the ability to testify, Alabama seemed to be moving in another by limiting it and reviving the old common law practice. Not only did the legislature fail to immediately rectify the situation, the state supreme court compounded the issue. In 1881 the Alabama Supreme Court held that a conviction for petit larceny—a nonfelony offense that was technically classified as "infamous"—was among those crimes that brought disqualification of testimony.[38] Limitations on testimony now extended to those convicted of misdemeanors.

Alabama also maintained a prohibition on defendant testimony later than many states. Legislators sought to find an elusive middle ground between prohibiting such testimony and allowing it, deciding in 1882 to allow defendants "to make a statement as to the facts in their own behalf but not under oath."[39] Two confused circuit courts wrestled with the implications of this soon after its passage, trying to determine the difference between evidence and unsworn statements and ascertain what weight juries should give such statements.[40] Three years later the legislature acted again, making people on trial in a criminal proceeding competent to testify if they desired to do so.[41] The law in Alabama was finally in line with the majority of the nation.

Florida, too, relegated the words of defendants to legally ambiguous statements rather than testimony, enacting legislation in 1865 that permitted defendants to make a statement, which, in contrast to Alabama, could be made under oath "when in the opinion of the court the ends of justice shall so require."[42] In practice this meant that defendants could make a sworn statement if the judge allowed it. Five years later, in 1870, the legislature changed the law again to allow defendants to make a statement without permission from the judge, but they still could not testify.[43] A series of cases clarified that defendants could not be asked questions, were not subject to the rules applicable to witnesses, and were not to be legally considered witnesses.[44] This remained the law in Florida until 1895, when the state joined the rest of the nation, except for Georgia, by allowing defendants to testify in their own trials under oath.[45]

Georgia was the only state in the nation to bar testimony by criminal defendants in the twentieth century. Under an 1866 law, all witnesses could testify regardless of prior convictions, but defendants were not "competent or compellable" to testify in their own criminal case.[46] In 1874 the legislature changed the code to allow defendants charged with felonies to make a statement, but the statement could not be under oath. How to weigh such testimony was up to the jury.[47] Furthermore, statements could not be guided by questions from counsel. Defendants were simply put in the witness chair and allowed to talk.

Over the next decades, Georgia courts would struggle with how to determine the weight and credibility of these statements, particularly with regard to how they compared to sworn testimony by other witnesses.[48] Because the value of these statements was unclear, they offered little, if any, help to the defense. One Georgia court described them as a "legal blank": "The jury are to deal with it on the plane of statement, and not on the plane of evidence, and may derive from it such aid as they can in reaching the truth. The law fixes no value upon it."[49]

In the late nineteenth century prohibiting defendant testimony was rare, but by the twentieth century it was a complete anachronism, even in the eyes of Georgia judges. In 1906 a speaker at the annual meeting of the Georgia Bar Association spoke out against the provision: "With such an overwhelming sentiment in favor of the defendant being sworn as a witness, Georgia should not remain the only State adhering to the obsolete custom of the defendant making a statement."[50] In 1909, in *Union v. State*, the Georgia Court of Appeals commented acerbically on the situation, calling the practice an "anomaly."[51]

Nonetheless, these restrictions in Georgia stayed on the books until 1961, when the US Supreme Court struck them down in *Ferguson v. State of Georgia*. Billy Ferguson, an African American man, was on trial for capital murder in Georgia. At his trial he offered an unsworn statement, during which his attorney endeavored to question him. The judge stopped the questioning, asserting that this was not allowed under Georgia law. Ferguson's attorneys argued that Ferguson's due process rights had been violated. The Supreme Court agreed. The majority opinion began with the scathing observation that "the State of Georgia is the only State—indeed, apparently the only jurisdiction in the common-law world—to retain the common-law rule that a person charged with a criminal offense is incompetent to testify under oath in his own behalf at his trial." However, the Court's decision was based on the defendant's right to counsel, not a due process right to testify in his own defense. The Court avoided weighing the validity of Georgia's statute denying defendants the right to testify, though it acceded that the attorney had the right to question defendants during these statements. The statute was not at issue in the case because Ferguson had not sought to testify. The US Supreme Court did not find a constitutional right for defendants to testify until the 1980s.[52]

In addition to maintaining prohibitions on testimony by the accused, southern states were also more likely to disallow testimony by people with prior convictions longer than the rest of the nation. By 1889 twenty-five of the thirty-eight states constitutionally or statutorily removed all limitations on testimony for prior convictions.[53] Six more states made those convicted of perjury incompetent as witnesses but allowed everyone else to testify.[54] Of the seven states that still imposed lifelong disqualifications from testimony for certain criminal convictions after 1881, six were in the South. In addition, courts administered under federal Indian law prohibited those convicted of certain crimes from testifying as witnesses in civil actions except by consent of both parties.[55]

These prohibitions persisted into the twentieth century in several southern states, including Florida and Texas. Under an 1845 Florida law, individuals convicted of a list of crimes could not testify as witnesses.[56] This law remained on the books there until 1901.[57] Texas held on to laws barring convicted felons from serving as witnesses even longer. The 1856 Code of Criminal Procedure in Texas codified common law, barring testimony by witnesses and defendants with prior criminal convictions by specifying that individuals who "have been or may be convicted of a felony" were incompetent to testify.[58] This changed with an 1889 law stating that defendants could testify in their own criminal cases.[59] But individuals convicted of a felony still were prohibited from testifying in any case.[60] This remained law until 1926, when the legislature removed bans on testimony by those with felony convictions.[61] The old statute, though, was not completely gone. A year after the legislature opened up the ability to testify to former felons, the state supreme court determined in *Underwood v. State* that the law applied only to those convicted after 1926. Individuals convicted prior to 1926 still could not testify as witnesses.[62] The impact of this decision reverberated for decades, at least until 1960, when an appeals court ruled a witness incompetent to testify because he had been convicted prior to the 1926 revision.[63]

Three other southern states joined Florida and Texas in banning witnesses with certain convictions. In 1874 Arkansas statutorily clarified common law by prohibiting testimony by witnesses previously convicted of a "capital offense, perjury, subordination of perjury, burglary, robbery, larceny, forgery, counterfeiting, or other infamous crimes."[64] This prohibition remained until the early twentieth century, though a growing number of legal authorities in the state believed the ban to be outdated and inefficient. In 1902 the Arkansas Supreme Court made a direct plea for ending barriers to testimony in its opinion in *Vance v. State*: "There are very few States that now retain such laws, and we think our legislators might well consider whether they should not be repealed in this state also."[65] Despite the court's entreaties, the prohibition on testimony lasted another decade, until 1913, when the legislature ended this disability with a statute allowing all to testify.[66]

South Carolina also denied those with infamous convictions the ability to testify as witnesses well into the twentieth century. In 1928 the South Carolina Supreme Court wrote an extensive opinion that noted that the state was one of the few remaining that followed this common law standard. The court cited judges in South Carolina and elsewhere that recommended abandoning the common law tradition.[67] In 1934 the legislature finally did exactly that, prohibiting disqualification from testimony for the "conviction and sentence for any crime."[68]

Tennessee's ban on testimony by those with certain kinds of criminal convictions lasted the longest. In 1887 the legislature allowed all defendants to testify in their own criminal cases but maintained the disqualification of individuals with infamous convictions from testifying in any other criminal case or any civil case.[69] Thirty-two offenses disqualified witnesses from testifying, and the list was expanded over the course of the nineteenth and twentieth centuries to encompass more crimes. For example, in 1932 the legislature made horse stealing an infamous crime. Such theft would have been considered larceny anyway, and thus an infamous crime, but this new legislation underscored that horse theft, in particular, brought disfranchisement and disqualification.[70]

This prohibition on testimony in Tennessee created a number of problems for prosecutors and law enforcement officials, some of which came to light when the state sought to prosecute crimes committed by individuals while in prison. In such cases, other prisoners might be witnesses, but testimony from these other prisoners would be greatly restricted, because only those felons who were not convicted of infamous crimes could testify.[71] In 1932 the legislature amended the code to allow incarcerated people to be witnesses against each other.[72] Some expressed concern that this law was unconstitutional, because while the prosecution could use such witnesses, the accused could not, creating an unequal burden for the defense.[73] Nonetheless, this revision remained, and disqualification for infamy remained the law in Tennessee for another twenty years, until 1953.[74]

The only nonsouthern state prohibiting those with criminal convictions from serving as witnesses after 1900 was Kansas. Kansas was the first state to depart from common law prohibitions on testimony by civil parties, allowing all to testify in civil actions regardless of "interest or conviction." A few decades later, the Kansas Supreme Court explained that this change was intended to "prevent the baffling of justice."[75] Though no statute barred defendant testimony in criminal trials, none allowed it either. As a result, courts followed common law, prohibiting defendant testimony in criminal trials.[76] This remained the practice until 1915, when the legislature revised the code of criminal practice so that the rule regarding testimony in criminal trials matched what had long existed in civil practice.[77]

Virginia's law governing testimony differed from the laws of other states. In a statute dating back to 1792, Virginia disqualified individuals convicted of felonies unless they had been "pardoned or punished."[78] The text of the law suggests that, unlike other states, the disability of disqualification would be incurred by convicted felons in Virginia only during incarceration; those released from incarceration as a result of a pardon or by completing their sentences would have their rights restored. In practice the law appears, at times, to have been interpreted more in line with procedures in other southern states whereby the disqualification extended beyond incarceration. Governor William Hodges Mann, who served from 1910 to 1914, instituted a gradation of pardons so that people could be released from prison without regaining the right to testify. Those pardoned "conditionally" could not testify in court. For them to gain that ability, another, separate order was required.[79]

Mann's system of gradations seemed to continue under the next governor, Henry Carter Stuart.[80] The question of which kind of pardons restored the right to testify would soon be resolved by the revised Code of 1919, which eliminated the disqualification from testimony for all individuals regardless of criminal record. After 1919 the fact of conviction could affect the credibility of testimony, but Virginia no longer barred convicted individuals from testifying altogether.[81]

Three southern states diverged from the nation in another way as well. During the 1880s, when most states were widening access to court testimony, Alabama, Arkansas, and South Carolina narrowed this access by extending barriers to court testimony to individuals convicted of minor property crimes, usually referred to as "petit larceny." An 1880 decision from the Arkansas Supreme Court ruled that petit larceny disqualified one from testimony in court, noting that the crime "is still larceny" and thus a disqualifying offense.[82] A year later, Alabama courts, too, ruled that laws barring witnesses with prior larceny convictions applied to those convicted of petit larceny.[83] That same year, the South Carolina Supreme Court also held that petit larceny disqualified witnesses from testifying.[84]

Traditionally, the denial of suffrage or court testimony was limited to those convicted of major, serious crimes, usually felonies, though that was not yet a standard, universal term. Lifelong disqualification from testimony due to a misdemeanor was unheard-of in the United States. With the national trend moving toward allowing all to testify, these three southern states doubled down, denying the ability to testify to those accused of small thefts, say, a chicken or a few ears of corn.

Maintaining bans on testimony by individuals with infamous convictions and relegating the testimony of criminal defendants to an unsworn statement was not simply a rejection of national norms but the repudiation of a recognized means of establishing truth and reaching justice. Why did southern states refuse to allow those with criminal convictions to testify in court, refusing to align with the national standard, in some cases for decades? Why did three southern states extend these barriers so they affected scores of people convicted of minor theft during the same decades that other states were eliminating them?

Beyond commentary in the handful of court opinions and legal journals discussed above, there is no evidence of debate or discussion over these exclusions of testimony. Rules of evidence are complex, and judicial processes are subject to less public scrutiny than other elements of public policy such as voting procedures, public spending, and even criminal law. Changes in rules governing testimony were often wrapped up in larger statutory revisions or worked out in case law. These rules affected only a small number of people in relatively rare circumstances. In short, they were not the stuff of headlines or public debate.[85] While legislative intent is hard to find, the absence of legislative action rarely leaves a historical record at all, making it even more difficult to ascertain why states failed to change their rules of evidence. Even the unparalleled expansion of these rules to affect those convicted of petit larceny in Alabama, Arkansas, and South Carolina does not seem to have evoked public comment. The vast majority of the population probably did not even know this expansion had happened.

With scant evidence indicating why southern states maintained these exclusions on testimony longer than other states, the debate over racial and ethnic barriers to court testimony earlier in the nineteenth century offers clues to a possible reason for these regional disparities. An unrestricted ability to testify in court was considered a privilege of citizenship, and white southern political leaders insisted, in the decades prior to the Civil War, that African Americans should not obtain it. In the 1840s testimony by African American sailors had been admitted in a military court in the trial of a white naval officer. This had been used to attack President Martin Van Buren; his opponents suggested that allowing such testimony in a military court indicated that the president was a secret supporter of abolition.[86] Soon afterward, the Methodist Episcopal Church came under fire from white southerners for allowing black persons to testify in an internal disciplinary tribunal.[87] In short, court testimony was believed to be an opening wedge to equal citizenship. The idea that allowing equal access to court testimony would justify demands for and facilitate the attainment of other kinds of legal and political rights was not limited to southerners. In 1854 the California Supreme Court affirmed a prohibition on Chinese testimony against whites, saying, "The same rule which would admit them to testify, would admit them to all the equal rights of citizenship, and we might soon see them at the polls, in the jury box, upon the bench, and in our legislative halls."[88] Access to testimony was understood to be a component of citizenship, and prohibiting racial minorities from obtaining it was a goal of white supremacy.

The ability to testify in court was guaranteed to African Americans at the end of the Civil War, when the Civil Rights Act of 1866 guaranteed equal rights in judicial proceedings. This act gave nonwhite individuals the same capabilities as white citizens to make and enforce contracts, sue and be sued, give evidence in court, and inherit property.[89] More broadly, the Thirteenth and Fourteenth Amendments represented efforts by northern Republicans to elevate African Americans from the same legal status as criminals—cast out from suffrage, testimony, and liberty—and grant them the full rights of citizenship.[90]

White southern political leaders resisted these changes, hoping to keep African Americans in a degraded legal status. One way to do this was to convict and punish African Americans for crimes, using the law to transform them from citizens into criminals with limited civil rights. The biased legal system, including black codes, discriminatory policing, and easily manipulable judicial processes, made it easy to disproportionately convict African Americans of crimes. Increasing the collateral consequences of these convictions limited the ability of African Americans to function as citizens. A clear example of this can be found in the expansion of restrictions on the voting rights of individuals with criminal convictions in southern states in the 1870s. The historical record demonstrates that this was a strategy aimed at reducing black suffrage. White southern Democrats hoped that these laws would erode the black electorate, and they lowered the bar for this collateral consequence, making minor property crimes punishable with disfranchisement. Although these actions were ostensibly race-neutral, they functioned to deny African Americans the right to vote, which had been granted to them by the federal government.[91]

The historical legacy of efforts to ban African Americans from testifying in court, coupled with the determination to restrict the voting rights of criminal convictions as part of an effort to limit black suffrage in the 1870s, suggests that the South's reluctance to expand court testimony in the 1870s and 1880s was part of a larger effort to restrict the civil rights of African Americans. White southern political leaders were uninterested in rationalizing judicial practices or guaranteeing due process in this period. To the contrary, a biased judicial system that frequently and reliably convicted African Americans of crimes served as a tool of white political and social dominance. Protecting accused individuals from wrongful conviction by allowing all possible testimony to be given had little value to those who used the courts to maintain racial hierarchies. Limiting the ability to testify in court could help increase criminal convictions, working alongside laws disfranchising for crime to maintain second-class status for African Americans. It was yet another way for southern states to push back against those who worked to promote equal citizenship. While political leaders in states outside the South celebrated the expansion of witness capacity because it promoted just legal outcomes, white southern leaders had little interest in such goals.

The fact that three southern states extended prohibitions on testifying in court to those convicted of petit larceny in the 1870s offers more evidence that the maintenance of bans on court testimony was part of a racial agenda. Increasing the penalties for petty theft was a celebrated part of the political and social agenda of white southern Democrats in the 1870s. Some states made all grades of larceny a felony so that petit larceny could be punished by incarceration (which usually involved being leased to a private employer of convict labor) and permanent disfranchisement. Others added petit larceny to the list of crimes that could bring lifelong disfranchisement. Increasing the punitive and collateral consequences of petty theft was rooted in assumptions about black criminality and the realities of a racially biased justice system.[92] Bans on court testimony for those with petit larceny convictions meant that African Americans would be subjected to an additional collateral consequence of criminal conviction and denied another privilege of citizenship that had been granted to them by federal authority during Reconstruction.[93]

The differing regional histories in the disqualification from court testimony for witnesses and defendants underscore the need for more studies of both the collateral consequences of criminal convictions and the historical exclusion of witnesses. Region offers one lens for evaluating these histories, because different parts of the nation have had different historical trajectories, particularly with regard to race and ethnicity. In this case, region offers an opening to consider a connection between the collateral consequence of criminal conviction and the systematic exclusion of African Americans from the rights of citizenship, but the larger logics behind restrictions on witness competence are likely more complex. More scholarship investigating the operation of these laws in lower courts and across the country can tell us more about how they shaped Americans' experience with the courts, citizenship, and justice. In particular, laws affecting Native American and immigrant court testimony, especially in western states, is an unexamined and potentially important area that could enhance the argument put forth here.

As George Teaster may have learned, Tennessee was the last state to end barriers for those with prior convictions to serve as witnesses. Change finally came in 1953. Likely contributing to the revision of the state code was an impassioned 1951 article in the *Tennessee Law Review*. Donald Halladay, a University of Tennessee law student and editor of the review, pointed out that the state had the strictest and most exclusionary law in the nation in this regard and called on the legislature to eliminate infamy as a barrier to competency. He asserted that the ban on testimony produced inequities across the state's justice system. Plaintiffs in civil suits had failed to receive justice, and prosecutors and attorneys had lost important cases when witnesses were disqualified for infamy.[94]

The *Tennessee Law Review* article spotlighted the impact of prohibitions on testimony by discussing both Teaster's case and another civil case, *Tom Love Grocery Co. v. Maryland Casualty Company*. In this 1933 case from Shelby County, Tennessee, a grocery store owner filed an insurance claim when his shop was robbed. The insurance company disputed that a robbery had occurred and demanded the grocer provide evidence of the crime. When the grocer called the man who had been convicted of robbing the store to testify that a crime had indeed been committed, the burglar's testimony was disqualified because he had been rendered infamous by the burglary conviction. With no evidence of burglary, the grocery store owner had no claim. At issue on appeal was whether the burglar's written confession was admissible as evidence, but the state supreme court ruled that it was not, and the insurance claim was denied.[95]

According to Halladay, *Tom Love Grocery Co.* offered evidence why ending this barrier to competency "would lift our law on this important point out of the fifteenth century into the twentieth."[96] Halladay's article, in conjunction with lobbying by legal scholars, prosecutors, and law enforcement officers, persuaded the legislature to lift this ban on testimony. The legislature acted in 1953, eliminating laws restricting competency due to prior convictions.[97]

No state today bars the testimony of witnesses based on a prior conviction, and criminal defendants may choose to testify in their own trials. But prior convictions still matter when witnesses come to court. Under federal rules of evidence, for example, a felony conviction can impact the credibility of witness testimony in some circumstances.[98] The rise in the number of individuals with such convictions in recent decades means that more people can be judged unreliable when they testify in courts. Rates of criminal conviction and incarceration today are racially and economically disproportionate. As a result, African Americans and Hispanics are more likely to have their testimony discredited, as are lower-income people of all races.[99] Recognizing the impact of this collateral consequence today and understanding its origins and implications in the past remind us that social and economic structures affect whose voices speak with authority and credibility in our justice system.

NOTES

I would like to thank George Fisher, Amy Louise Wood, Natalie J. Ring, and the anonymous reviewers for the University of Illinois Press for commenting on various drafts of this chapter.

1. Cambria Coal Co. v. Teaster, 167 S.W.2d 343 (Tennessee Supreme Court, 1943); *Clinton (TN) Courier-News,* September 18, 1941, 1; *George Teaster v. Cambria Coal Company,* Anderson County Circuit Court, Civil Minutes, vol. 11, Tennessee State Library and Archives (hereafter cited as TSLA), Nashville; *Cambria Coal Company*

v. George Teaster, Tennessee Supreme Court Records, TSLA; *Clinton (TN) Courier-News,* October 1, 1936, 1; Donald L. Halladay, "Infamy as Ground of Disqualification in Tennessee," *Tennessee Law Review* 24, no. 4 (1951–53): 544–57.

2. Anderson County Circuit Court, Criminal Minutes, vol. 5, TSLA; *Cambria Coal Co.,* 167 S.W.2d 343.

3. Restrictions on testimony by individuals who had been convicted of perjury persisted in some states. See, for example, chap. 23, art. XI, sec. 2225, in *The Revised Laws of Oklahoma: 1910* (St. Paul, MN: Pioneer Company, 1912), 1:559; chap. 12, sec. 8708, in *The Revised Codes of the State of North Dakota, 1905* (Bismarck, ND: Tribune Co., 1905), 1432.

4. Kimberly S. Smith, "The Death of Discretion: Prior Felony Convictions Automatically Admissible in Civil Actions," *Campbell Law Review* 12, no. 2 (1990): 319–42.

5. Mary Bell Hammerman, "Criminal Defendant's Constitutional Right to Testify," *Villanova Law Review* 23, no. 4 (1978): 678–87; Robert Popper, "History and Development of the Accused's Right to Testify," *Washington University Law Review* 1962, no. 4 (1962): 454–71; George Fisher, "The Jury's Rise as a Lie Detector," *Yale Law Journal* 107, no. 3 (1997): 575–708.

6. Fisher, "The Jury's Rise," 656–97, quote at 658.

7. For a discussion of the difference between legal practice in "localized law" and in state law, see Laura Edwards, *The People and Their Peace: Legal Culture and the Transformation of Inequality in the Post-Revolutionary South* (Chapel Hill: University of North Carolina Press, 2009).

8. John William Salmond, *Essays in Jurisprudence and Legal History* (London: Steven and Hayes, 1891), 27–35.

9. Simon Greenleaf, *A Treatise on the Law of Evidence,* 14th ed. (Boston: Little, Brown, 1883), 1:465; James Q. Whitman, *Harsh Justice: Criminal Punishment and the Widening Divide between America and Europe* (New York: Oxford University Press, 2003).

10. Samuel March Phillipps and Andrew Amos, *A Treatise on the Law of Evidence* (London: Saunders and Benning, 1838), 1:43–137. A history of barriers to testimony by the accused can also be found in Ferguson v. State of Ga., 365 U.S. 570 (1961); and Popper, "History and Development," 454–71.

11. Popper, "History and Development," 458.

12. People v. Tyler, 36 Cal. 522 (1869).

13. *The Spectator: A Weekly Review of Politics, Literature, Theology, and Art,* March 8, 1884, 310. For a US perspective, see "Testimony of Persons Accused of Crime," *American Law Review* 1, no. 3 (1867): 443; Boston v. State, 94 Ga. 590 (1894); People v. Thomas, 9 Mich. 314 (1861); Baker v. U.S., 1 Minn. 207 (1854).

14. William Stoebuck, "Reception of English Common Law in the American Colonies," *William and Mary Law Review* 10, no. 2 (1968): 393–426.

15. Chap. 23, sec. 71, in *Acts of the State of Tennessee, 1829* (Nashville: Allen A. Hall, 1829), 253.

16. Pt. IV, title 7, sec. 23, in *Revised Statutes of the State of New York* (Albany: Packard and Van Bentruysen, 1836), 2:586.

17. No. XIV, in *Acts and Resolutions Passed by the Legislative Council of the Territory of Florida* (Tallahassee: Star of Florida, 1845), 43.

18. Gabriel J. Chin, "'A Chinaman's Chance' in Court: Asian Pacific Americans and Racial Rules of Evidence," *University of California Irvine Law Review* 3, no. 4 (2013): 965–72; Alfred Avins, "Right to Be a Witness and the Fourteenth Amendment," *Missouri Law Review* 31, no. 4 (1966): 471–504.

19. Henry Potter, *The Office and Duty of a Justice of the Peace* (Raleigh: Joseph Gales, 1816); see also State v. Yeates, 4 Hawks 187 (1825).

20. Overviews of state rules governing witness competence circa the 1880s can be found in Stewart Rapalje, *A Treatise on the Law of Witnesses* (New York: Banks and Brothers 1887), 16–25, 249–65; and Greenleaf, *A Treatise*, 730–816. While this work relies on Greenleaf's and Rapalje's generalizations, I confirmed the account of each state mentioned here by consulting state constitutions, legislation, and case law.

21. Christopher J. W. Allen, *The Law of Evidence in Victorian England* (Cambridge: Cambridge University Press, 1997), 183.

22. Sec. 243, *The Revised Statutes of the State of Indiana, 1852* (Indianapolis: J. P. Chapman, State Printer, 1852), 83, clarified and quoted in Stocking v. State, 7 Ind. 326 (1855).

23. Title 1, chap. 10, sec. 141, in *The Revised Statutes of the State of Connecticut* (Hartford, CT: Case, Tiffany, 1849), 86.

24. See also title XXII, chap. 102, in *Revised Statutes of the State of Michigan* (Detroit: Bagg and Harmon, 1846), 99; art. 2388, in *The Code of Iowa: Passed at the Session of the General Assembly of 1850–1851* (Iowa City: Palmer and Paul, 1851), 322.

25. "Massachusetts," *American Law Review* 1, no. 2 (1867): 396.

26. US v. Sims, 161 F.1008 (Circuit Court, N.D. Alabama, Southern Division 1907).

27. State v. Connor, 7 La. Ann. 379 (1852).

28. Ibid.

29. Act 29 of the session of 1886, cited in Solomon Wolff, *Revised Laws of Louisiana* (New Orleans: F. F. Hansel and Bro., 1897), 276.

30. Vance v. State, 70 Ark. 272 (Ark. 1902).

31. Rapalje, *A Treatise*, 247–49. See, for example, Le Baron v. Crombie, 14 Mass. 234 (Mass. 1817); People v. Whipple, 9 Cow. 707 (New York 1827); Popper, "History and Development," 463; *Ferguson*, 365 U.S. 570. For a consideration of the motivations for this movement, see Fisher, "The Jury's Rise," 662–72.

32. Chap. 37, in *Revised Statutes of the United States* (Washington, DC: US Government Printing Office, 1881), 1:312.

33. "Testimony of Persons Accused of Crime," *American Law Review* 1, no. 1 (1866): 443–50. On liberal opponents of the expansion of testimony, see Popper, "History and Development," 460.

34. Yerachmiel E. Weinstein, "Criminal Procedure: Fifth Amendment: Judicial Comment on Failure to Testify Allowed (*Lakeside v. Oregon*)," *Marquette Law Review* 62, no. 74 (1978): 74–89; Popper, "History and Development," 463.

35. Popper asserts that Pennsylvania maintained laws barring testimony by defendants until 1885, but that is incorrect. See act 43, in *Laws of the General Assembly of the State of Pennsylvania* (Harrisburg: B. F. Meyers, 1877), 45.

36. Art. 1, chap. 10, sec. 2302, in *The Code of Alabama* (Montgomery: Brittan and De Wolf, 1852), 427. See also State v. McCall, 4 Ala. 643 (Ala. 1843) on rights of defendants.

37. Taylor v. State, 62 Ala. 164 (Ala. 1878).

38. Sylvester v. The State, 71 Ala. 17 (Ala. 1881).

39. *Acts of the General Assembly of the State of Alabama Passed at the Session of 1882–83* (Montgomery: W. D. Brown and Company, 1883), 4. Allowing unsworn statements by defendants had occurred in sixteenth-century England. See Fisher, "The Jury's Rise," 603–5. This may have been practice in lower courts in the United States as well.

40. Chappell v. State, 71 Ala. 322 (1883); Blackburn v. State, 71 Ala. 321 (1883).

41. No. 80, in *Acts of the General Assembly of the State of Alabama Passed at the Session of 1884–1885* (Montgomery: Barrett and Company, 1885), 139.

42. Chap. 1472, sec. 4, in *Acts and Resolutions Adopted by the General Assembly of Florida* (Tallahassee: Office of the Floridian, 1866), 36.

43. Chap. 1816, in *The Acts and Resolutions Adopted by the Legislature of Florida at Its Extra Session Beginning May 23, 1870* (Tallahassee: Charles H. Walton, 1870), 13.

44. Hawkins v. State, 29 Fla. 554 (1892); Miller v. State, 15 Fla. 577 (1876).

45. Chap. 4400, in *Acts and Resolutions Adopted by the Legislature of Florida* (Tallahassee: Tallahassean Book and Job Office, 1895), 16.

46. No. 189, in *Acts Passed by the General Assembly of Georgia, November and December 1866* (Macon: J. W. Burke and Co., 1867), 138. See also Brown v. State, 60 Ga. 210 (1878); Brunswick and W. R. Co. v. Clem, 80 Ga. 534 (1888).

47. I have been unable to locate the 1874 act, but it is referenced as chap. XLIX, art. 10, in *The Code of the State of Georgia*, comp. N. E. Harris (Macon: J. W. Burke and Co., 1878), 93. See also pt. 4, title 1, div. xiii, in *The Code of the State of Georgia* (Atlanta: J. P. Harrison, 1882), 1214; Ross v. State, 59 Ga. 248 (Ga. 1876).

48. *Brown*, 60 Ga. 210 (1878).

49. Vaughn v. State, 88 Ga. 731 (Ga. 1892).

50. William W. Gordon Jr., "Defects in Our Criminal Procedure and the Remedies Therefor," in *Report of the Annual Session of the Georgia Bar Association* (Atlanta: Franklin Turner Company, 1906), 254–56. See also Bird v. State, 50 Ga. 585 (1874).

51. Union v. State, 7 Ga. App. 27 (Ga. Appeals 1909).

52. *Ferguson*, 365 U.S. 570; Hammerman, "Criminal Defendant's Constitutional Right."

53. Rapalje, *A Treatise*, 256. Rapalje does not discuss the following states: Kentucky, Louisiana, Nevada, Nebraska, Ohio, and Oregon. Information on Kentucky is from chap. 107, sec. 5, in *The Revised Statutes of Kentucky*, comp. Richard H. Stanton (Cincinnati: Robert Clark, 1867), 2:471; Commonwealth v. McGuire, 7 Ky. L. Rptr. 814 (1886); chap. 37, in *The General Statutes of Kentucky*, comp. Joshua Bullitt and

John Feland (Louisville: Bradley and Gilbert, 1887), 548. On Louisiana, see act 29, "An Act Declaring the Competency of Witnesses in Criminal Proceedings," in *Revised Laws of Louisiana, 1870–1896* (New Orleans: F. F. Hansel and Bro., 1897), 276; State v. McManus, 42 La. Ann. 1194 (La. 1890). Nevada and Nebraska had statutes giving defendants the right to testify, but the law did not clarify the position of other witnesses. With no appellate court decisions prior to the 1880s on these questions, my assumption is that they followed common law. On Ohio, see chap. 1710, art. 2, sec. 139, in *The Statutes of the State of Ohio* (Cincinnati: Robert Clarke, 1876), 3:2160. On Oregon, see chap. 4, secs. 722–24, in Oregon Laws of 1862, *The Codes and Statutes of Oregon* (San Francisco: Bancroft Whitney Company, 1901), 1:366–67.

54. The six states were Kentucky, Mississippi, Maryland, Ohio, Pennsylvania, and Vermont.

55. Moore v. Adams, 26 Okla. 48 (Okla. 1810); chap. 25, sec. 1974, in *Annotated Statutes of the Indian Territory* (St. Paul, MN: West Publishing Co., 1899), 346. The territory of Montana barred felons from testifying, though the injured party in a criminal case could testify even with a prior felony. See chap. 2, sec. 649, in *Compiled Statutes of Montana* (Helena: Journal Publishing Company, 1888), 230.

56. No. XIV, in *Acts and Resolutions Passed by the Legislative Council of the Territory of Florida* (Tallahassee: Star of Florida, 1845), 43.

57. Chap. 4966, in *General Acts and Resolutions Adopted by the Legislature of Florida* (Tallahassee: Tallahassee Book and Job Print, 1901), 111.

58. Chap. 151, "An Act Supplemental to and Amendatory of an Act to Establish a Code of Criminal Procedure for the State of Texas," approved August 26, 1856, in *The Laws of Texas, 1822–1909*, comp. H. P. N. Gammel (Austin: Gammel Book Co., 1898), 4:240.

59. Chap. 43, in *General Laws of the State of Texas, 1889* (Austin: State Printing Office, 1889), 37.

60. Art. 768, in *The Penal Code and Code of Criminal Procedure of the State of Texas*, comp. Sam A. Wilson (St. Louis: Gilbert Book Company, 1896), 263.

61. Chap. 13, in *Acts of the 39th Legislature of Texas*, 20, cited in Underwood v. State, 111 Tex. Crim. 124 (Court of Criminal Appeals of Texas 1927).

62. *Underwood*, 111 Tex. Crim. 124.

63. Marshall v. State, 168 Tex. Crim. 569 (Court of Criminal Appeals of Texas 1960).

64. Sec. 2482, in *A Digest of the Statutes of Arkansas*, comp. Edward W. Gantt (Little Rock: Little Rock Printing and Publishing, 1874), 491.

65. *Vance*, 70 Ark. 272.

66. Arkansas Statutes, secs. 28-605, 28-707, cited in Holcomb v. State, 238 S.W.2d 505 (1951).

67. State v. Jeffcoat, 148 S.C. 322 (S.C. 1928).

68. Act no. 632 of 1934, 38 Statutes at Large 1193, cited in State v. Merriman, 287 S.C. 74 (S.C. Ct. App. 1985).

69. Chap. 79, sec. 1, in *Acts of the State of Tennessee, 1887* (Nashville: Marshall and Bruce, 1887), 158.

70. Chap. 23, sec. 71, in *Acts of the State of Tennessee, 1829*; sec. 11762, in *Code of Tennessee, 1932* (Kingsport, TN: Southern Publishers, 1931).

71. Noninfamous felonies were crimes that involved violence, such as murder and assault.

72. Sec. 12179, in *Code of Tennessee, 1932.*

73. Halladay, "Infamy"; Hambrick v. State, 181 Tenn. 544 (Tenn. 1944).

74. Halladay, "Infamy," 547; chap. 194, in *Public Acts of the State of Tennessee* (Nashville: Rich Printing Company, 1953), 701; *Nashville Tennessean,* April 11, 1953, 9. A 1948 Tennessee Supreme Court decision limited disqualification to those convicted in Tennessee courts. Burdine v. Kennon, 186 Tenn. 200 (Tenn. 1948).

75. Title X, chap. 1, in *General Laws of the State of Kansas . . . 1862* (Topeka: J. H. Bennet, 1862), 176; State v. Clark, 60 Kan. 450 (Kansas 1899).

76. *State,* 60 Kan. 450.

77. Cited in State v. Marshall, 95 Kan. 628 (1915). For a longer comparison of the relationship between civil party competency and defendant testimony, see Fisher, "The Jury's Rise," 656–97.

78. Chap. 78, in *Statutes at Large of Virginia* (Richmond: Samuel Shepherd, 1835), 196; chap. 10, sec. 19, in *Acts and Joint Resolutions Passed by the General Assembly of the State of Virginia* (Richmond: R. F. Walker, 1878), 314.

79. *Journal of the Senate of the Commonwealth of Virginia, 1914* (Richmond: Davis Bottom, 1914), 47.

80. *Journal of the Senate of the Commonwealth of Virginia, 1916* (Richmond: Davis Bottom, 1916), 13, 21.

81. Sec. 4779, in *Virginia Code of 1919* (Richmond: D. Bottom, Superintendent of Public Printing, 1919); D. W. Woodbridge, "The Effect in Virginia of Conviction of Crime on Competency and Credibility of Witnesses," *Virginia Law Review* 23, no. 470 (1936–37): 470–80. The case of Virginia demonstrates that using published appellate opinions to establish how rules of evidence functioned on a day-to-day level in local courts has limited value.

82. Hall v. Doyle, 35 Ark. 445 (1880).

83. *Sylvester,* 71 Ala. 17.

84. State v. James, 15 S.C. 233 (1881).

85. Fisher confirms the difficulty of finding legislative or public discussion in the historical record: "The issue of defendant testimony . . . rarely disturbed the public consciousness" ("The Jury's Rise," 683).

86. *The Northern Man with Southern Principles, and the Southern Man with American Principles: Or a View of the Comparative Claims of Gen. William H. Harrison and Martin Van Buren, Candidates for the Presidency* (Washington, DC: Peter Force, 1840).

87. Charles Elliott, *History of the Great Secession from the Methodist Episcopal Church in the Year 1845* (Cincinnati: Swormstedt and Poe, 1855), 220–23.

88. People v. Hall, 4 Cal. 399 (1854), quoted in Chin, "'A Chinaman's Chance,'" 968.

89. A. Leon Higginbotham Jr., *Shades of Freedom: Racial Politics and Presumptions of the American Legal Process* (New York: Oxford University Press, 1996), 76–80.

90. Pippa Holloway, *Living in Infamy: Felon Disfranchisement and the History of American Citizenship* (New York: Oxford University Press, 2013), 17–32, 159–60.

91. Ibid., 54–78.

92. Ibid.

93. I have been unable to locate any critiques of these new evidentiary practices from leaders of the African American community, North or South. This may be in part because, as I note above, changes to rules of evidence were a technical legal matter that rarely encountered public scrutiny. A racist national discourse linking race and criminality began to emerge in the 1890s, but in those years the pushback by African American intellectuals such as W. E. B. Du Bois and Kelly Miller focused on challenging explanations for this perceived disparity rather than the criminal justice processes that produced it. I have not located any discussions of racial injustice in southern courts that critiqued the rules of evidence examined here. In 1870s Virginia some African American leaders did speak out against punishing black voters with larceny convictions with disfranchisement by framing petit larceny as a morally valid tactic for survival rather than an immoral crime, but they did not extend this analysis to a critique of the rules of evidence limiting witness testimony for those with prior convictions. See ibid., 73–77; Khalil Gibran Muhammad, *The Condemnation of Blackness: Race, Crime, and the Making of Modern Urban America* (Cambridge, MA: Harvard University Press, 2010), 58–87.

94. Halladay, "Infamy," 550.

95. Tom Love Grocery Co. v. Maryland Casualty Company, 166 Tenn. 275 (Tenn. 1933).

96. Halladay, "Infamy," 553, quoting An Act for Improving the Law of Evidence, 6 & 7 Vict. 85 (1843).

97. Chap. 194, in *Public Acts of the State of Tennessee; Nashville Tennessean,* April 11, 1953, 9.

98. Prior convictions may affect the credibility of defendant testimony in more limited circumstances. See Glen Weissenberger and James J. Duane, *Federal Rules of Evidence: Rules, Legislative History, Commentary and Authority,* 7th ed. (Newark, NJ: LexisNexis, 2012), chap. 609.

99. Marc Mauer and Nazgol Ghandnoosh, "Incorporating Racial Equity into Criminal Justice Reform," The Sentencing Project, 2014, www.sentencingproject .org/doc/rd_Incorporating_Racial_Equity_into_Criminal_Justice_Reform.pdf; Bernadette Rabuy and Daniel Kopf, "Prisons of Poverty: Uncovering the Pre-incarceration Incomes of the Imprisoned," Prison Policy Initiative, PrisonPolicy.org., July 2015.

CHAPTER 6

Sewing and Spinning for the State

Incarcerated Black Female Garment Workers in the Jim Crow South

Talitha L. LeFlouria

On August 29, 1897, in Haywood County, Tennessee, Hannah Merriweather, a "colored woman," was sentenced to life imprisonment for allegedly poisoning her father. One night, the man started to show signs of being "violently sick." According to Bate Bond, the defense attorney in the case, "No one at that time suspected he had been poisoned. A short time thereafter, Hannah's conduct in some way excited suspicion. It developed that she had, a day or two prior to the old man's death, bought a box of Rough on Rats [rat poison]."[1]

Merriweather lived with her father on the farm of "Major" Shaw and worked for shares. According to Shaw, the woman's relationship with her father "had not been pleasant." He alleged that Merriweather "admitted" to giving the man Rough on Rats on the night of his death. Based on Shaw's claims and Merriweather's reportedly "suspicious behavior," her father's body was exhumed. As recorded in attorney Bond's letter to Nashville judge William A. Carter, a "chemical examination of the contents of his stomach [was] made, which disclosed the fact that the old man died from arsenical poisoning."[2]

Following her father's autopsy, Merriweather was arrested, charged, tried, and convicted. She was later transferred from the local jail, where she had been detained, to the Tennessee State Prison in Nashville, about 150 miles east of Haywood County. There she was joined by approximately forty-two other women, thirty-seven of whom were African American and five of whom were white.[3] All of these women, including Merriweather, were put to work in the prison hosiery mill. They were tasked with making stockings and expanding the growth of the state's newly emerging contract labor system. In neighboring Alabama, at the women's prison in Wetumpka, known as the

Walls, female inmates were required to do the same. However, in Alabama, clothing manufactures extended beyond hosiery to include pants, shirts, blouses, roller towels, union suits, belts, underwear, pillowcases, and a host of other wares to be sold on the open market and used by prisoners.

By the turn of the twentieth century, when convict leasing began to dematerialize in the southern states, new systems of convict labor were established in its place.[4] Convict leasing permitted private companies to lease felony inmates from the state and assume total control over their lives, welfare, and working bodies. In some southern states, namely, Alabama and Tennessee, the contract system, whereby private investors were allowed to build and operate factories on the grounds of state-run prison facilities, arose as an alternative mode of labor exploitation.

The 1896 shift from convict leasing to contract labor in Tennessee resulted from the problem that convict leasing created competition with free labor. Miners protested that they could not secure jobs or fair wages because convicts could be forced to do twice the work for half the pay.[5] In Alabama contract labor was adopted as a way to extract greater profits from the female prison labor force; more money could be derived from using them to sew in the sweatshop than to sow the fields of the state prison farm. Unlike in Tennessee, where contract labor served as a replacement for convict leasing, contracting and convict leasing existed in tandem in Alabama. Convict leasing was not abolished in Alabama until 1928.

This chapter examines how incarcerated black female garment workers contributed to the contract labor systems of Tennessee and Alabama and explores how their lives and labors were fashioned within these states' newly established apparel industries during the late nineteenth and early twentieth centuries. By homing in on the plight of black women workers in particular, this chapter challenges the dualistic constructions during this period of southern black women's labor, which has been primarily categorized as agricultural or domestic in nature. Through the execution of new forms of specialized industrial work that remained off-limits to most black women in the free labor market, female felons contributed to the modernization of the Jim Crow South.[6]

Whether sewing garments, making bricks, building roads, laying railroad tracks, felling trees, plowing fields, or picking crops, imprisoned women workers added to the economic growth of southern Jim Crow carceral regimes. This chapter situates imprisoned female garment workers in the broader historical and historiographical discourse on women and work in the Jim Crow South and calls attention to the ways in which this particular class of black female convicts aided in the development of the region's industrial economy.

Historian Michelle Haberland's pioneering study, *Striking Beauties: Women Apparel Workers in the U.S. South, 1930–2000*, reveals the contributions working-class women made to the twentieth-century southern apparel industry, an enterprise that has gained little attention among historians, who have tended to focus more on the textile industry instead.[7] By directing attention to the apparel industry, *Striking Beauties* sheds light on an overlooked area of southern industrialization. It gives voice to the women, most of whom were white, who "sewed clothes and claimed a distinctly feminine space in the history of America's working classes."[8] Expanding on Haberland's work, this chapter places the imprisoned black female garment worker at the center of the southern industrialization experiment. In doing so, it breaks new ground by showing how the southern apparel industry profited from the use of convict women workers, who helped advance industrial capitalism in the Jim Crow South, aiding in the shift from an agrarian economy to a diversified economic system.

The same occupations African American women were denied outside of prison were impressed upon them by the state. In this way, prison expanded the compass of southern black women's labor. Nevertheless, in all other ways, the same racial divisions that were being codified beyond the walls of the sweatshops were firmly reinforced on prison grounds. Black and white women prisoners were required to sleep in separate quarters and occupied opposite corners of sewing rooms. In this way, the everyday lives of female felons in Tennessee, Alabama, and nearby Georgia were one and the same.

My book, *Chained in Silence: Black Women and Convict Labor in the New South*, has shown that black women were a central part of the prison labor force. Like men, they were required to work in brickyards, sawmills, railroads, mines, and plantations and on chain gangs. The prison sweatshop was another critical site where female prisoners labored and experienced work-related oppression, bodily commodification, and gendered forms of exploitation. Yet for the many similarities that existed between the experiences of imprisoned women workers who occupied these various spaces, there were some marked differences as well. When we look at the social aspects of involuntary servitude in Tennessee and Alabama in particular, it becomes evident that prison officials and contractors respected gender conventions and did not utilize black female laborers to perform "men's work," as was the practice in neighboring Georgia. In other words, they did not practice "compulsory defeminization," a term I use to describe how some prison contractors forcefully ungendered black women's work (and dress) as a form of punishment and as a way to satisfy financial and work-related needs.[9] Instead, these women's energies were preserved for what was considered the most feminine of industries: sewing and spinning for the state. Yet even in the absence of compulsory defeminization, African American women prisoners in Tennessee and Alabama were still prone to other forms of work-related mistreatment and race-based discrimination that, in many ways, mirrored the conditions faced by working-class black women in the Jim Crow South. White female inmates received preferential treatment: some were prescribed lighter or "better" labor assignments, and black women were commonly excluded from the politics of protection afforded to white women prisoners. ·

Jim Crow logics of "separate and (un)equal" extended to the free labor marketplace. Race was used as a delimiting factor that determined the level of access that wage-earning black women had to certain occupations. Factory jobs and specialized trades were held in reserve for white women, rendering black women a negligible part of the labor force.[10] When they did secure employment, they were usually given menial jobs (such as sweeping and cleaning) and provided unequal pay.[11]

In 1910 roughly ten thousand African American women were employed in cigar and tobacco factories in the Upper South, where, according to the Women's Bureau of the US Department of Labor, they "held a monopoly on the heavy and dusty labor."[12] A lesser number worked in other industries throughout the United States. As shown in table 6.1, 4,749 black women were employed in nonagricultural forms of industrial production.[13] During World War I (1914–18) and in the decade afterward, the population of black women engaged in industrial jobs in the Upper South and in certain parts of the North and Midwest significantly increased. Wartime labor demands and the withdrawal of men from the labor pool allowed black women in these areas to obtain factory positions. According to a 1922 joint report entitled "Negro Women in Industry," issued by the Women's Bureau of the US Department of Labor in conjunction with the bureau's Division of Negro Economics, African American women made up 16.8 percent (11,812) of the total 70,409 industrial workers employed in the following nine states: New York, Pennsylvania, Ohio, Illinois, Michigan, Indiana, Virginia, West Virginia, and North Carolina. Of the 1,473 women employed in clothing manufactures, 41.5 percent (710) were African American.[14]

Not unlike their peers in the North, Midwest, and Upper South, working-class African American women in the Deep South sought employment in the region's textile mills and garment factories. In Alabama and Tennessee, black women entered these industries in small numbers and were usually

Table 6.1. Black Women in Labor Industries, 1910

Industry	Number of Black Women Workers
Bag-making plants	296
Candy factories	126
Canneries	124
Glass factories	77
Hosiery mills	327
Meatpacking plants	173
Nut sorting and packing plants	1,017
Textile mills (cotton and knitting)	1,157
Wood industry (boxes, furniture, sawmills)	1,452

Source: James J. Davis, Secretary, US Department of Labor, and Mary Anderson, Director, US Women's Bureau, *Negro Women in Industry in 15 States*, Bulletin of the Women's Bureau, No. 70 (Washington, DC: US Government Printing Office, 1929), 15–26. Unfortunately, this report excludes any mention of the specific states where black women were working in 1910. Nevertheless, the report is important for showing the occupational distribution of black female industrial workers during this period.

limited in the types of work they could perform. According to the Women's Bureau of the US Department of Labor, "the occupations of negro women in textiles, except those in hosiery and knit goods, were concerned chiefly with cleaning, with the simpler performances, with the traditional hand occupations, or with the heavier or dirtier parts of the work." They did the scrubbing, sweeping, sorting, and picking of waste matter from raw cotton. A smaller fraction engaged in more specialized tasks, such as spinning and weaving. In the knitting mills, some worked as "knitters, loopers and top-pers, inspectors, and sewers and sewing-machine operators." In the hosiery mills, black women were routinely "engaged upon parts of the work that bore a considerable degree of importance in the manufacturing process": power-machine sewing, running winders, seaming, spinning, mending, and inspecting, among other tasks.[15]

To fully grasp the diverse and dynamic nature of black women's labor in the southern apparel industry, one must take into account the lesser-known experiences of working-class incarcerated women. When the convict female worker is included in the historical conversation and her sweat, strife, strain, and attempts toward survival in the region's prison-based garment factories are accounted for, an alternative outlook emerges. It becomes apparent that these women, too, contributed to the southern industrialization experiment of the late nineteenth and early twentieth centuries.

The rise of the southern apparel industry had implications for how some southern states, namely, Tennessee and Alabama, went about restructuring their penal systems. These states maneuvered to erect "factories with fences" to replace the decentralized method of hiring out prisoners to private companies. Contracting firms continued to purchase the services of convicts from the state, but they worked them from within the walls of the prison, as opposed to outside the penitentiary. As stated in a report from the Board of Prison Commissioners of the State of Tennessee, "The buildings, power, heat, light, water, convict labor, guards, and provisions was [*sic*] supplied by penal officials at a given price per day, per piece, pound or quantity, for a satisfactory term of years to manufacturers."[16] The manufacturers, in turn, provided the working capital, machinery, and technical supervision necessary to run the garment factories.

In 1896, the year convict leasing was abolished in Tennessee (making it the first southern state to do away with the system), Jacob May, founder of Rock City Hosiery Mills (later renamed May Hosiery Mills), broke new ground when he became the first entrepreneur to establish a garment factory inside the walls of the Tennessee State Prison (TSP). His entry into the hosiery business began after he responded to an advertisement in a Boston newspaper announcing that the state was taking bids for convict labor. After his initial bid for "50 men at approximately 50 cents per day" was accepted, May, his wife, two sons, and a small group of "fixers"—men he hired to help repair knitting machines—moved from Boston to Nashville and started the hosiery mill.[17]

Between 1896 and 1908—the year May's contract with the state of Tennessee was suspended—Rock City Hosiery employed an average of 211 prisoners each year to labor in its knitting mill, as well as the mill's dyeing and finishing departments. Two buildings, Nos. 2 and 6, were reserved for the manufacture of women's and children's hose, while the remaining eight buildings were used for foundry labor and the manufacture of harnesses and saddles, paper boxes, shoes, rattan chairs, and baby carriages.[18] Through their partnership with these diverse manufacturing entities, TSP officials expressed the hope that "more net revenue will come into the state treasury after the year 1897 from the penitentiary system than was received under the general wholesale lease system."[19]

Unlike Alabama, where the prison-based apparel industry was exclusively dominated by women, Tennessee prison officials and contractors most heavily relied on "lame, young, and weaker male" *and* female convicts to do "feminine" work.[20] The labor demands imposed by the contract labor system and the state's and manufacturer's mutual goal to turn a sizeable profit resulted in the unmaking of racialized gender norms. Consequently, male and female work roles were collapsed—but only when it came to men;

women prisoners were rarely if ever impressed to perform "men's work" in the Tennessee coalfields. Yet male inmates could easily be found sewing, spinning, stitching, and knitting hosiery.

Working separately but at the same trade, male and female hosiery mill workers made up a considerable fraction of the TSP labor force. By 1898 Jacob May & Co. and Leo Kaufman & Co. (a partner company) had contracted 198 convicts, 52 of whom were women, to work in the Rock City Hosiery Mills. According to the second biennial report of the Board of Prison Commissioners, 99 inmates were used for knitting hosiery, while the remainder were put to work "dyeing, finishing, manipulating and handling hosiery." Laboring from "sun to sun," these individuals churned out a remarkable "7,000 pair of hose daily."[21]

The everyday routine of incarcerated garment workers began before daybreak, when male and female inmates (who lived and worked at separate ends of the prison grounds) were lined up in the yard and ushered into their respective dining quarters for breakfast. On Monday, Wednesday, Thursday, and Saturday they could expect to receive a stingy helping of "beef stew and onions, coffee, cornbread or flour bread." Tuesday's, Friday's, and Sunday's rations were a little more plentiful, consisting of "fried bacon and gravy, coffee, and corn or flour bread," with an occasional side of fried apples.[22] After their morning meal, the laborers were rounded up and escorted to the factory buildings, where they spent the next twelve to fourteen hours churning out hosiery, with breaks only for dinner and supper.

The grind at Rock City mimicked the work routines played out by sweatshop operatives all over the South. In the mills, hosiery workers engaged in a complex, collaborative, and multilayered sequence of tasks that included each of the following: roving, doffing, winding, knitting, looping, turning, boarding, pairing, and stamping. Rovers performed the initial duty of twisting and strengthening fibers not yet formed into yarn, then winding the fibers onto a bobbin. Those tasked with operating the frame spinner were required to place full bobbins on the machine and keep watch as the fibers were transferred to a small spinning bobbin. This process was known as "setting in roving." In this stage of the hosiery-making process, a worker was made to walk up and down the aisle between the frames to see which bobbins were empty and piece together broken yarn ends.[23]

The doffers stood watch over the bobbins until they were full of yarn, then quickly removed them from the spinning frame. The full bobbins were then transferred to cones by a group of winders. It was the job of the winding crew to ensure that the cones were properly positioned and the yarn smoothly and evenly wound. The cones were then passed off to the knitters.

Once the yarn had cycled through the knitting machine and the stockings were composed, the loopers stepped in to close the toes and heels, which had been left open. As described in a report from the US Department of Labor, "stitch by stitch, they [the loopers] place together, on a series of fine needles or quills, the corresponding opposite loops of the open edges of a stocking, so that the looping machine can catch each stitch and complete a perfect seam." While this process by itself was not a dangerous one, it did place considerable strain on the eyes and was known to "produce nervous tension when done at high speed."[24]

Prisoner Fred Moore, a "Negro" man, experienced firsthand the effects of physical overexertion and eyestrain caused by standing for long periods of time and working at an intense pace. Convicted of rape in March 1898 and sentenced to serve a life term in the TSP, Moore spent the first year of his sentence working in the Rock City Mills as a looper. But to the displeasure of management, Moore was "excused by the prison doctor from doing this work on account, as he [the doctor] claimed it was injuring his eyes."[25] Shortly after being removed from the mills, he was "put into the shoe shop [and] was put on stitching work." But Rock City officials complained that the work he was performing in the shoe shop was far more injurious to his eyes than looping. They also bemoaned the loss of their investment, claiming, "We paid $75.00 to $100.00 to the state for his services and learned him to do the work and when he reached the point of proficiency where his services were of some value to us he was . . . taken away from us. Now Mr. Nixon [the prison commissioner] you can not help but see the unjustness of such action and we respectfully request that you order him back to our mills."[26]

In 1899 TSP generated $96,219.40 from the use of convict labor in its various industries (see table 6.2).[27] The majority of these profits were derived from the production of hosiery. The following year, TSP's returns were even higher. Of the $110,814.93 earned in 1900, $28,786.47 worth of profits was derived from hose production. Hosiery manufacturing was a lucrative business, and TSP officials came to appreciate the proceeds derived from industry sales. Yet as they reaped the fiscal benefits to be had through the apparel trade, prison commissioners and contractors alike deeply discounted the humanity of those individuals who were forced to make the hose. In response, both male and female convict workers maneuvered to decommodify their bodies, choosing to express their discontent through the act of stealing. In 1899 a complaint was sent from a Rock City official to the Board of Prison Commissioners:

> We have notified you many times that your convicts steal on an average 5 doz pairs of our stockings per day and have asked you as often to put a stop to it.

Your final decision was that all convicts must wear regulation red socks but this decision has not been put in force. As we cannot stand this stealing and as we have no power over the convicts to stop it we will for the last time ask you to stop the convicts from wearing stockings. If this stealing of our goods is not stopped we shall have to ask our lawyer what course we shall pursue to receive the value of the stolen goods.[28]

The historical record is incomplete in its documentation of women prisoners' unique experiences of labor, confinement, and resistance in the state of Tennessee. Nevertheless, it appears that the lived and laboring experiences of incarcerated garment workers in this state mirrored those of Alabama's prisoners. In both sites, sweat, strife, and strain characterized the day-to-day struggles of male and female inmates. Yet even with the parallels, there are some stark economic and gendered differences that existed between the Tennessee model of contract labor and other prison-based manufacturing entities. When the Tennessee model is contrasted against the Alabama penitentiary system in particular, these distinctions become widely apparent. In Alabama, women inmates, not men, were the predominant labor force in the state's prison-based apparel industry. Gender conventions in the "heart of Dixie" were rarely unheeded in the carceral sector. Because of Alabama officials' strict and concrete devotion to preserving gender norms and the resulting abundant documentation of women's working lives, scholars are left with a much fuller picture of the contributions female prisoners made to the apparel trade in this state.

Prior to 1888 the female prison population in Alabama was leased out to a series of mining companies and private farms. Under the convict lease system, these women worked as cooks, domestics, and the private servants of wardens and other officials. But in 1888 the practice of leasing out

Table 6.2. TSP Revenue from Convict Labor in Seven Industries, 1899

Industry	Earnings
Metal making (foundry)	$20,544.46
Harness and saddlery	$11,768.92
Hosiery mill	$27,267.47
Paper box factory	$2,290.20
Chair factory	$7,538.32
Shoe factory	$18,792.28
Brickyard	$7,997.75

Source: Third Biennial Report of the Board of Prison Commissioners of the State of Tennessee, 1898–1900, 14, TSLA.

female felons was banned, and the Alabama attorney general ordered women prisoners sent to the Walls in Wetumpka.[29] The primary purpose of this relocation to a centralized space was to reduce "lapses in discipline" that stemmed from integrating the sexes and to somehow attend to the welfare of female prisoners and their children.[30]

At the Walls, female inmates worked on a state farm under the supervision of an inspector. Approximately fifty women and fifteen children labored in the fields, growing food for prisoners to eat. A handful of others were put to work washing, sewing, cooking, and cleaning. For a short time, the Walls primarily housed female inmates. But with nowhere to house its supposedly "disposable" or "unprofitable" prisoners, the state began dumping sick youths and elderly convicts at the site. Along with the existing duties they were required to perform, able-bodied female inmates were tasked with caring for those too injured, sick, or enfeebled to work.[31]

In the years preceding the eradication of convict leasing, state officials found it necessary to provide for new industries under its newly formed contract labor system. Convict leasing had proved profitable, and state officials wanted to continue to draw revenue from imprisoned workers. To accommodate the penal system's changing structure, the old prison (the Walls) was renovated into a women's reformatory and garment factory. A fully equipped tailor shop with facilities for the manufacture of clothing and bedding was placed where there were formerly "gloomy dungeons."[32]

In 1922 the new women's prison and tailor shop opened at Wetumpka, and a contract was established between the Litewear Manufacturing Company and the Alabama prison system. Incorporated by A. O. Brent, Bernard W. Scheer, and F. K. Mann, the company specialized in the production of men's and boys' underwear.[33] At the Litewear plant, sweatshop operatives were responsible for making clothing for the prisons and other state institutions, in addition to manufacturing garments for Litewear to be sold on the open market.

As of September 19, 1923, there were 113 women incarcerated in the Alabama prison system. Roughly 35 percent of the female population worked in the garment factory at Wetumpka, while a smaller number labored in the cotton mill at Speigner, a male prison. Compared to Speigner, the Litewear factory at Wetumpka was a manageable space. In a letter to then governor William M. Brandon, female inmates pleaded to remain at the Walls: "Governor why we come to you is because you are the only protection we have on earth and we feel that it is our duty to come to you. We are lots better women here than we were at Speigner. . . . When we were in the cotton mill at Speigner there was some one cut near to death almost every day both white and colored. . . . [L]et us stay here because we can make our time better here to ourselves than we can at Speigner with all those men."[34] There is much to be said about the fears, vulnerabilities, afflictions, and terrors that circumscribed black women's lives in Alabama's prison-based textile mills. The abovementioned letter provides access to the interiority of incarcerated women's lives and their desires to be seen and heard. One clear wish was to be viewed as redeemable by the state, capable of reform, and worthy of protection. Protection for the authors of this letter meant removal from sex-integrated camps, where violence was rife, into an enclosed gender-segregated setting.

Daily operations at the Wetumpka tailor shop were similar to the day-to-day practices carried out by garment workers in the TSP. Women prisoners worked overtime in the tailor shop making pants, shirts, pillows, aprons, jeans, union suits, mattress covers, skirts, "middie blouses," dresses, sheets, and pillowcases.[35] Black women workers were placed in charge of running the machines. White women (fewer than five in number) worked as packers, cutters, and button sewers. To ensure the "expeditious and economical" manufacture of Litewear (and prison) garments, the factory was equipped with "modern cutting tables, machinery, and appliances." A supervisor from the company was put in charge of managing the workers and maintaining and repairing the equipment. The state furnished the "light, heat, and power for the operation of the plant." In exchange, the prison was set to receive a fixed price for the manufacture of the garments while retaining control and management of the inmates.[36]

For the year 1924 (excluding missing months), Litewear Manufacturing Company paid $14,345.09 for garments produced in the tailor shop: $1,920.38 was paid in January; $1,803.04 in April; $1,804.65 in May; $1,376.93 in June; $1,618.65 in July; $1,282.05 in August; $1,778.66 in September; $1,404.50 in October; and $1,355.63 in November.[37] As for the volume of garments produced on February 4 alone, twenty-five (reported) women workers turned out 18 pairs of pants, 42 shirts, 2 drawers, 680 union suits, 697 pillowcases, 2 skirts, 2 middies, and 1 gown.[38]

Albeit an improvement when compared to Speigner, the strain of life in the tailor shop produced strife among female inmates. In a split second, a verbal sparring match between two overworked, fatigued, and frustrated operatives could turn into a physical confrontation. For example, when Ethel May Turk and Ruth Brown could not orally resolve their differences, they decided that "fighting it out" was the best solution. According to Turk, "Ruth Brown kept picking on me." After allegedly starting an argument with

Brown that resulted in a fight, Turk was "hit over the head with a poker."[39] In a similar instance, Mary Jackson stabbed Linnie Holt for working too slowly. According to Holt, "I was sitting at my machine sewing when the difficulty started, and Mary Jackson was insisting that I speed up my work on collars which I was making." An argument ensued, and "Mary Jackson cut Linnie Holt . . . then Linnie cut her."[40]

There are a number of potential explanations for why Mary Jackson stabbed Linnie Holt. In the violent milieu in which the women labored, where their lack of productivity could result in a flogging, it is quite plausible that Jackson's fears of punishment drove her to stab Holt. Perhaps Mary had suffered before because of Linnie's "slowness." It is also possible that Linnie consciously decided to take her time. Or Linnie may have slowed down for retaliatory purposes, drawing violent consequences (a flogging) to Mary in response to previous threats of violence. Mary Jackson may not have been policing Linnie's labor in this context; instead, Linnie may have been punishing Mary.

While most reported cases of infighting among female inmates were intraracial in nature, sometimes conflicts transcended racial lines. After several alleged run-ins with the "colored girls" at Wetumpka, one white female prisoner wrote to then governor Bibb Graves to express her concerns about the "matter of the 'colored' and 'white' mixing." In her statement to Graves, she claimed that "the officials allow it in the presents of thair eyes and hearing of thair ears for the 'colored' girls to call us 'white girls' 'white hoer's' and 'B—s.' Pardon being so plain but its positive facts. Gov. Graves, we have ask them kindly to have it stoped [stopped]." She continued, "We would appreciate your help. They will take a colored girl word in preference to us white girl and reaed [*read*] us for their lies."[41]

The abovementioned letter is critical for two reasons. First, it clearly illuminates the racial tensions that existed between black and white female inmates. Second, it reveals clues regarding how white women prisoners understood their position of privilege within the prison community. For a white official to take a "colored" woman's word over that of a white woman was as injurious (if not more injurious) as the profane insults allegedly hurled at the complainant(s). As a rule, southern officials were disproportionately sympathetic toward the plight of white women prisoners. Claims of abuse or mistreatment at the hands of penal authorities were sometimes strong enough to persuade affirmative clemency rulings. Yet these legal exemptions from punishment did not exist for black female prisoners. In Alabama and throughout the South, African American women prisoners were the principal recipients of punishment and violence when compared to white women.

The mode and frequency of abuse meted out against female inmates are detailed in a series of letters between Hamp Draper, associate member of the Board of Administration, and Thomas A. Walls, acting warden at Wetumpka. In a conduct report dated October 1, 1928, through October 7, 1928, Walls informed Draper that he punished Clara Jackson, a "Negro female," by placing her in solitary confinement for six hours. In the same report, Walls reported having given Bertha Lee Golden, another "Negro female," twenty-one lashes for "doing bad work and refusing to work." In a similar fashion, he gave Lula May Edwards ten lashes for "failing to get task."[42]

Overall, whipping and other forms of punishment were used as a way to control and force incarcerated workers to engage in labor. In response to the violence and exploitation they experienced, some women prisoners opted to run away. On January 23, 1928, Annie Davis and Clara Jackson escaped from Wetumpka by "breaking locks on the gate in the rear of the prison," according to a letter from the warden. When the night guard went to the cell at 2:00 a.m. to "awake them to cook breakfast," they were missing. "We went in search of them immediately with the dogs and trailed them for 3 or 4 miles and lost track of them," the warden reported. "We also hunted for them during the day and at 6:30 P.M. yesterday . . . captured Annie Davis and returned her to the prison." The following day, the night guard allegedly "carried the dogs and went about 10 miles north . . . and soon located Clara Jackson in the loft of a Negro's house and captured her and returned her to the prison."[43]

By running away, women prisoners at Wetumpka sought to decommodify their bodies, regain some sense of autonomy and power, and have their humanity recognized. They vocalized this desire in a letter to Governor Bibb Graves: "Dear Sir. We the inmates of this prison camp most humbly ask, plead and beg of you to please see into our welfare. . . . We all realize that we are unfortunate convicts and expect to be treated as convicts but yet we all are humans and want to be treated as humans."[44]

Imprisoned women's quest to be "treated as humans" and to have their humanity affirmed is a consistent theme that runs through the historical record yet rarely appears on the pages of scholarly texts. The overemphasis on black men's experiences of confinement within the South's carceral regimes has obscured the lived and laboring realities of imprisoned black women in the Jim Crow South. Hence, the purpose of this chapter is to draw visibility to an otherwise obscure population of women workers and to account for the less familiar narratives of incarcerated black female garment workers. In doing so, it raises critical questions regarding the extent to which imprisoned apparel workers advanced the development of industrial capitalism not only in Tennessee and Alabama but also in other localities. Did other southern states adopt the contract labor system? Were these systems also deeply reliant on the energies of black female prisoners? If so, did the interior lives of these apparel workers complement or contrast with the experiences of female laborers in the Tennessee state penitentiary system or at the Wetumpka Walls? It is hoped that future scholars will take up these questions, among others, and continue to respond to incarcerated women's requests for recognition of their humanity.

NOTES

1. Bate Bond, Attorney at Law, Brownsville, Tennessee, to Hon. Wm. A. Carter, Nashville, Tennessee, August 10, 1904, Fifth Biennial Report of the Board of Prison Commissioners of the State of Tennessee, 1902–4, 271, Tennessee State Library and Archives, Nashville (hereafter cited as TSLA).

2. Ibid.

3. Second Biennial Report of the Board of Prison Commissioners of the State of Tennessee, 1897–98, 185, TSLA.

4. For a broader discussion of convict leasing in the southern states, see Matthew Mancini, *One Dies, Get Another: Convict Leasing in the American South, 1866–1928* (Columbia: University of South Carolina Press, 1996); David M. Oshinsky, *"Worse Than Slavery": Parchman Farm and the Ordeal of Jim Crow Justice* (New York: Free Press, 1996); Alex Lichtenstein, *Twice the Work of Free Labor: The Political Economy of Convict Labor in the New South* (New York: Verso, 1996); Mary Ellen Curtin, *Black Prisoners and Their World, Alabama, 1865–1900* (Charlottesville: University of Virginia Press, 2000); Vivien Miller, *Crime, Sexual Violence, and Clemency: Florida's Pardon Board and Penal System in the Progressive Era* (Gainesville: University Press of Florida, 2000); Douglas A. Blackmon, *Slavery by Another Name: The Re-enslavement of Black Americans from the Civil War to World War II* (New York: Anchor, 2008); Milfred Fierce, *Slavery Revisited: Blacks and the Southern Convict Lease System, 1865–1933* (New York: Africana Studies Center, Brooklyn, 1994); Karin A. Shapiro, *A New South Rebellion: The Battle against Convict Labor in the Tennessee Coalfields, 1871–1896* (Chapel Hill: University of North Carolina Press, 1998); Edward L. Ayers, *Vengeance and Justice: Crime and Punishment in the Nineteenth-Century American South* (New York: Oxford University Press, 1984); Martha A. Myers, *Race, Labor, and Punishment in the New South* (Columbus: Ohio State University Press, 1998); Paul Ortiz, *Emancipation Betrayed: The Hidden History of Black Organizing and White Violence in Florida from Reconstruction to the Bloody Election of 1920* (Berkeley: University

of California Press, 2005); Vivien Miller, *Hard Labor and Hard Time: Florida's "Sunshine Prison" and Chain Gangs* (Gainesville: University Press of Florida, 2012); Robert Perkinson, *Texas Tough: The Rise of America's Prison Empire* (New York: Picador, 2010); Talitha L. LeFlouria, *Chained in Silence: Black Women and Convict Labor in the New South* (Chapel Hill: University of North Carolina Press, 2015); and Sarah Haley, *No Mercy Here: Gender, Punishment, and the Making of Jim Crow Modernity* (Chapel Hill: University of North Carolina Press, 2016).

5. For further reading, see Shapiro, *A New South Rebellion*.

6. LeFlouria, *Chained in Silence*, 9, 62. This argument is an extension of an idea that was initially introduced in my study, *Chained in Silence*, the first history of black, working-class, incarcerated women in the post–Civil War South. Southern modernity in this context applies to the movement from agrarianism toward an agroindustrial economy.

7. For further reading on the southern textile industry, see Mildred Gwin Andrews, *The Men and the Mills: A History of the Southern Textile Industry* (Macon, GA: Mercer University Press, 1987); Gary M. Fink, *The Fulton Bag and Cotton Mills Strike of 1914–1915: Espionage, Labor Conflict, and New South Industrial Relations* (Ithaca, NY: Cornell University Press, 1993); Jacqueline Dowd Hall, James Leloudis, Robert Korstad, Mary Murphy, Lu Ann Jones, and Christopher B. Daly, *Like a Family: The Making of a Southern Cotton Mill World* (Chapel Hill: University of North Carolina Press, 2000); Glenn T. Eskew, ed., *Labor in the Modern South* (Athens: University of Georgia Press, 2001); Douglas Flamming, *Creating the Modern South: Millhands and Managers in Dalton, Georgia, 1884–1984* (Chapel Hill: University of North Carolina Press, 1992); Clifford M. Kuhn, *Contesting the New South Order: The 1914–1915 Strike at Atlanta's Fulton Mills* (Chapel Hill: University of North Carolina Press, 2001); Michelle Brattain, *The Politics of Whiteness: Race, Workers, and Culture in the Modern South* (Athens: University of Georgia Press, 2004).

8. Michelle Haberland, *Striking Beauties: Women Apparel Workers in the U.S. South, 1930–2000* (Athens: University of Georgia Press, 2015), 2, 8–9.

9. LeFlouria, *Chained in Silence*, 14.

10. In the absence of factory jobs, city-dwelling, wage-earning, southern black women worked as cooks, maids, child nurses, and laundresses. Some found work in the informal economy as sex workers, bootleggers, and gamblers. For a more comprehensive discussion of working-class black women's lives and labors, see Tera Hunter, *To 'Joy My Freedom: Southern Black Women's Lives and Labors after the Civil War* (Cambridge, MA: Harvard University Press, 1998); Jacqueline Jones, *Labor of Love, Labor of Sorrow: Black Women, Work, and the Family, from Slavery to the Present* (New York: Vintage, 1986); Sharon Harley, *Sister Circle: Black Women and Work* (New Brunswick, NJ: Rutgers University Press, 2002); Elizabeth Clark-Lewis, *Living In, Living Out: African American Domestics in Washington, D.C., 1910–1940* (Washington, DC: Smithsonian Institution Press, 1994); LaShawn Harris, *Sex Workers, Psychics, and Numbers Runners: Black Women in New York City's*

Underground Economy (Urbana: University of Illinois Press, 2016); and Cynthia Blair, *I've Got to Make My Livin': Black Women's Sex Work in Turn-of-the-Century Chicago* (Chicago: University of Chicago Press, 2010).

11. Jones, *Labor of Love*, 135.

12. James J. Davis, Secretary, US Department of Labor, and Mary Anderson, Director, US Women's Bureau, *Negro Women in Industry in 15 States*, Bulletin of the Women's Bureau, No. 70 (Washington, DC: US Government Printing Office, 1929), 15. See also Dolores Janiewski, *Sisterhood Denied: Race, Gender, and Class in a New South Community* (Philadelphia: Temple University Press, 1992).

13. Statistics derived from Davis and Anderson, *Negro Women in Industry in 15 States*, 15–26.

14. James J. Davis, Secretary, US Department of Labor, and Mary Anderson, Director, US Women's Bureau, *Negro Women in Industry*, Bulletin of the Women's Bureau, No. 20 (Washington, DC: US Government Printing Office, 1922).

15. Davis and Anderson, *Negro Women in Industry in 15 States*, 20, 21.

16. Report of the Board of Prison Commissioners of the State of Tennessee, 1895–96, TSLA. For a comprehensive reading on the history of convict labor in Tennessee, see Shapiro, *A New South Rebellion*.

17. "May Hosiery Mills," a paper read at the Green Hills Branch of the Nashville Public Library, May 14, 1973, TSLA.

18. Second Biennial Report, 1897–98, 6, TSLA.

19. Report of the Board of Prison Commissioners of the State of Tennessee, 1895–96, 34.

20. Second Biennial Report, 1897–98, 23.

21. Ibid., 186. As of December 1, 1898, a total of 1,525 inmates were detained at the TSP: 400 white males, 8 white females, 1,066 "colored" males, and 51 "colored" females.

22. Ibid., 188.

23. Davis and Anderson, *Negro Women in Industry in 15 States*, 22.

24. Ibid.

25. W. M. Nixon to the Rock City Hosiery Mills, June 19, 1899, RG 25, State Prison Records, 1831–1992, box 4, folder 6: Correspondence: Board of Prison Commissioners, 1899, TSLA; Third Biennial Report of the Board of Prison Commissioners of the State of Tennessee, 1898–1900, 190, TSLA.

26. Rock City Hosiery Mills to W. M. Nixon, June 19, 1899, RG 25, State Prison Records, 1831–1992, box 4, folder 6: Correspondence: Board of Prison Commissioners, 1899, TSLA.

27. Information obtained from the Third Biennial Report, 14.

28. Rock City Hosiery Mills to the Board of the Prison Commissioners, Tennessee, July 10, 1899, RG 25, State Prison Records, 1831–1992, box 4, folder 7, TSLA.

29. Curtin, *Black Prisoners*, 123. In the 1920s convict leasing began to wane in Alabama. Reforms and political outcries connected to the 1924 torture and murder of a prisoner who was "lowered into a vat of boiling water" until he perished

prompted an investigation of the system and likely added to its demise. With the inauguration of Governor Bibb Graves (1927–31), a staunch opponent of convict leasing, the system was eventually abolished. In 1928 Alabama's prisoners were placed on state highway projects and state farms. For further reading, see Blackmon, *Slavery by Another Name*; and Robert David Ward and William Warren Rogers, *Convicts, Coal, and the Banner Mine Tragedy* (Tuscaloosa: University of Alabama Press, 1987).

30. Curtin, *Black Prisoners*, 124.

31. Ibid.

32. Quadrennial Report of the Board of Control and Economy, Convict Department, 1919–22, 9, Alabama Department of Archives and History, Montgomery, Alabama (hereafter cited as ADAH).

33. Manufacturers Record Exponent of America, September 7, 1922, Baltimore, MD; *Annual Report of the Commissioner of Patents for the Year 1924* (Washington, DC: US Government Printing Office, 1925).

34. Female inmates to Honorable Wm. M. Brandon, Montgomery, Alabama, December 20, 1923, Board of Convict Supervisors, ADAH.

35. Daily Tailor Shop Report, Wetumpka, 1923, Board of Convict Supervisors, ADAH.

36. Quadrennial Report, 1919–22, 19.

37. J. A. Howle, Warden, to Hon. Roy L. Nolen, Montgomery, Alabama, February 5, 1924, Board of Administration, ADAH.

38. Daily Tailor Shop Report, Wetumpka, 1924, Board of Convict Supervisors, ADAH. The Litewear Manufacturing Company apparently relied on a quota of eighty-five workers per day for 1923. Yet it is unclear in the historical record whether or not this quota was maintained in 1924 or in subsequent years. Daily Tailor Shop Reports only show the presence of female inmates. No males are cited in these reports. But reports do indicate that patients confined in the Tubercular Hospital did work in the tailor shop.

39. Board of Administration, State of Alabama, Convict Department, Preliminary Report of Accident, December 5, 1932, ADAH.

40. Board of Administration, Preliminary Report of Accident, September 3, 1934, ADAH.

41. Female inmate to Governor Bibb Graves, Wetumpka, Alabama, July 15, 1929, Board Administration, ADAH.

42. L. D. Carlton, Warden, to Hon. Hamp Draper, Montgomery, Alabama, January 25, 1928, Board of Administration, ADAH.

43. Ibid.

44. Inmates of the Wetumpka Prison Camp to Governor Bibb Graves, Wetumpka, Alabama, July 15, 1929, Board of Administration, ADAH.

CHAPTER 7

COLE BLEASE'S PARDONING PEN

State Power and Penal Reform in South Carolina

Amy Louise Wood

South Carolina governor Cole Blease created a firestorm when he offered a brazen defense of lynching at the 1912 Governors' Conference. "I have said it all over the state of South Carolina, and I say it again now," he declared. ". . . I will never order out the militia to shoot down its neighbors and protect a brute who commits the nameless crime against a white woman." His colleagues rose to rebuke him. The following day, the governor of Wyoming asked Blease if he had not taken an oath to uphold the law and defend the Constitution, to which Blease replied, "When the Constitution steps between me and the defense of the white women in my state, I will resign my commission and tear it up and throw it to the breezes. I have heretofore said, 'To hell with the Constitution!.'"[1] Blease's incendiary remarks dominated coverage of the meeting as newspapers across the country, including many in the South, condemned him and called upon South Carolinians to impeach him. The *New York Evening Post* coined the verb "to blease" to refer to "doing a great number of obnoxious things at the same time or in quick succession." Many South Carolinians cringed in embarrassment, even though, as the *Washington Times* pointed out, Blease was simply saying openly what other governors probably tacitly believed.[2] In turn, Blease claimed he had been misrepresented, and he denounced news editors across the state who printed condemnations from "Yankee hoodlums and little newspaper pimps" while withholding "hundreds of telegrams and letters" of commendation.[3]

The events in Richmond cemented Blease's national reputation as a race-baiting demagogue—a reputation already well established in his home state. The controversy, however, overshadowed the rest of Blease's speech, which deplored the conditions at the state penitentiary; in fact, his remarks on lynching were really offered only as a careless aside.[4] Blease spoke of a recent visit to the state penitentiary in Columbia, which he described as a "tuberculosis institution where poor devils were dying at their tasks, making money for other people, poor devils who had no choice but to stand and work or take the lash." One black prisoner had told Blease that he had been in the penitentiary for twenty-two years for stealing a watch. Another had served almost twelve years for stealing three dollars. These conditions, Blease claimed, had compelled him to use his pardoning power liberally. In his first twenty-two months in office, he had pardoned or paroled some four hundred convicts, and he promised to double that number in his second term.[5]

Blease exceeded his own expectations. During his four-year tenure, he extended executive clemency to at least 1,740 prisoners, both black and white, the most of any governor to that point.[6] That number does not count the over 1,000 convicts paroled on good behavior to whom he offered full pardons just before leaving office in January 1915. By comparison, his predecessors averaged about 16 pardons a year.[7] At the end of his tenure, only about 180 prisoners remained in the state penal system, and fewer than 100 of those were confined to the penitentiary—a number down from 935 prisoners in 1910.[8] At the 1915 Governors' Conference, Blease boasted that he had been "heralded to the world as 'the pardoning governor.'"[9]

As he indicated in Richmond, Blease used executive clemency as a tool to reform the state penitentiary, which had become an overcrowded incubator of disease, an inhumane dungeon where overworked inmates were regularly brutalized. In addition to releasing prisoners, Blease pushed for a number of systemic reforms to improve prisoners' lives, some successfully. How can we reconcile Cole Blease, the prolynching firebrand and unapologetic Negrophobe, with this passionate critic of a draconian criminal justice system? To his critics, his defense of lynching and his liberal use of the pardoning pen, paired together, revealed his basic disrespect for law and order. Yet both may say much more about the nature of Blease's political appeal, which was rooted in a skepticism toward a certain kind of progressive-minded, centralized state power. In his supporters' minds, governmental elites sought to inhibit white citizens' rights to defend their homes and families against "brutes," while the penal system they created confined other helpless citizens unjustly in state institutions. In both cases, the wheels of justice were slow and crooked. Blease offered himself as the premier advocate for the downtrodden against the authority of professional administrative elites. His reform of the penal system ultimately worked to decentralize the system and weaken state bureaucracies while bolstering his own authoritarian power. In that sense, he adhered to a premodern, prebureaucratic approach to criminal justice that reinforced a dynamic of benevolence and deference between the governor and his supporters. Although he adopted the language of Progressive Era penal reform, he did so to enact what was essentially a revolt against progressive ideals, that is, the use of bureaucratic state power—modern, efficient, and scientific—to ameliorate social problems.

Blease represented a political extreme, even among other demagogues in the South, yet his extremism puts in stark relief the distinct ways penal reform played out in the Jim Crow South. A wave of penal reform known as the "new penology" cascaded across the country in the early twentieth century. Reformers sought to improve sanitary conditions and expand educational, recreational, and spiritual activities for inmates in order to promote their rehabilitation. Corporal punishments were banned in many states, and practices such as parole and probation were introduced, as was indeterminate sentencing, which gave the state discretion to release prisoners on good behavior and offered prisoners incentives to redeem themselves. The new penologists combined clinical approaches to criminology with humanitarian rhetoric, and although their actions often failed to live up to their articulated ideals or had unintended consequences, they initiated a host of new state institutions and agencies to oversee the treatment of potential offenders, prisoners, and ex-convicts.[10]

Southern states were comparatively slow to adopt penal reform; nevertheless, vigorous reform movements existed in them to end abuses and promote these kinds of reforms. Many state officials and prison administrators were attuned to the new penology and readily adopted its rhetoric. Yet as Blease's pardoning pen suggests, penal reform took on a different texture in the South. It had appeal when it relied upon localism rather than a centralized state and when it played to popular prejudices and traditions rather than furthering neutral bureaucratic governance advocated by elites. And, importantly, reform conformed to and reinforced the racial hierarchy of Jim Crow. In fact, Blease's racism—a mix of Negrophobia and paternalism—furthered reform rather than hindering it. Blease's history of pardons thus reveals the ironies of southern penal reform, in which progress was laden with antimodern tendencies. In that way, it played out much like other reforms in the South, revealing what William Link has called the "paradox of southern progressivism."[11]

Blease began his political career as a Tillmanite legislator in the South Carolina General Assembly in 1890.[12] After an unsuccessful bid for the governorship in 1908, he was elected governor in 1910 and reelected in 1912 with the strong support of the rising industrial working class, as well as poor and struggling rural whites.[13] Millworkers, in particular, felt a kinship with Blease, despite his middle-class upbringing, his Georgetown University education, and his early career as a criminal defense lawyer. Blease did much to cultivate their loyalty by appealing to their racism, to be sure, but also by appealing to their class anxieties, in particular, their distrust of middle-class and elite townspeople. As David Carlton and others have argued, Blease successfully channeled workers' wholesale rejection of the modern and progressive forces that they believed were threatening to upend their self-sufficiency. This thesis counters earlier assessments of Blease that have dismissed his populism as empty rhetoric. In that view, he indulged his supporters' racial paranoia while doing nothing to serve their economic interests. He resisted measures to promote social equality, such as regulations on the mill industry and attempts to ally textile unions with national labor organizations.[14]

Workers' support for Blease might have been more rational, however. In particular, they were suspicious of elite authority and viewed progressive reforms through that lens. Even as New South boosters promoted industry as the means to modernize the state and build economic prosperity, they bemoaned the lawlessness and vice of the industrial working class. Their solution was moral uplift via the abolition of child labor, public health campaigns, and compulsory education. Through state intervention, it was hoped, social order, class stability, and labor discipline could be imposed on the unruly lower classes. Workers, however, resented these attempts to elevate them, believing them to be a further encroachment on their independence. In their view, government agencies could not be trusted; they were corrupt institutions that bolstered the interests of the wealthy at the expense of workers. Compulsory education, for instance, represented an intrusion upon parental authority in the home and was an elite mechanism to inculcate alien values in workers' children. Blease thus gained a lot of political traction by rejecting compulsory education, public health measures, and laws against child labor. Poor whites' racism only furthered their resistance to government authority, as they particularly objected when state resources might be funneled toward African Americans.[15]

This attack on reform was very much in line with progressivism as it played out in the South more generally. Southern progressivism was, as C. Vann Woodward notably deemed it, "for whites only" in the sense that reform not only failed to challenge white supremacy but served to reinforce it.[16] But progressivism was also inseparable from class politics, in which rural white farmers and industrial laborers rejected the paternalism of town elites. They also, as Link has argued, held to a prebureaucratic sensibility that was suspicious of concentrated state power and instead embraced a culture of localism that prized self-reliance.[17]

Blease's use of executive clemency and his approach to penal reform comport with this larger story of southern progressivism. Prisons in the early twentieth century were abysmal places, but they were arguably even more abysmal in the South. Convict leasing and contract labor still persisted in many states, and abuses like corporal punishments and dark cells were practiced with impunity long after they had officially been discontinued in many northern states. Southern states were slower to improve health and sanitary conditions; introduce chapels, libraries, and gymnasiums into their penitentiaries; and establish separate reformatories for juveniles. Indeterminate sentencing, parole, and probation also came late to the South. And when the private contracting of prison labor was abolished, a number of southern states replaced it with notoriously brutal county chain gangs. South Carolina was no different. The sluggishness of southern penal reform was due, in good part, to the dominance of white supremacy in the region. The rehabilitative ideal gained little traction in a climate in which the majority of prisoners were black and most whites, including southern reformers, accepted the prevailing view that African Americans were incorrigibly and instinctively criminally minded. The southern penal system had long operated as an effective form of racial control that even reformers were loath to disrupt.[18]

Nevertheless, southern reformers sought to end abuses and improve prisoners' health and lives. The South Carolina state legislature launched investigations into inhumane practices and conditions in the state penitentiary in 1899, 1915, 1923, and 1925, as did other southern states in the early decades of the twentieth century. In 1915 the state created the Board of Charities and Corrections, which considered prisoners as a larger class of people who required state charity. Throughout the next decade, the board repeatedly pressed, albeit in vain, for significant reforms, such as abolishing the chain gang, eliminating corporal punishment, and paying prisoners a wage for their labor. It adopted a typically progressive-minded approach to the penal system, recommending increased state supervision to correct abuses in the system and ensure its efficient management.[19]

Blease, in some ways, was in the vanguard of southern penal reform. He styled himself a humanitarian, pardoning convicts in the name of Christian mercy. "Nothing has given me more genuine pleasure than the privilege of exercising the power of forgiveness and of saying to down-trodden humanity, 'Arise! Cast off your shackles, look up, remember that there is a God, and that there is a future. . . . I propose to give you another chance in life,'" he wrote in his 1912 report to the state legislature.[20] Most notably, Blease used his pardoning power to abolish the last vestiges of convict leasing in South Carolina.[21] The state had begun to unravel the convict leasing system in the 1880s by placing all privately leased convicts under the supervision of state officers in what was known as a contract labor system. In 1901 all private leases were terminated except for that of a hosiery mill, which employed two hundred men within the state penitentiary, manufacturing stockings and other knit goods.[22] In his first year in office, Blease successfully pressured the General Assembly to close the mill in part by threatening to pardon every prisoner working in it.[23]

The closing of the mill directly benefited his working-class constituents, who would no longer have to compete with cheap prison labor. Indeed, opponents of convict leasing and contract labor commonly argued that these practices distorted the labor market. In addition, they emphasized the fiscal gains to the state if it used prison labor for public works. And they consistently made humanitarian pleas against the abuses of prisoners, the corruption of state officials, and the ethics of using prison labor for profit.[24] In his opposition to the private contracting of prison labor, Blease made all these arguments, but he tended to focus on the inhumanity of the system. In a 1911 speech to cotton mill workers in Spartanburg County—the very workers who would have a vested interest in abolishing a mill worked by prison labor—he railed against the hosiery mill by lamenting its harsh conditions. Prisoners with no experience, he said, were expected to do the work of "skilled operatives" and were whipped severely when they could not measure up. This kind of argument against the mill appealed both to workers' sense of class injustice and to their sense of pride as "skilled operatives."[25] Blease also opposed the use of the penitentiary for profit, and for that same reason, he called for the closing of the state's penal farms.[26]

Instead, Blease supported the use of county chain gangs in the construction of roads and bridges. Chain gangs exemplify the skepticism toward centralized bureaucracy that characterized southern progressivism. Reformers across the South touted them as a humanitarian alternative to both convict leasing and contract labor under the mistaken assumption that the supervision of prisoners by county and municipal authorities would prevent the kinds of abuses that occurred under private lessees or at the state penitentiary. Chain gangs had the added benefit of allowing states to profit directly from prison labor by modernizing their infrastructure as a form of capital investment. They did so, as Tammy Ingram has noted, with the "illusion of a democratized labor system," since, unlike with convict leasing, in which private businesses reaped the benefits of prison labor, all citizens supposedly benefited from improved infrastructure.[27]

South Carolina had begun using county chain gangs on public roads in 1885, but under Blease's leadership, their use greatly increased, so that by

1915 the state held only a small portion of prisoners at the penitentiary. The General Assembly had passed laws in 1911 and 1914, respectively, giving judges authority to sentence convicts to labor on public works as an alternative to imprisonment and allowing county supervisors to take any prisoner convicted in his county from the penitentiary to work in a road gang.[28] The use of prison labor on public highways, in the governor's view, was not exploitative, since it benefited a higher purpose than mere profit: good roads. Roads would offer families better access to churches and schools and farmers better access to markets. In that sense, Blease was not against modernizing the state, as long as these efforts did not infringe upon the independence of his working-class constituents. For Blease, chain gangs also had the benefit of decentralizing state power. He wanted the counties to be responsible for the "humane treatment" of their prisoners rather than the state, which he did not trust with that responsibility.[29]

There was nothing humane about chain gangs, however, and they soon became a national symbol of the benighted and barbaric South. That was due in part to the fact that chain gangs *did* represent a decentralized form of power. The State Board of Charities and Corrections soon came to bemoan the unsanitary conditions at the county camps; the lack of sufficient diets and housing; and the harsh treatments accorded to prisoners, including shackling, whippings, and other forms of torture. The board was frustrated that county sheriffs ignored state constitutional decrees against corporal punishment, as well as laws requiring that prisoners be segregated by race and gender. And they lamented that bookkeeping accounts and convict records were almost nonexistent, a sign, in their view, of inefficient management. Yet without centralized oversight, there was little the board could do. The board repeatedly called for state management of the gangs or, at the very least, the establishment of state standards and regular inspections.[30]

Blease's greater legacy, however, was his liberal use of pardons. Like his predecessors, Blease used his power of executive clemency to extend mercy to convicts whose cases warranted it or for whom extenuating circumstances had shifted the grounds of justice. What made Blease's use of executive clemency remarkable, however, was not simply the sheer numbers of prisoners he pardoned but the attention he paid to the process and the political import he placed on it. It also epitomized his approach to reform, which was not only seemingly democratic and compassionate, addressing injustices and appealing to the values of his constituents, but also authoritarian and paternalistic. Although the State Board of Pardons had been established in 1906 to oversee governors' use of their pardoning power and make recommendations, Blease largely acted alone. In fact, in 1911 he ignored the board completely, claiming its members were political enemies with whom he could not work. Though he stopped short of dismissing them, he encouraged them to resign. The following year, he vetoed the legislature's appropriation for their salaries because, he said, there would be nothing for them to do. When the legislature overrode his veto, he replaced two members of the board with political supporters. In the next two years, he at times consulted with the board, especially in the face of public criticism, but he also claimed repeatedly that all clemency decisions were his own.[31]

Indeed, Blease delved into cases, reading trial transcripts and sometimes interviewing convicts himself. His annual pardon reports ran into hundreds of pages. In them, he offered detailed and often vehement explanations for his decisions. Despite charges that he handed out pardons haphazardly, he did adhere to certain administrative standards. Prisoners who simply wrote for mercy without a formal petition were invariably denied their requests. He favored petitions that included testimonials from citizens closest to the case: judges, solicitors, and jury members who had come to regret their decisions. As was common, he offered pardons to convicts whose testimony was needed in other cases, as South Carolina did not allow convicted felons to testify in court.[32] But his motive, most often, was to overturn what he deemed to be unjust rulings. In some cases, he questioned the decisions of judges or the intelligence of juries even as he insisted he was not criticizing the courts.[33] He was at times direct that his experience as a criminal defense lawyer had informed his decisions. "I have practiced law more than twenty-two years and made a specialty of criminal cases," he wrote in a 1911 case, ". . . and I think from my experience that I am as competent to judge the testimony as that jury and as well posted on criminal law as the lawyer who presided."[34]

He was particularly lenient in cases of personal honor. He pardoned an elderly white man, Harvey Smith, sentenced to two years for fatally shooting his son-in-law after he caught the man beating Smith's daughter. Blease concluded that Smith had done "just what he should have done and just what any decent, self-respecting man would have done."[35] The jury members had agreed, as had the presiding judge, but their hands were tied by the letter of the law. Blease, however, had the discretionary power to counter the rule of law when it contravened community values. He paroled another white man, Otis Hilton, serving a life sentence for killing a young black man, who apparently had threatened Hilton and called him an "s.o.b." To justify his decision, Blease referenced the thirty-six affidavits from local citizens testifying on Hilton's behalf and then added, "I think if any man calls another a s.o.b. and he shoots him, that the verdict should not be greater than manslaughter, and if a negro calls a white man a s.o.b. then I won't say here what I think the verdict ought to be, but other people can draw their own inference."[36] In these cases and others, Blease not only reflected the white supremacy of his constituents but also upheld the principle that the state should not interfere with what were deemed private matters of honor. In this regard, Blease's use of executive clemency was in line with his views on lynching. A reportedly emotional man himself, Blease believed that crimes of passion and reprisal, especially to avenge black transgression, were justified.[37]

Blease was also, in many cases, explicitly humanitarian. He was partial to convicts who were sick, especially if they had become incapacitated and could no longer work. In these cases, his pardoning pen became a tool for prison reform. He was particularly appalled by the tuberculosis cases in the prison, which he attributed to unsanitary conditions, especially in the hosiery mill. The State Board of Health confirmed his impressions in its 1911 report, recommending that tubercular patients be confined to a separate hospital and condemning the mill. On a subsequent visit to the penitentiary, Blease spoke to many prisoners and promised to release all those suffering from chronic diseases.[38] His motive here was also pragmatic. In pardoning sick prisoners, he was relieving the state of the burden for caring for men who could not pull their weight.

In other cases, Blease unabashedly reported that he was moved by compassion to release certain prisoners who, he believed, had suffered enough or, alternatively, whose families had suffered enough. He frequently released convicts whose labor and income were needed to support their wives or mothers. In the case of John Ellison, for instance, a white man sentenced to the chain gang for manslaughter, Blease was moved by a doctor's report that Ellison suffered from "neurasthenia and nervous indigestion" and was possibly in "the incipient stages of tuberculosis." He then reported, "Now comes his wife with six little girl children and states to me, not in dishonor, not in shame, but in the matter of the love of her children and in humiliation that she and her six little children and her poor mother are actually suffering in need and in want. These little children come and plead for their father."[39] Blease's reasoning in this case and others was in line with modern penologists who advocated for parole and probation as a means to maintain the family structure and hold men accountable to their families; such accountability, it was hoped, would further their rehabilitation.[40] Blease even suggested in 1915 that a wage be paid to a prisoner's dependents in compensation for his labor while he was incarcerated, a novel concept at the time. If such a system had existed in South Carolina while he was governor, he claimed, he would not have felt it necessary to release prisoners so they could care for their families.[41]

Blease made this contention in a speech at the 1915 Governors' Conference, some eight months after his term had ended, a speech in which he elaborated on his views on prison reform, presumably to shore up his legacy in this area. Offenders must be punished, he conceded; yet society should treat them with kindness and mercy not only because it was the Christian thing to do but because it was the most effective way to prevent crime. It would also make fiscal sense. He advocated that prisoners receive fresh air, healthy food, comfortable surroundings, and access to literature and newspapers and that whippings be exacted only in cases of "willful disobedience or acts of insubordination," and then only in front of "disinterested" witnesses "of good repute."[42] Despite his advocacy for corporal punishment, Blease's speech echoed progressive penology in its arguments that society and its penal institutions actually create crime and that prisoners deserve humane treatment, which would restore their dignity and their sense of obligation as law-abiding citizens.

Blease's liberal use of executive clemency might thus appear to epitomize a Progressive Era optimism about the positive function of modern state power, except that, in practice, it recalled a prebureaucratic form of governance. In premodern cultures, pardons played a vital role in compensating for criminal codes that were especially severe or that did not yet, in law, distinguish between gradations of crimes—say, for example, the difference between premeditated murder and manslaughter. Pardons could, in theory, foster more equality under the law by rectifying the disparities in sentencing for similar crimes.[43] Yet, rather than operating within the judicial system, such justice lay in the hands of ruling elites. Moreover, premodern peoples wanted justice, but they did not expect the law itself to be consistent or unerring. That is, there was no conception of a "rule of law." Rather, people understood justice as something that operated through personal discretion rather than abstract principles. As Douglas Hay has written, "Justice in the sense of rational, bureaucratic decisions made in the common interest is a peculiarly modern conception." In this context, a ruler's use of discretion in the application of criminal justice made sense. His paternalistic benevolence shored up his power by reinforcing the lower classes' bonds of obedience and deference to him and by making it seem as if the law was merciful when it was, in fact, quite draconian.[44]

Blease operated within this model of power, even as he shrouded his use of executive clemency in the trappings of bureaucratic processes and modern penology. Executive clemency enhanced his stature as a generous paternalist. Indeed, the loyalty he earned from released prisoners, their families, and their friends was unwavering. The mother of a paroled white convict wrote to the governor: "I have always praised you no matter what people said about you. But now I don't think I can ever praise you enough. You have made this poor aching hearted mother rejoice and how could I forget you. . . . [A]s the bible says blessed are the merciful for they shall obtain mercy."[45] A former prisoner, George Barnes, a white man released because he had become too sick to work, likened Blease to Jesus, because through his kindness he was doing God's work. Barnes also thanked the governor for working to close the hosiery mill, which would "be one of the greatest things that you can do in your life for it is killing men and women."[46]

Blease, in turn, reveled in the role of savior to the people. He compared his use of clemency to a form of missionary work, helping "the people that were spoken of in the expression, 'The least of these.'"[47] This was a not uncommon stance toward pardons, as many governors saw themselves as human agents of God's mercy, since, after all, only God could offer forgiveness. Blease saw himself as a martyr to his cause for the political blowback he received. "When I have granted pardons and paroles . . . to poor human beings, instead of receiving a reward, up to this time I have suffered as the Savior did on earth," he wrote to a minister friend in 1914.[48]

Enlightenment and post-Enlightenment liberal thinkers, from Montesquieu to Immanuel Kant to Jeremy Bentham, decried the use of clemency for this reason: it reinforced and indulged an executive's absolute power. Pardons also created injustice, for they undermined equality before the law, and for utilitarian thinkers like Bentham, they weakened the central goal of punishment—deterrence. Though wary of absolute power, the framers of both the US Constitution and state constitutions allowed for pardoning power because they viewed it as a tool for correcting injustices.[49] At the turn of the twentieth century, progressives similarly lamented its use as archaic, more appropriate to monarchies than democratic states. In a humane system, they believed, acts of mercy would be unnecessary. In turn, most states established pardon boards, which they trusted would operate as modern bureaucratic agencies, with accountability and transparency. Reformers further hoped that penal reform would render executive clemency redundant, as indeterminate sentencing and parole, both of which were meant to foster the convict's reformation, would come to replace pardons.[50] In most states, parole did replace pardons to a certain extent, though both pardons and commutations continued in part because, as in the case of Blease, it served governors' interests to apply that power.[51]

Blease, who was the first governor of the state to parole prisoners to any great degree, defended parole by saying it gave him more control over the prisoners, and he used the language of the rehabilitative ideal in doing so. In his 1913 report to the General Assembly, he deemed parole "the best system ever devised for the handling of convicts" because it offered released prisoners an incentive to reform themselves.[52] Blease liked to attach conditions upon parole, such as abstaining from drink, and he at times released convicts on the condition that they report to him directly on a certain date, making himself into a de facto parole officer. Yet there were no mechanisms in place for Blease to actually monitor the behavior of parolees, except for future convictions. Although the General Assembly gave the governor authority to parole any prisoner in 1909, it did not create a parole board that would oversee the release of prisoners until 1941.[53] That did not stop Blease from boasting that not one man he had paroled had been returned to prison. "These one-time convicts have reformed and are leading good lives and making substantial citizens," he declared in his 1915 speech to the Governors' Conference, although, without a bureaucracy of parole officers, he would have had no systematic way of knowing this.[54]

In effect, then, parole was simply a modified version of a pardon with all the same premodern inflections; the principal difference was that pardons restored a convict's citizenship rights. Historians who have studied the institution of parole in the North have interpreted it as a particularly modern form of state power. Parole extended the disciplinary regime of the modern penitentiary beyond the prison walls, allowing the state to police not only the offender but also his community—his family, friends, and associates. It relied upon individualized attention to the convict, but the process itself was impersonal and intrusive.[55] Southern governors, however, may have exerted social—and racial—control in granting parole, but not through the apparatus of a modern state, that is, not through administrative structures that allowed for the surveillance and policing of offenders. Rather, parole, much like pardons or commutations, operated through older, personal modes of transaction and could serve as benevolent acts of grace to compensate for an otherwise brutal system.[56] Although Blease spoke often of reforming the state penal system and in some ways did—by the closing of the mill, for instance—he did little to improve the prison hospital or further educational or recreational opportunities for prisoners, nor did he address injustices in the judicial system. Instead, like a monarchial ruler, Blease ruled over a penal system that, for the most part, remained draconian but that through his liberal use of mercy could appear benevolent.

Blease's critics, many of them urban elites and boosters who would have found common cause with northern progressives, viewed his use of paroles and pardons in just this light: as an arbitrary and self-serving use of state power. These detractors did not object to penal reform, but they saw Blease as using penal reform to consolidate monarchial power for himself. *The State*, for instance, called for a "more humane and scientific penal method" that would emphasize rehabilitation, but it believed the administration of such a system should not "be the function of any one man" who had expanded his executive power "in an elaborate scheme of penal reform."[57] Blease, in *The State*'s view, was committing an assault on law and order, making deterrence meaningless. "Convicted criminals go back to their communities to laugh in the faces of just judges and conscientious jurymen and, incidentally, to vote for Blease," the paper intoned.[58]

One of the most damning critiques of executive clemency was that the process was plagued with corruption. The wealthy could offer bribes to secure the release of their friends and relations. Or clemency operated as a form of peonage, whereby prisoners would be paroled to landowners to work off their debt. The system was particularly lucrative for lawyers, since petitions were more likely to succeed if filed by an attorney.[59] Many viewed Blease's pardon record as evidence of his desire to benefit his friends and supporters. Even his former mentor, Ben Tillman, castigated him as a "lunatic" in a public letter for "emptying the penitentiary" and turning the "criminals, murderers and cut-throats" loose. Blease's claim to mercy, Tillman claimed, was merely a "pretense," for "nothing but venality and greed of money can make him place the pardoning power in the hands of a lawyer who charges big fees to obtain pardons."[60] Blease was sensitive to these charges, particularly during the heat of campaigns. He told a judge in June 1914 that he would not consider a petition for pardon until after the Democratic primary. In 1912 he rejected a petition on the grounds that he was not considering any cases at the time due to the pushback he had received during his recent reelection campaign.[61]

Still, some of Blease's supporters expected that he would use his pardoning power to repay them. Mr. W. L. Cooper contacted Blease several times to secure the release of his "man" John Anderson, an African American laborer, an "obedient and respectful worker," who had been sentenced to a chain gang for twelve years on manslaughter charges. After Blease rejected his first petition, Cooper became increasingly agitated, stressing that everyone who had signed the petition was the governor's friend. "We have always believed and still believe that you will take care of your friends . . . and all your enemies can't make me believe anything else," he wrote.[62] Similarly, Blease received letters from friends and family of Thurston Vaughn, a white man sentenced to death for sexually assaulting girls under his care as superintendent of an orphanage in Greenville, asking him to reduce his sentence due to its severity toward a man they deemed not fully sane. One supporter in Greenville wrote to Blease that the governor had "thousands of friends in this county" who were "extremely anxious that the sentence be changed." He then named several Greenville people "who are all died [*sic*] in the wool bleasites and thousands of others." They "are entitled to some consideration at your hands," he continued. "We know that one of the noblest traits that characterize your Excellency is that you stick to your friends."[63] Yet even his fiercest critics could find no evidence that Blease benefited financially by granting clemency. There were charges that Blease was able to repay political favors through pardons, but again, the evidence was not firm. If Blease profited, it was through the boosting of his status among his supporters as a benevolent leader who understood the suffering of the poor and dispossessed.[64]

Indeed, his supporters viewed his release of prisoners as an expression of Blease's understanding of their values and the hardships they faced, and Blease, in turn, defended his use of clemency as a reflection of popular will. He regularly drew comparisons between his constituents and the unfortunates he had released from prison. "There are good men in the penitentiary," he told cotton mill workers in Spartanburg County, "men of as good families as yours or mine."[65] While it was appropriate for governors to defer to the judgment of community members where a crime had taken place, especially prosecutors and judges, Blease was criticized for going even further by deferring to popular opinion. In a rousing speech to supporters that summer, he promised the crowd he would pardon any prisoner they wanted. The crowd asked for the release of William Mills, a local man convicted of murder and serving a life sentence. Blease told the crowd he would pardon Mills if their district ensured the defeat of a political rival in the upcoming primary election. When his rival lost the election, Blease pardoned Mills, along with thirty-two other convicts, on Thanksgiving Day. His critics deemed this a gross form of pandering that undermined the solemnity of pardoning powers.[66]

Though his core constituents were white workers, Blease seemed to relish playing the role of savior to African American convicts, who also benefited from his liberal use of executive clemency. Blease claimed that 75 percent of the convicts he pardoned or paroled were African American.[67] Though that is probably an exaggeration, he reportedly released more black prisoners than all other governors since Reconstruction.[68] The pardoning or paroling of African American convicts was not unheard-of, even in the Jim Crow South, though clemency always operated within the bounds of racial paternalism. White landowners, for instance, commonly petitioned on behalf of their laborers, testifying that the convict in question was a "good negro" or a hard worker, obedient and trustworthy. Release, however, came at a cost, as it required that prisoners and their families subordinate themselves to powerful whites.[69]

Blease's use of clemency evinced this same kind of paternalism. He was especially moved by the plight of black prisoners whom he had met personally in prison or elsewhere. He paroled Franklin McAllister, convicted of murder, who, after escaping from the State Farm, appeared at Blease's office and "threw himself on [the governor's] mercy." His mother had gone blind and could no longer tend to her farm or care for McAllister's younger sisters.[70] In another case, Blease released Josh Gadsen, serving life imprisonment for burglary and larceny, whom he had met when Gadsen worked on the statehouse grounds. Blease was moved by this case because Gadsen had been "a good and faithful prisoner" who had already served ten years and who, with a poor and "aged mother," could not afford a lawyer.[71] In 1913 he paroled Simeon Ellis, a black man convicted of murder and sentenced to life imprisonment, after Ellis had spoken to Blease on the street in Columbia, where he was working on a chain gang. For that perceived impudence, Ellis's guards whipped him, and the prison physician tortured him with an electric battery. When an anonymous letter alerted Blease to this punishment, the governor was horrified. In a long message to the General Assembly, Blease expressed his sympathies for the "poor, ignorant Negro," whose "screams and cries and piteous appeals for mercy could be heard all over the Penitentiary grounds," and he impressed upon the assembly that prison officials were violating the state constitution's prohibition against corporal punishment.[72]

Many black prisoners wrote to Blease directly with their pleas for release in voices resounding with subservience. Natalie Zemon Davis, in her study of royal pardon petitions in sixteenth-century France, notes the fictional quality of these petitions not in their falseness but in their storytelling quality. These petitions, she argues, serve as rare documents in which the voices of the lower classes can be heard, providing a counternarrative to the stories of their crimes told in official court documents.[73] But such a distinction between fiction and documentation is nearly impossible to discern in letters from black prisoners, who regularly performed a kind of racialized obsequiousness to elicit the governor's goodwill. In that sense, their letters can be read as theater. In a letter to Blease, a convict named John Allen, serving two years for manslaughter, calls himself a "poor negro" who, if the governor releases him, "will try and be a better negro."[74] Another assured Blease that he had "bin a trusted hand for 5 years" and begged to be released, as, he wrote, "I am a Prisoner now and got no one to help me and I ant got no Body to ask for help But you and I believe that you will help me."[75]

Like many white constituents, black convicts and their families offered their unwavering support and blessings to Blease in exchange for his benevolence. Joe Adams, sentenced to twenty years for arson and working at the hosiery mill, wrote to Blease that he believes that "god will bless you for the good your doing the prisoners in this state and I am going to hope and trust in god. . . . for their wont be no more Prisoners Friend like you and Please sir Be a friend to me as well as them." Although he proclaimed his innocence, he signed his letter "from your truly Criminal Negro friend."[76] On behalf of her brother, serving time for assault, a young woman wrote to Blease that "we are poor colored people and ignorant and had no one to instruct us what to do" to explain why her brother was sentenced to the chain gang for what she describes as a minor assault. Her brother had no lawyer serving in his defense. If Blease can help, she says, "the Lord will bless you for your care for the poor and distressed."[77] Since these kinds of letters came without formal petitions, Blease did not pardon these prisoners.

The paternalistic compassion he evinced toward certain prisoners might seem at odds with his fierce Negrophobia. After all, this was a man who, in defending lynching, referred to African Americans as "apes and baboons."[78] But his Negrophobia and his paternalism were actually two sides of the same coin. In many cases, the former swayed him to release prisoners. Like most white southerners, Blease viewed African Americans as inherently immoral and irredeemable, but this meant that he held black convicts to a different standard than he did white convicts. "On the order of the lower animals . . . the negro race has absolutely no standard of morality," he wrote, defending his parole of a black man convicted of manslaughter of another black man. "They are, in that respect, a class by themselves."[79] He was thus often persuaded by petitions on behalf of black convicts imprisoned for assaults on or murders of other African Americans. Clemency in these cases was not unusual for southern governors, who placed certain crimes under what was called "negro law."[80] Blease, in fact, often expressed appreciation for African Americans who had murdered other black men for the service they had done to the state, particularly if the victim was reported to be a malevolent or disreputable character. His racism also led him to release white men convicted of raping black women or girls, a crime he thought impossible. "I have heretofore stated that I do not believe that a white man would commit rape on a negro," he wrote in his report justifying his parole of a white boy convicted of sexually assaulting a black girl. "I certainly see no necessity for it, by which he runs the risk of being sentenced to the Penitentiary or possibly to the electric chair for possibly what he could usually get from prices ranging from 25 cents to $1."[81]

This kind of flippant reasoning was common in Blease's annual pardon and parole reports. Despite his professed regard for administrative norms—heeding the opinions of judges and other community leaders, ignoring prisoners without formal petitions—Blease tended to make decisions emotionally. He was easily moved by compassion, racist sentiment, or his own self-regard. In 1913, in a case that made national news, he pardoned his own chauffeur, a black man who was sentenced, in lieu of paying a fine he could not afford, to the chain gang for thirty days for speeding because Blease viewed the conviction as payback from the police.[82] In other words, like all authoritarian leaders, he demanded obedience and lashed out at those who challenged his authority. The power of executive clemency reinforced that sense of authority for Blease, especially as it elicited deference and loyalty from prisoners and their families, both black and white.

That Blease used this power to advocate for penal reform reveals how that reform played out in the South. The measures that Blease enacted to make life more tolerable for prisoners, from the closing of the hosiery mill to shorter sentences through pardons and parole, were taken not through the administrative power of the modern state or the expansion of due process and the rule of law; rather, they happened through retrogressive forms of power. With the chain gangs, power was decentralized, as county sheriffs and judges regained control over the criminal justice system. Inversely, with executive clemency, it was highly centralized in the governor's authority, but an authority that was more autocratic than democratic, tempered by his reputed beneficence. In both cases, what was deemed "reform" stood at odds with many principles of the new penology, from the application of abstract scientific principles to criminal justice to the expansion of state bureaucracies to oversee the penal system. Instead, reform followed the pattern of southern progressivism more broadly: populist and personal, and inextricably bound to Jim Crow norms.

NOTES

I would like to thank Margaret Storey and Carole Emberton for planting the seed of my argument in this chapter and Natalie J. Ring for her comments on an early draft.

1. *Outlook*, December 21, 1912, 843; *Chicago Tribune*, December 7, 1912, 7; *San Francisco Call*, December 6, 1912, 1–2.

2. *Outlook*, December 21, 1912, 843; *State* (Columbia, SC), December 10, 1912, 10. Both *Outlook* and *The State* reprinted editorial responses from around the country.

3. Letter of transmittal, in "Statement of Pardons, Paroles, and Commutations Granted by Cole L. Blease, 1912–1913," in *Reports and Resolutions of the General Assembly by the State of South Carolina* (Columbia, SC: Gonzales and Bryan, 1913), 3:524. Hereafter cited as 1913 Pardon Report.

4. *Outlook*, December 21, 1912, 843; *State*, December 4, 1912, 1.

5. *State*, December 4, 1912, 1.

6. *State*, January 15, 1915, 10; *New York Times*, January 15, 1915, 1; Ronald Dantan Burnside, "The Governorship of Coleman Livingston Blease of South Carolina, 1911–1915" (PhD diss., Indiana University, 1963), 183. Burnside claims that this number, reported in *The State*, might be a low estimate, since Blease never published official tallies, and in 1914 he failed to submit an official report to the state legislature.

7. Burnside, "The Governorship," 183–85. Blease pardoned these parolees to counter his successor's threat to return them to the penal system by forcing them to break parole.

8. These numbers do not include prisoners on the county chain gangs. *State*, January 15, 1915, 10; *Annual Report of the Board of Directors and Superintendent of the South Carolina Penitentiary for the Fiscal Year, 1910* (Columbia, SC: Gonzales and Bryan, 1911), 10; *Annual Report of the Board of Directors and Superintendent of the South Carolina Penitentiary for the Fiscal Year, 1914* (Columbia, SC: Gonzales and Bryan, 1915), 3.

9. *State*, September 2, 1915, 1.

10. David J. Rothman, *Conscience and Convenience: The Asylum and Its Alternatives in Progressive America* (New York: Aldine de Gruyter, 1980); Jonathan Simon, *Poor Discipline: Parole and the Social Control of the Underclass, 1890–1990* (Chicago: University of Chicago Press, 1993), 17–38; Michael Willrich, *City of Courts: Socializing Justice in Progressive Era Chicago* (New York: Cambridge University Press, 2003); Rebecca M. McLennan, *The Crisis of Imprisonment: Protest, Politics, and the Making of the American Penal State, 1776–1941* (New York: Cambridge University Press, 2008), 193–416.

11. William A. Link, *The Paradox of Southern Progressivism, 1880–1930* (Chapel Hill: University of North Carolina Press, 1992).

12. Tillmanite refers to followers of Ben Tillman, an advocate of populist policies and a fierce white supremacist who served as governor of South Carolina from 1890 to 1894 and then represented the state in the US Senate from 1895 to 1918.

13. David L. Carlton, *Mill and Town in South Carolina, 1880–1920* (Baton Rouge: Louisiana State University Press, 1982), 215–16; Bryant Simon, "The Appeal of Cole Blease in South Carolina: Race, Class, and Sex in the New South," in *Sex, Love, Race: Crossing Boundaries in North American History*, ed. Martha Hodes (New York: New York University Press, 1999), 376; Burnside, "The Governorship," 5–6. Blease lost the governor's race in 1914. He continued to run for office for years and was elected to the US Senate in 1924. He served until 1930, when he lost his reelection bid.

14. On earlier critiques of Blease, see W. J. Cash, *The Mind of the South* (New York: A. A. Knopf, 1941), 245; V. O. Key Jr., *Southern Politics in State and Nation* (New York: Vintage Books, 1949), 144. On revisionist interpretations of Blease, see Carlton, *Mill and Town*, 215–72; Simon, "The Appeal," 373–98; Clarence N. Stone, "Bleaseism and the 1912 Election in South Carolina," *North Carolina Historical Review* 40, no. 1 (1963): 54–74.

15. Carlton, *Mill and Town*, 224–25, 234–39; Simon, "The Appeal," 377–78; Stone, "Bleaseism," 71.

16. C. Vann Woodward, *Origins of the New South, 1877–1913* (Baton Rouge: Louisiana State University Press, 1951), 369–95; Jack Temple Kirby, *Darkness at the Dawning: Race and Reform in the Progressive South* (Philadelphia: Lippincott, 1972); John Dittmer, *Black Georgia in the Progressive Era, 1900–1920* (Urbana: University of Illinois Press, 1977).

17. Link, *The Paradox*.

18. On the southern penal system as a form of racial control, see Douglas A. Blackmon, *Slavery by Another Name: The Re-enslavement of Black Americans from the Civil War to World War II* (New York: Anchor Books, 2008); David M. Oshinsky, *"Worse Than Slavery": Parchman Farm and the Ordeal of Jim Crow Justice* (New York: Simon & Schuster, 1996); Alex Lichtenstein, *Twice the Work of Free Labor: The Political Economy of Convict Labor in the New South* (London: Verso, 1996); Mary Ellen Curtin, *Black Prisoners and Their World, Alabama, 1865–1900* (Charlottesville: University Press of Virginia, 2000); Talitha L. LeFlouria, *Chained in Silence: Black Women and Convict Labor in the New South* (Chapel Hill: University of North Carolina Press, 2015).

19. "Report of the Joint Committee to Investigate the Affairs of the State Penitentiary (1899)," in *Reports and Resolutions of the General Assembly of the State of South Carolina at the Regular Session Commencing January 9, 1900*, vol. 2 (Columbia, SC: Bryan Printing Company, 1900); "Report of the Legislative Committee on Penal and Charitable Institutions to the General Assembly of the State of South Carolina at the Regular Session of 1915," in *Reports and Resolutions of the General Assembly of the State of South Carolina, Regular Session Commencing January 12, 1915*, vol. 3 (Columbia, SC: Gonzales and Bryan, 1915); "Report of the Special Joint Legislative Committee to Investigate Conditions at the State Penitentiary," in *Reports of the State Officers Boards and Committees to the General Assembly of the State of South Carolina, Regular Session Commencing January 9, 1923*, vol. 2 (Columbia, SC: Gonzales and Bryan, 1923); "Report of the Joint Legislative Committee to Investigate the State Penitentiary," in *Reports of the State Officers Boards and Committees to the General Assembly, Regular Session Commencing January 12, 1926*, vol. 2 (Columbia, SC: Printed under the Direction of the Joint Committee on Printing, General Assembly of South Carolina); *Second Annual Report of the State Board of Charities and Corrections of South Carolina, 1916* (Columbia, SC: Gonzales and Bryan, 1916); Albert D. Oliphant, *The Evolution of the Penal System in South Carolina from 1866–1916* (Columbia, SC: State

Company, 1916), 13–14. Oliphant was the assistant secretary of the State Board of Charities and Correction.

20. Cole Blease, letter of transmittal, in "Statement of Pardons, Paroles, and Commutations Granted by Cole L. Blease, 1911–1912," in *Reports and Resolutions of the General Assembly by the State of South Carolina* (Columbia, SC: Gonzales and Bryan, 1912), 3:891. Hereafter cited as 1912 Pardon Report.

21. Other reforms included the following: convicts sentenced to more than six months were given a 10 percent reduction in their sentences for good behavior; counties were authorized to establish female houses of correction, separating male and female prisoners; and the state moved away from execution by hanging, under the jurisdiction of counties and often still public, to executions by electrocution, performed privately at the state penitentiary. Burnside, "The Governorship," 179–84; Oliphant, *The Evolution*, 6–12.

22. Oliphant, *The Evolution*, 7–8.

23. A chair factory temporarily replaced the mill, but conditions were supposedly better in it, and it went out of business in 1915, ending private contracts for prison labor once and for all. Burnside, "The Governorship," 176; *State*, July 20, 1912, 1; Oliphant, *The Evolution*, 7–13.

24. Historians have tended to devalue opponents' humanitarian arguments, focusing instead on their pragmatic fiscal or political incentives. Yet humanitarian arguments were just as, if not more, prevalent in abolitionist rhetoric and literature. See Donald R. Walker, *Penology for Profit: A History of the Texas Prison System, 1867–1912* (College Station: Texas A&M University Press, 1988), 76; Martha A. Myers, *Race, Labor, and Punishment in the New South* (Columbus: Ohio State University Press, 1998), 16–20; on the historiography on this point, see Vivien Miller, *Crime, Sexual Violence, and Clemency: Florida's Pardon Board and Penal System in the Progressive Era* (Gainesville: University of Florida Press, 2000), 49.

25. *State*, July 6, 1911, 1.

26. "Annual Message of Governor Cole L. Blease to the General Assembly of South Carolina, January 13, 1914," in *Reports and Resolutions of the General Assembly of the State of South Carolina* (Columbia, SC: Gonzales and Bryan, 1914), 3:21.

27. Tammy Ingram, *Dixie Highway: Road Building and the Making of the Modern South, 1900–1930* (Chapel Hill: University of North Carolina Press, 2014), 140. See also Lichtenstein, *Twice the Work*, 152–85.

28. Burnside, "The Governorship," 181–82; Oliphant, *The Evolution*, 8, 12; *Annual Report of the Board of Directors and Superintendent of the South Carolina Penitentiary for the Fiscal Year, 1913* (Columbia, SC: Gonzales and Bryan, 1914).

29. "Annual Message of Governor Cole L. Blease, 1914," 21–22.

30. *Second Annual Report of the State Board of Charities and Corrections of South Carolina, 1916*, 4–5; *Fourth Annual Report of the State Board of Charities and Corrections of South Carolina, 1918, to the Governor* (Columbia, SC: Gonzales and Bryan, 1919), 6–7; "Fifth Annual Report of the State Board of Charities and Corrections of South Carolina, 1919, to the Governor," in *Reports of State*

Officers, Boards, and Committees to the General Assembly to the State of South Carolina, Regular Session Commencing January 13, 1920 (Columbia, SC: Gonzales and Bryan, 1920), 92–96. To these reformers, their humanitarian progressivism did not conflict with their white supremacy. Oliphant advocated that no white prisoners should be sentenced to the county chain gangs; instead, they should be sent to the state penitentiary, where presumably they would receive better treatment (*The Evolution*, 14).

31. *State*, February 10, 1906, 6, February 25, 1911, 1, March 23, 1911, 9; Burnside, "The Governorship," 185–86.

32. On this issue, see Pippa Holloway, "Testimonial Incapacity and Criminal Defendants in the South," in this volume.

33. For example, 1912 Pardon Report, 920; 1913 Pardon Report, 537.

34. 1912 Pardon Report, 898.

35. Ibid., 937.

36. Ibid., 977–78.

37. Burnside, "The Governorship," 190; Stone, "Blease," 72.

38. Burnside, "The Governorship," 174–77; *Annual Report of the Board of Directors and Superintendent of the South Carolina Penitentiary for the Fiscal Year, 1910* (Columbia, SC: Gonzales and Bryan, 1911), 42.

39. "Statement of Pardons, Paroles, and Commutations Granted by Cole L. Blease, Governor of South Carolina, 1913," in *Reports and Resolutions of the General Assembly of the State of South Carolina, Regular Session Commencing January 13, 1914* (Columbia, SC: Gonzales and Bryan, 1914), 3:258. Hereafter cited as 1914 Pardon Report.

40. Willrich, *City of Courts*, 65–66.

41. *State*, September 2, 1915, 9. The State Board of Charities and Corrections made this same recommendation for the same reason. See "Fifth Annual Report," 15.

42. *State*, September 2, 1915, 9.

43. Kathleen Dean Moore, *Pardons: Justice, Mercy, and the Public Interest* (New York: Oxford University Press, 1989), 7, 17–19.

44. Douglas Hay, "Property, Authority, and the Criminal Law," in *Albion's Fatal Tree: Crime and Society in Eighteenth-Century England*, ed. Douglas Hay et al. (New York: Pantheon Books, 1975), 17–63; see also Carolyn Strange, introduction to *Qualities of Mercy: Justice, Punishment, and Discretion*, ed. Carolyn Strange (Vancouver: UBC Press, 1996), 5–6.

45. Victoria Barton to Gov. Blease, April 1, 1913, box 3, folder "Posey Barton," Gov. Coleman L. Blease, Pardons, Paroles, and Commutations, 1911–15, South Carolina Archives and History, Columbia, SC. Hereafter cited as Blease Pardons.

46. George Barnes to Gov. Blease, June 4, 1911, box 3, folder "George Barnes," Blease Pardons.

47. 1912 Pardon Report, 892–93.

48. Gov. Blease to Reverend D. G. Phillips, October 31, 1914, cited in Burnside, "The Governorship," 101.

49. Moore, *Pardons*, 23–45.

50. Ibid., 55–65; Miller, *Crime*, 4.

51. Moore, *Pardons*, 61–62.

52. 1913 Pardon Report, 525.

53. Oliphant, *The Evolution*, 12.

54. *State*, September 2, 1915, 9.

55. Simon, *Poor Discipline*, 44–59; Rothman, *Conscience and Convenience*, 3–6, 159–204.

56. Stephen Garton, "Managing Mercy: African Americans, Parole, and Paternalism in the Georgia Prison System, 1919–1945," *Journal of Social History* 36, no. 3 (2003): 677, 687, 691. Rothman argues that although parole was designed as a rational, therapeutic system of rehabilitation, it was, in practice, "arbitrary and capricious," and it never effectively succeeded in controlling or reforming offenders (*Conscience and Convenience*, 173). In that case, these regional differences might not be so pronounced.

57. *State*, January 14, 1915, 4.

58. *State*, December 30, 1911, 4.

59. Garton, "Managing Mercy," 683–84; Miller points out that pardon applications were lucrative business for lawyers, as the filing of one would cost a laborer several months' wages. For that reason, most petitions were paid for by landowners or other employers on behalf of their workers (Miller, *Crime*, 136).

60. Tillman's letter was published in full in *The State*, September 1, 1912, 1, 10.

61. Gov. Blease to Hon. J. E. Beamguard, June 5, 1914, box 1, folder "Malachi Alger," Blease Pardons; Gov. Blease to D. D. McColl, September 16, 1912, box 1, folder "Essex Alford," Blease Pardons.

62. Affidavit of W. L. Cooper, April, 2, 1913, and W. L. Cooper to Gov. Cole Blease, May 27, 1913, box 1, folder "John Anderson," Blease Pardons.

63. G. W. Piegler to Gov. Cole Blease, December 18, 1914, box 58, folder "T. U. Vaughn," Blease Pardons.

64. Burnside, "The Governorship," 189–92.

65. *State*, July 6, 1911, 1.

66. James D. Barnett, "The Grounds of Pardon," *Journal of Criminal Law and Criminology* 17, no. 4 (1927): 507n91.

67. *State*, September 2, 1915, 9.

68. Burnside, "The Governorship," 190.

69. Some historians have concluded that African American convicts did not benefit from executive clemency. See Leon Litwack, *Trouble in Mind: Black Southerners in the Age of Jim Crow* (New York: Vintage Books, 1998), 270; Miller, *Crime*, 115. Other historians, however, have argued that while pardons were rarer, African Americans were regularly paroled, but largely only to serve white paternalistic sentiment or economic need. See Oshinsky, *Worse Than Slavery*, 179–204; Garton, "Managing Mercy," 675–99; Myers, *Race*, 188–97.

70. 1912 Pardon Report, 990.

71. 1914 Pardon Report, 277.

72. Ibid., 254–55.

73. Natalie Zemon Davis, *Fiction in the Archives: Pardon Tales and Their Tellers in Sixteenth-Century France* (Stanford, CA: Stanford University Press, 1987), 3–5.

74. John Allen to Gov. Blease, April 1, 1914, box 1, folder "John Allen," Blease Pardons.

75. Willie Abney to Gov. Blease, December 22, 1914, box 1, folder "Willie Abney," Blease Pardons.

76. Joe Adams to Gov. Blease, July 7, 1912, box 1, folder "Joe Adams," Blease Pardons.

77. L. Harrison to Gov. Blease, December 23, 1914, box 3, folder "Elliot Barnes," Blease Pardons.

78. *State*, July 6, 1911, 1.

79. 1914 Pardon Report, 328–29.

80. Litwack, *Trouble in Mind*, 269; Garton, "Managing Mercy," 689–90.

81. 1914 Pardon Report, 305–6. He likewise frequently exonerated white men convicted of raping white women if they were women of ill repute.

82. 1914 Pardon Report, 194; *Life*, March 27, 1913, 614.

CHAPTER 8

Hanging, the Electric Chair, and Death Penalty Reform in the Early Twentieth-Century South

Vivien Miller

By 1930 most states in the southern region, stretching from Maryland to Texas, had switched from hanging to the electric chair to carry out state-sanctioned or legal executions. Beginning with Virginia in 1908, followed by Tennessee, North Carolina, Kentucky, South Carolina, Arkansas, and Oklahoma, the first group had adopted electrical execution prior to the United States' entry into World War I. Governor J. C. W. Beckham told Kentucky legislators in 1906: "The hanging of a man in the community where he is tried produces a sensation, a nervousness and excitement upon the part of the people, and it has a brutalizing effect upon the large numbers, in spite of the law, who witness it."[1] All Kentucky executions were to be carried out in the electric chair at Eddyville penitentiary from June 1910.[2]

New execution laws were enacted in Maryland, Florida, Texas, Georgia, and Alabama during a second period of death penalty reform in the 1920s.[3] Texas legislators observed in 1923 that "hanging is antiquated and has been supplanted in many states by the more modern and humane system of electrocution."[4] In an era when electricity inspired popular awe and community pride and was considered integral to advancing industrialism and civilization, journalists and politicians frequently contrasted the "antiquated" and "barbaric" practice of hanging with the superior method of electrical execution.[5] Only Louisiana and Mississippi resisted change, until 1940.[6]

Local conditions shaped death penalty reform and the adoption of new execution technology, and each state's journey from public to private execution was rarely linear or straightforward. In contrast to the prison systems in states such as Kentucky and Virginia, Florida's prison system did not have the industrial capacity to support electrical execution in the 1890s and 1900s, when there was no central penitentiary. However, changing social and cultural sensibilities, greater scrutiny of the conduct and professionalism of local law enforcers, and technological developments all coalesced behind calls for reform in the early 1920s. Florida was the fifteenth US state to embrace electrical execution.[7] From January 1, 1924, capital offenders were to be executed in a newly constructed electric chair at the state prison farm.[8]

This chapter focuses on the transition from hanging to electrical execution in Florida, when the older gallows rituals associated with hanging were replaced with the time-managed, gendered, and racialized death penalty procedures that were emblematic of the modernizing industrial state. Many officials sought an end to public executions and to curtail lynchings during the post–World War I years, when the state was reinventing itself as a tropical tourist paradise for predominantly white elite vacationers and tin-can tourists and seeking vital business and real estate investors, as well as increasing numbers of migrants and settlers. By the early twentieth century, several county and state officials were troubled by the size and conduct of execution crowds and the ways in which salutary messages of deterrence, penitence, order, and due process of law were being interpreted. County officials were also vexed by the rising costs of policing hangings. Further, execution reforms in Florida, as in states across the southern region, were embedded within a wider set of changing local, state, and regional judicial, political, and popular relations and the increasing centralization and bureaucratization of state governments. More robust regulatory and social efficiency frameworks were established to address perennial southern "problems" of poverty, illiteracy, and poor health.[9] State management and regulation of capital punishment were also increasing; in Florida these changes occurred largely under the direction of the Board of Commissioners of State Institutions.

This chapter focuses also on the figure of the sheriff. The main custodians of hanging rituals were local sheriffs, as they oversaw the treatment of the condemned from their arrest through to their execution, managed the construction and testing of the gallows, performed the execution, and supervised the disposal of the corpse. As the chief law officer in all Florida counties, the sheriff also oversaw the policing of execution crowds. Early twentieth-century photographs, like the ones included here, underscore the often rudimentary technology of locally constructed gallows, as well as the public theater of execution day itself. They also help chart the continuities and transformations in sheriffs' roles and responsibilities as executions ceased to take place in the counties of conviction. Even after the inauguration of the electric chair in 1924, Florida sheriffs continued to perform executions until 1941 and so preserved a degree of local authority amid state centralization and control. Consequently, despite the veneer of greater professionalism that surrounded electrical execution in the interwar years, the executioner remained an untrained amateur. Nevertheless, the adoption of electrical execution was an important marker in Florida's slow embrace of penal modernism.

In several southern states, execution reform was promoted by one adept politician who could mobilize crucial legislative and gubernatorial support for change, often amid key moments of community disorder and county mismanagement. Leon County representative and House Speaker Fred H. Davis prepared the legislative bill to establish Florida's electric chair in the spring of 1923 against the backdrop of the Rosewood Massacre in January that year and during a specially convened legislative investigation into a series of well-publicized incidents of prisoner mistreatment.[10] Revelations of lessee corruption and cruelty to convicts generated national condemnation and the threat of consumer boycotts and thus provided the pivotal moment in which prison reformers secured significant changes: abolition of convict leasing, of corporal punishment of prisoners, and of hanging.[11]

Death penalty historian John Bessler situates the adoption of the electric chair within a broad complement of death penalty reforms taking place in different US regions between the 1830s and 1930s, as the public spectacle of execution was increasingly out of step with the disciplinary needs of the modern industrial nation-state.[12] These reforms included the shift from public to private execution and the consequent denial of public access, centralization of capital punishment in state penitentiaries, staging of executions at or after midnight, restrictions on the numbers of witnesses, and passage of press gag laws. A lexicon of penal humanitarianism, which highlighted the unnecessary suffering of the condemned at the hands of inexperienced executioners and on faulty scaffolds, infused elite and middle-class criticism of hanging throughout the nineteenth century.[13] Support for a more merciful and less spectacular death came also from medical and political quarters.[14]

The electric chair first appeared in New York (1889), followed by Ohio (1896), Massachusetts (1898), and New Jersey (1907). Several newspaper reports and scientific publications therefore equated electrical execution with the ostensibly more inventive and progressive northern state penal systems, particularly as southern spectacles of public execution, vigilantism, and the suffering of the condemned persisted well into the twentieth century.[15] To many fin-de-siècle commentators, the South remained a stagnant, backward, underdeveloped, less industrialized, and largely peripheral region.[16] It was also extraordinarily lethal, as interracial and intraracial black and white murder rates, for example, were higher in the South than in other regions.[17] Sociologists James Massey and Martha Myers calculate there were over six thousand deaths from legal execution and lynching in the southern region between the 1880s and early 1930s.[18] Yet the rhetoric of death penalty modernization percolated through the South, and many state politicians, sheriffs, and prison officials were as willing to embrace electrical execution as their northern counterparts.

Even so, death sentences and executions were, then as now, relatively intermittent events. Myers found that 2 percent of African American offenders and 1 percent of white offenders convicted of a violent crime in Georgia between January 1870 and December 1940 received a death sentence. Thus, the 415 executions over a seventy-year period in that state amounted to 1.7 percent of total convictions, from a total of 46,566 offenders.[19] The 213 executions in Florida between 1870 and 1920 equate to a similarly small percentage of the convictions for first-degree murder and rape.[20] There were generally between two and eight hangings per year, except for 1901, 1907, 1910, 1912, and 1915, when numbers reached double figures.[21] As has been well documented, African Americans accounted for a disturbingly high proportion of those condemned to death and those executed in all southern states.[22] Most of the condemned in late nineteenth- and early twentieth-century Florida were young African American men convicted of murder.[23] Florida's death chamber was also an overwhelmingly male-dominated space, as there were no state-sanctioned executions of women between 1846 and 1997.[24]

Legal executions in Florida during the hanging period (1824–1923) were usually carried out in the county of conviction and under the control of local sheriffs. These men determined whether private execution laws were wholly, partially, or barely complied with. They were responsible for the construction and positioning of the gallows; they controlled the number of spectator passes that enabled privileged witnesses into the jail yard or execution enclosure; and they determined the information or access granted to local journalists. By the early twentieth century, county jails in larger cities such as Jacksonville, Duval County (which also had the highest number of executions), had permanent scaffolds within an enclosed jail yard or jailhouse.[25] In rural counties, where legal executions were much rarer events, temporary wooden structures were constructed as required and situated next to the jailhouse, as illustrated in figures 8.1 and 8.2.[26] As a result, there would be no gallows procession, a traditional feature of many early northern executions, as the condemned would simply step from the cells to the platform.[27]

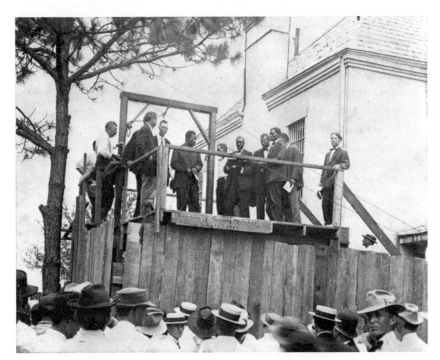

Figure 8.1. Execution of Hersey Mitchell, Bradford County Jail, Starke, Florida, 1913. Image No. RC03432. Black-and-white photoprint, 7 by 9 inches, State Archives of Florida, Florida Memory, www.floridamemory.com/items/show/25518. Courtesy of the State Archives of Florida.

In late November 1914 Will Moore was hanged at Starke, Bradford County, for the first-degree murder, nine months previously, of a deputy sheriff who had been called to an altercation involving Moore and three other African American men during a late-night crap game. Moore had been removed to the Alachua County jail in Gainesville, thirty miles away, as threats of lynching reverberated through the local white communities. A special term of the Bradford County Circuit Court was convened in March 1914 to consider the murder charges against Moore. As was anticipated in local news reports, he was swiftly convicted and sentenced to hang.[28]

His execution on November 27, 1914, functioned as an important forum for public consumption and community censure. Even though the gallows were constructed within the jail yard, Moore's execution was witnessed by a crowd of several hundred spectators "from all sections of the county" that included "two hundred women and children," according to the local newspaper, the *Bradford County Telegraph*.[29] There was a certain novelty about the macabre spectacle, which dominated the front pages of the *Telegraph*. Moore was only the second person to be executed in Bradford County; Hersey Mitchell, also convicted of murder, was the first, in 1913. Photographic firms were specially commissioned to record both executions.[30]

State and local responsibilities for capital punishment were clearly demarcated by law and custom: the governor set the execution date, but the details were left to the local sheriff, who was also master of ceremonies on execution day itself. Hanging included a host of traditional, often meaningful, rituals, which began with the formal reading of the death warrant to the prisoner. According to the local paper, Moore "listened breathlessly to the reading and gazed in a fascinated manner at the legal document with its solemn black ribbons and glistening, gold seal" as Sheriff S. B. Denmark read its contents. Moore then sighed, "'All right, sir. I have nothing to say. Pray for me.'"[31] At 11:15 a.m. on November 27, Moore, dressed in a new blue serge suit, white shoes, and white gloves, mounted the scaffold, which was crowded with sheriffs from neighboring counties, Denmark's deputies, several trial jurors (who had offered no recommendation of mercy), and local clergy. Hymns and prayers followed.[32]

The scene depicted in the *Bradford County Telegraph* substantiates Michael Trotti's argument that "the typical public execution of a southern black man was two different events occurring in the same place at the same time. It was the display of (white) state power upon a (black) criminal; it was also the display of African-American piety and religious terror in front of a vast black and white congregation." The gathering of members of the black community at the gallows, resembling a church congregation, "made the moment more meaningful" for the condemned. However, this gathering also stoked the hostility of white officials and observers.[33] At Denmark's signal, Moore addressed the crowd, thanked the jailer "'for his kindness to me,'" paid tribute to his spiritual advisors, and warned: "'Young men, when you start to a crap game take a second thought and go to church.'" The sheriff then placed the noose around Moore's neck and sprung the trap. Readers were assured that "Moore met his doom in a courageous manner. He never flinched nor faltered."[34]

The positioning of the Bradford County scaffold meant that the spectacle of the condemned man dangling at the end of the rope under the platform, perhaps choking from asphyxiation, would not be visible to the spectators. Yet the proximity of the crowd to the wooden partition meant that many spectators would likely have been within earshot of the condemned man's final death throes. When Ebenezer Tobin was executed in Pinellas County in October 1915, the *Evening Independent* noted that the fence around the jail enclosure was only six feet high and "would not obstruct the view of anybody on the outside of the enclosure and the hanging practically will be public." (Sheriff Whitehurst complained that he lacked the funds to build a higher fence.) In fact, the accompanying headline—"Everybody Who Wants to Can See Tobin Hanged by Neck until Dead"—seemed more of an invitation rather than a criticism.[35] By contrast, black fabric was placed around the scaffold for the 1920 execution of a white defendant in Okaloosa County.

Photographs of executions in Florida in the 1910s and 1920s indicate that sheriffs used gallows with lever-operated trap doors, which required some technical knowledge and expertise. There were undoubtedly experienced gallows builders in the United States, but it is not clear whether any were employed in Florida; sheriffs were more likely to rely on local carpenters.[36] In his broad study of crime and punishment in British colonial North America and the United States, legal historian Lawrence Friedman describes justice in the colonial period as the "business of amateurs," a description that remained pertinent through the nineteenth century, especially in Florida.[37] Further, men without special training, relevant educational achievements, or strong commitment to crime control continued to win appointments or elections to the office of sheriff in the early twentieth century. These men also brokered the leasing of misdemeanants and oversaw the county prison farms and road squads, which were vital mechanisms in local racial, social, and crime control. Most rural sheriffs in Florida were not paid a regular salary until the 1940s; they earned their living from the collection of local taxes and fines. Fees were paid to them for a range of duties, including providing bed and board to state prisoners being transported from the county of conviction to the state prison.[38] They would also receive a fee for performing an execution, a responsibility for which they were given no instruction.[39]

Therefore, if Hersey Mitchell was the first person whom Sheriff Denmark had actually hanged, how did he know what to do? Professional hangmen were employed in the northeastern United States and Canada by the late nineteenth century and seem to have been largely peripatetic, often employed by several states or provinces within the same region.[40] It is possible that several experienced or "professional" executioners were operating throughout the southern region in the early twentieth century, perhaps as consultants, offering advice on knots, how to test the drop, and operating the trap door mechanism rather than engaging in neck breaking, but I have not found evidence of this in Florida so far.[41] However, it was customary for the sheriffs of neighboring Florida counties to attend a hanging, and these men were the most likely custodians of a body of informal knowledge for first-time executioners. Former sheriffs with hanging experience were available for hire: Daviess County sheriff Florence Thompson engaged a retired sheriff to hang Rainey Bethea in Kentucky in 1936.[42] Expertise with knots and the position of the noose (often prominently displayed in lynching photographs) may also have been borrowed from illegal executions: at least 250 persons were lynched in Florida between 1882 and 1930, including two black men in early twentieth-century Bradford County.[43]

Many historians view legal execution as a functional replacement for lynching.[44] However, in their study of lynching and executions in Georgia, Massey and Myers found the relationship between lynching, incarceration rates, and execution rates to be much more complex than one of simple substitution. They concluded that there were indications of compensatory social and racial control but found "no evidence that changes in lynching rates have any significant effect on the rate at which black males are either executed or incarcerated" in early twentieth-century Georgia.[45] Criminologist Margaret Vandiver also found no evidence for the replacement thesis in her study of Tennessee counties but a clearer connection in her case study of interwar Marion County, Florida, where three black men, each accused of raping white women, were rushed to execution to prevent lynchings from taking place.[46] Arthur Johnson, one of the last men to be hanged in Florida in July 1923, was saved from local rough justice by the sheriff of Putnam County and then taken to Duval County for safekeeping until his trial in Alachua County and subsequent execution.[47]

There were many instances when black defendants were convicted within a matter of hours by unsympathetic and prejudiced jurors and judges who heard cases based on weak, fabricated, or purely circumstantial evidence. The accused were defended by uninterested and uncommitted court-appointed lawyers, and all-white juries acquiesced in the prosecutor's demand for the death penalty. Such cases offered a veneer of legal formalism. Historian Michael Pfeifer analogizes the persistent tensions between local lower- and working-class proponents of "rough justice" and elite and middle-class promoters of legal formalism and due process. Both camps demanded the reinforcement of white supremacy over the criminal justice apparatus and the perpetuation of a racial hierarchy in discipline and punishment, particularly of nonwhites, but rough justice advocates resented and resisted the encroaching power of the market and the modern state.[48] Due process advocates also demanded that local law enforcers preserve law and order, and by the early 1920s, the loyalties and professionalism of county officials, especially sheriffs, were clearly under scrutiny in several states.[49]

In Florida, local irritation over the financial burdens of maintaining public order also framed the transition from hanging. Three legal hangings in

Okaloosa County in 1920 and 1921 had each cost $25,000 to police. Ten thousand spectators were reported to have witnessed the double hanging at Crestview of white murderers Jake Martin and Putnam Ponsell in September 1921.[50] The Okaloosa County commissioners expressed considerable irritation at the expense of maintaining public order and controlling the crowds, particularly as two of the three men were from other states, and the third had been resident in Florida for only a short period of time.[51] The point is that while establishment of a single central place of execution reflected the increasing bureaucratization of state governments and government institutions in the early twentieth century, local officials also had to be willing to relinquish authority over parts of the criminal justice apparatus. Further, if the goal was to merely supplant lynching with state-sanctioned capital punishment, then this could have been achieved through more robust enforcement of private execution laws or the centralization of hangings at state prisons, as had occurred in Louisiana in the 1910s, rather than recourse to expensive technology.[52]

By the 1920s there was growing political appetite for death penalty reform in Florida from legislators, the Florida Federation of Women's Clubs, and local sheriffs. R. H. Weaver of Liberty County introduced Davis's electric

Figure 8.2. Crowd Gathered for the Execution of Eddie Broom, Kissimmee, Florida, 1912. Image No. RC13770. Black-and-white photoprint, 8 by 10 inches, State Archives of Florida, Florida Memory, www.floridamemory.com/items/show/36063. Courtesy of the State Archives of Florida.

chair bill in the House, where it passed 43–15 without amendment, and Senator W. W. Phillips of Columbia County introduced the bill in the upper chamber, where it passed 21–9.[53] Florida's state legislature was notoriously malapportioned, stuffed with representatives from the more rural northern and central counties at the expense of the burgeoning southern half of the state. It was perhaps no accident that the recent history of the counties that Weaver and Phillips represented had been marred by extralegal violence. The bullet-ridden bodies of six black men, illegally removed from the Columbia County jail in Lake City, had been found in the outskirts of the city in May 1911. In 1920 the Liberty County grand jury indicted local law officers for the lynching of two black prisoners.[54]

The 1923 Davis bill abolished hanging in favor of electrocution, centralized executions, restricted the numbers of witnesses, and set out the timetable for the issuance of the death warrant and transport of the condemned prisoner to the state prison. With the bill's adoption, control of the execution process shifted from local counties to the state prison bureaucracy, but the governor retained the prerogative to issue a death warrant. He also determined the week in which an execution would take place, although the state prison superintendent decided on the day and hour. As of January 1, 1924, capital offenders were to be executed within the walls of a permanent death chamber at the state prison farm rather than in the county of conviction.[55]

Yet there was considerable overlap between the hanging and electric chair periods in the 1920s. Convicted murderer Lawrence Revels was hanged in November 1923 after the execution reforms had already been signed into law, and the last hanging in Florida took place in April 1927, when Charles Browne was executed in the Deland jail yard within view of a reported crowd of over two thousand persons.[56] Large crowds continued to gather at these hangings, perhaps to acknowledge their significance as the final acts in the theater of public execution, as community cultural and legal traditions and local authority were being eclipsed by a seemingly more impersonal criminal justice system.

To replace hanging with electrocution, it was crucial that the Florida state prison system had the industrial capacity and scientific expertise to support the installation of an electric chair. In 1914, the year that Will Moore was hanged outside the Bradford County jail, a new state prison farm opened at nearby Raiford. The electric power station inside the prison estate lit up cellblocks, offices, and workshops; powered the arc lights that illuminated the prison compound at night; and eventually fired the movie theater that offered screenings for prisoners and county residents.[57] The same generators that powered prison industrial plants and delivered electric lighting to the cellblocks could animate an electric chair.

By the 1920s most southern cities, major towns, and many mill towns had central electric power stations of some sort, even though industrial and scientific innovation also accentuated class and racial technological gaps.[58] Historians David Nye and Jürgen Martschukat have demonstrated how electrification of public spaces and buildings denoted prestige and status, while artificial illuminations generated community excitement and pride. Noteworthy buildings, such as courthouses and jails in southern county seats and emerging urban centers, were often the first to be equipped with electric lights, telephones, and other modern conveniences, whereas lower-class white and African American areas were usually the last.[59] The location of state prisons could ensure that the prestige and status associated with the electrification of public spaces and buildings extended beyond rural county seats.

Electrical execution also required that an electrician oversee the operation and maintenance of the dynamo and the current required to kill the condemned. The emergence of a new class of technological "expert" was emblematic of the Progressive Era industrial United States.[60] According to the minutes of the Board of Commissioners of State Institutions, during the summer months of 1924 C. S. Hammatt, Florida state engineer and the electrician based at the state prison, took advice from officials at Sing Sing prison in New York and the General Electric Company on the design of the chair and its electrical circuitry.[61] Exchanging information with electricians and executioners in other states on helmet design, electrodes for the leg and back, and leather straps for the wrists also seems to have been fairly common. North Carolina officials paid for the professional services of New York state electrician Edwin Davis, who installed the new electric chair and attended the first electrical execution in March 1910.[62] In early August 1924 Hammatt announced that Florida's electric chair was ready for use. He also requested that a GE representative should be present at the first electrical execution in case of any problems.[63]

Ten months after Florida's electric chair law came into effect, African American inmate Frank Johnson was the first person to be executed on October 7, 1924. Convicted of the first-degree murder of a white railroad engineer during a late-night boardinghouse burglary and gun battle in Jacksonville in December 1923, Johnson was sentenced to death in March 1924. On the day of his execution, Johnson was accompanied by Superintendent J. S. Blitch, the prison chaplain, and several guards as he made the short walk from the holding cell for condemned prisoners to the newly constructed death chamber. He was then strapped into the wooden electric chair, electrodes were attached to his head and leg, and, in keeping with centuries-old execution rituals, he made a "gallows confession" of his guilt and forgave those responsible for his conviction and execution. A lethal electric charge was administered by the sheriff of Duval County, and Johnson was pronounced dead by the prison physician. The times of the switch being thrown, of death, and of the removal of the corpse were all recorded as part of the shift to the modern, bureaucratic, and time-managed rituals of capital punishment.[64]

In their respective studies, Michael Trotti and Amy Louise Wood argue that many white southerners in the early twentieth century believed that public hangings had "failed as an effective instrument of legal and racial terror"; thus the more "cold-blooded and business-like" rituals of the execution chamber were deemed to be "a more effective tool of terror" for black capital offenders in particular.[65] Historians often refer to an article published in the *Richmond Times-Dispatch* in 1908 that drew on phrenology, social Darwinism, eugenics, and black inferiority to argue for the benefits of privatization and electrocution on the grounds that they would instill more fear in condemned African Americans.[66] However, it is difficult to gauge whether the condemned in 1920s Florida were more fearful of death by hanging or in the electric chair, particularly as execution news reports became shorter, more factual, and less concerned with the "human interest" aspects of capital punishment because of post-1923 restrictions.[67]

Frank Johnson's views on his impending execution were not recorded, and virtually all the surviving information on the inauguration of the electric chair comes from a privileged white male perspective. The prison superintendent informed Governor Cary A. Hardee that the state's first electrical execution "was carried out yesterday on time without a hitch. It required about four minutes from the time we began to strap him in the chair until the doctors pronounced him dead. We had a splendid representation of citizens as witnesses, and two newspaper correspondents with a number of others." Blitch's communication did not mention Frank Johnson by name; he was simply the medium for the implementation of new state policy and the guinea pig for the new method. Hardee congratulated Blitch on "your" success.[68]

Superintendent Blitch may have taken over the role of master of ceremonies on execution day but, significantly, did not perform the actual execution. Under the 1923 law, the prison superintendent could delegate the task of performing executions. Consequently, the sheriff of the county in which the offender had been convicted became the superintendent's deputy and continued to execute offenders until a sole state executioner was appointed in 1941. Thus, Sheriff W. H. Dowling rather than Superintendent Blitch pulled the switch at Frank Johnson's execution and was paid a fee for doing so.[69] Under the new method, the sheriff was a machine operator who pulled the lever or pressed the button to ensure the electric current reached the condemned but had no role in determining whether the current was sufficient to kill. Yet the practice between 1924 and 1941 also emphasized the liminality of the sheriff as an agent of modernization as well as a curator of community authority and local criminal justice matters.

As in the hanging period, sheriffs from Duval and Dade Counties, which were dominated by the cities of Jacksonville and Miami and which generated larger numbers of committals to the state prison system, performed a greater number of executions than their rural counterparts. Some sheriffs therefore became more experienced operators of the electric chair than others. For example, Sheriff Dan Hardie of Dade County was required at four executions in 1926, those of white rapist Henry Harry Scrimm in May and black murderers Philip Taylor, Willie Green, and Arthur Williams in October, November, and December, respectively.[70] In the 1920s and 1930s few Florida sheriffs refused to either attend or carry out an execution, and rarely was the task delegated to another.[71] By contrast, the role of state executioner proved too much for Capt. R. F. Coleman in Huntsville, Texas, who resigned on January 1, 1923, rather than perform the first electrical executions scheduled for January 16. His replacement, Walter Monroe Miller, expressed fewer qualms: "I hanged several men while I was sheriff and to touch the button or pull the switch means no more to me than pulling the lever on the gallows. At any rate it's more humane—the chair."[72]

Restrictions on the numbers of witnesses and the use of a designated death chamber, housed in the middle of a sprawling prison farm estate in a remote part of a rural north Florida county, ensured that executions became tightly controlled private events for privileged white male consumption and gaze and thus directly bolstered gendered and racialized state power and authority over black (and lower-class white) prisoners. Further, five black men were executed in Florida's electric chair ahead of the first white man in May 1926 (and Scrimm was the only white defendant to be executed for rape until 1960). This racial pattern defined both the hanging and electric chair periods, but the practice of executing black men in front of audiences composed only of white men also characterized the early electric chair period.[73]

The overt whitening and gendering of the execution audience are underlined by the information in the death warrants themselves. The names of the twelve execution witnesses, often prison guards and county officials, were typed on the back of many of the warrants, which had to be returned to Florida governors after an execution had taken place.[74] Florida's attorney general and the commissioner of agriculture (who oversaw the prison system) were among the select group of witnesses invited to Johnson's execution in October 1924 to see the new electric chair in action for the first time.[75]

In conclusion, despite the slower retreat from public punishment, by 1930 most states in the homicidal, racially segregated, provincial, poverty-stricken, and less industrial southern region had discarded their low-tech method of capital punishment and embraced the most technologically advanced method of the day. Harriet Frazier suggests that state legislators in Missouri pressed for the replacement of hanging with electrocution in the later 1920s because they wanted "to be as up-to-date" as other states.[76] The electric chair fused technology, progress, and a quest for perfection with a superior view of civilization that was as keenly felt in the South as in other regions. That is not to say that the execution reforms were unchallenged; every state supreme court received challenges to the change of method and the designation of the executioner.[77] Yet in the early twentieth century, electrocution was a distinctively, indeed exceptional, American method of execution that was rooted in the celebration of technological innovation and scientific prowess, both of which were integral to regional and national identities.

Intriguingly, the new execution technology was adopted by the same southern prison bureaucracies that maintained penal regimes characterized by outdoor labor, corporal punishment, limited investment in education and vocational training for white inmates, and lack of investment for African Americans.[78] The growing industrial operations in central penitentiaries and sprawling prison farms signaled that there was the technological capacity to support electrical execution in the same period when there was sufficient political will to promote reform. In many ways, this was an important victory for due process advocates over rough justice adherents. Nevertheless, privatization, centralization, and restrictions on the spectacle of execution could have been achieved even if state legislators in Florida and other southern states had voted to retain hanging. The relocation of executions from county jail yards to central death chambers within the bowels of state prisons did not have to be accompanied by a sizeable investment in an electric chair; thus the allure of the new technology and its association with modernity were clearly important to reformers.

Punishment in a modern, progressive, and civilizing society necessitated private and efficient capital punishment that was carried out by machine, which offered a more depersonalized relationship between the executioner and the condemned. The rituals and responsibilities, as well as the decorum, expected inside the execution chamber were bound up with notions of industrial efficiency, modernity, and civilized sensibilities, but they were also imbued with white social norms on racial and gender hierarchy, white superiority, and black subordination. Privatization, centralization, and the maintenance of white supremacy were all served by the introduction of electrical execution in Florida. The privileging of white male execution audiences extended the racial and gender exclusion that had begun with the removal of black criminal justice officials, who had first gained office during Reconstruction, the New South, and the early Jim Crow decades. Jim Crow justice and modernity in Florida necessitated white dominance of all criminal justice offices—justices of the peace, constables, sheriffs, police, jurors, judges—and finally execution witnesses.[79]

NOTES

1. Quoted in Hamilton Mercer, *The Reproach of Capital Punishment* (Greensburg, IN: Greensburg Democrat Publishing, 1915), 22.

2. *Atlanta Constitution*, January 30, 1911, 5.

3. See William J. Bowers, Glen L. Pierce, and John F. McDevitt, *Legal Homicide: Death as Punishment in America, 1864–1982* (Boston: Northeastern University Press, 1984); Stuart Banner, *The Death Penalty: An American History* (Cambridge, MA: Harvard University Press, 2002), 190; Trina N. Seitz, "Electrocution and the Tar Heel State: The Advent and Demise of a Southern Sanction," *American Journal of Criminal Justice* 31, no. 1 (2006): 103–4; Timothy S. Kearns, "The Chair, the Needle, and the Damage Done: What the Electric Chair and the Rebirth of the Method-of-Execution Challenge Could Mean for the Future of the Eighth Amendment," *Cornell Journal of Law and Public Policy* 15, no. 1 (2005): 204, 204n65.

4. Quoted in Banner, *The Death Penalty*, 189.

5. Jürgen Martschukat, "'The Art of Killing by Electricity': The Sublime and the Electric Chair," *Journal of American History* 89, no. 3 (2002): 920; E. Anthony Spitzka, "Observations Regarding the Infliction of the Death Penalty by Electricity," *Proceedings of the American Philosophical Society* 47, no. 188 (1908): 41; Mark Essig, *Edison & the Electric Chair* (New York: Walker & Company, 2003), 279–82.

6. Louisiana and Mississippi continued to carry out executions at the local level until the 1950s, yet they also adopted the new technology in the form of the portable electric chair and generator. The last state to adopt the electric chair in 1949 was West Virginia, where it was used for the first time in March 1951. See Craig Brandon, *The Electric Chair: An Unnatural History* (Jefferson, NC: McFarland & Company, Inc., 2009), 235–36. The gas chamber was adopted in four states in the

region: North Carolina, 1936; Missouri, 1937; Mississippi, 1954; and Maryland, 1955. Three of these states had experimented first with electrical execution.

7. *St. Petersburg (FL) Independent*, March 11, 1924, 3; *Newsweek*, August 19, 1940, 46. In 1924 twenty-two states continued to use hanging, one had adopted lethal gas, and seven had abolished capital punishment. Utah had two methods, and the condemned could choose. Two other states had "conditional executions." For example, Kentucky used its electric chair for executions that did not involve convicted rapists following a post-1908 amendment to its electric chair laws.

8. Florida, Acts of 1923, chap. 9169.

9. See, for example, Dewey W. Grantham, *Southern Progressivism: The Reconciliation of Progress and Tradition* (Knoxville: University of Tennessee Press, 1983); William A. Link, *The Paradox of Southern Progressivism, 1880–1930* (Chapel Hill: University of North Carolina Press, 1997); Anne-Marie Szymanski, "Beyond Parochialism: Southern Progressivism, Prohibition, and State-Building," *Journal of Southern History* 69, no. 1 (2003): 107–36; Christopher Waldrep, "National Policing, Lynching, and Constitutional Change," *Journal of Southern History* 74, no. 3 (2008): 589–626; Natalie J. Ring, *The Problem South: Region, Empire, and the New Liberal State, 1880–1930* (Athens: University of Georgia Press, 2012).

10. Vivien Miller, "The Icelandic Man Cometh: North Dakota State Attorney Gudmunder Grimson and a Reassessment of the Martin Tabert Case," *Florida Historical Quarterly* 81, no. 3 (2003): 270–315. The Rosewood Massacre began when false rumors spread that a black man had sexually assaulted a local white woman. A group of white men with connections to the local Ku Klux Klan believed the culprit was a recently escaped convict hiding in Rosewood. The men pursued the culprit to seek "justice" for the alleged victim. A mob of over two hundred white men attacked the town and its residents, buildings, and livestock. Residents were forced to flee for their lives. See Maxine D. Jones, "The Rosewood Massacre and the Women Who Survived It," *Florida Historical Quarterly* 76, no. 2 (1997): 193–208; Edward González-Tennant, "Intersectional Violence, New Media, and the 1923 Rosewood Massacre," *Fire!!!* 1, no. 2 (2012): 64–110; Jessica Glenza, "Rosewood Massacre a Harrowing Tale of Racism and the Road toward Reparations," *Guardian*, January 3, 2016, http://www.theguardian.com/us-news/2016/jan/03/rosewood-florida-massacre-racial-violence-reparations (accessed February 19, 2016).

11. *Florida Times Union*, May 2, 1923, 8; *Miami Herald*, November 8, 1936, MS94-2, Newspaper Clippings 1936–38, Leonard F. Chapman Papers, 1933–56, Florida State Library and Archives, Tallahassee. (Hereafter cited as FSLA.)

12. John D. Bessler, *Death in the Dark: Midnight Executions in America* (Boston: Northeastern University Press, 1997), 63–65. For a full discussion of the modern power to punish, see Michel Foucault, *Discipline and Punish: The Birth of the Prison*, trans. Alan Sheridan (New York: Vintage Books, 1995); and David Garland, *Peculiar Institution: America's Death Penalty in an Age of Abolition* (New York: Oxford University Press, 2010).

13. Louis P. Masur, *Rites of Execution: Capital Punishment and the Transformation of American Culture, 1776–1865* (New York: Oxford University Press, 1989), esp. chap. 5.

14. See, for example, Samuel J. Barrows, "Legislative Tendencies as to Capital Punishment," *Annals of the American Academy of Political and Social Science* 29 (May 1907): 180; Spitzka, "Observations," 40, 45–46.

15. See, for example, *Bradford County Telegraph*, May 31, 1918, 3, and March 21, 1919, 2; Michael A. Trotti, "The Scaffold's Revival: Race and Public Execution in the South," *Journal of Southern History* 45, no. 1 (2011): 195–224.

16. Grantham, *Southern Progressivism*, 132; Ring, *The Problem South*, 55.

17. See Randolph Roth, *American Homicide* (Cambridge, MA: Belknap Press / Harvard University Press, 2009), 386–434; Edward L. Ayers, *The Promise of the New South: Life after Reconstruction* (New York: Oxford University Press, 1992), 155. In 1920 Florida's homicide rate was recorded as 19.9 per 100,000 of population (8.7 per 100,000 for the white homicide rate and 42 per 100,000 for the "colored" homicide rate) and thus was not dissimilar to that of Mississippi (19.7 per 100,000) or South Carolina (15.3 per 100,000), but the national average in 1922 was 8.4 homicides per 100,000 of population. See US Department of Commerce, Bureau of the Census, *Mortality Statistics* (Washington, DC: Government Printing Office, 1935), 33:46; E. H. Sutherland, "Murder and the Death Penalty," *Journal of Criminal Law & Criminology* 15, no. 4 (1924–25): 523.

18. James L. Massey and Martha A. Myers, "Patterns of Repressive Social Control in Post-Reconstruction Georgia, 1882–1935," *Social Forces* 68, no. 2 (1989): 459.

19. Martha A. Myers, *Race, Labor and Punishment in the New South* (Columbus: Ohio State University Press, 1998), 45.

20. At this time, first-degree murder (specifically when a trial jury did not recommend mercy), rape, and treason were punishable by death in Florida. See Raymond T. Bye, "Recent History and Present Status of Capital Punishment in the United States," *Journal of the American Institute of Criminal Law and Criminology* 17, no. 2 (1926): 241–42.

21. Based on the numbers of surviving death warrants, there were eleven hangings in 1901, twelve in 1907, twelve in 1910, sixteen in 1912, and twelve in 1915.

22. Howard W. Allen and Jerome W. Chubb, *Race, Class, and the Death Penalty: Capital Punishment in American History* (Albany: State University of New York Press, 2008), 68–72; Margaret Wener Cahalan, *Historical Corrections Statistics in the United States, 1850–1984* (Rockville, MD: Westat, 1986), 10–15; *St. Petersburg Times*, August 14, 1965, 3A; Margaret Vandiver, "The Quality of Mercy: Race and Clemency in Florida Death Penalty Cases, 1924–1966," *University of Richmond Law Review* 27, no. 2 (1992–93): 336.

23. Using Cahalan, *Historical Corrections Statistics*, 10, table 2-1: Executions per Decade under Civil Authority and Illegal Lynchings, 1890–1984, and Ken Driggs's "Florida Executions List," compiled October 1993, located in the FSLA. I calculated

that 183 men were hanged for murder between 1870 and 1920 (inclusive) and 19 men for rape.

24. Vivien Miller, "'The Last Vestige of Institutionalized Sexism'? Paternalism, Equal Rights, and the Death Penalty in Twentieth and Twenty-First Century Sunbelt America: The Case for Florida," *Journal of American Studies* 38, no. 1 (2004): 391–424.

25. Vivien M. L. Miller, *Crime, Violence and Sexual Clemency: Florida's Pardon Board and Penal System in the Progressive Era* (Gainesville: University Press of Florida, 2000), 230–31.

26. An elevated platform was usually necessary to accommodate the drop and prevent the condemned crashing into the ground below.

27. See, for example, Steven Wilf, *Law's Imagined Republic: Popular Politics and Criminal Justice in Revolutionary America* (New York: Cambridge University Press, 2010), 95.

28. The murder victim was also the son of a prominent local white businessman. Moore fled to Jacksonville (where his parents lived) but was forced to flee again following a gunfight with Duval County deputy sheriffs. Shortly after he was arrested at Yulee by a special agent of the Seaboard Railway Company and taken to Fernandina on a concealed weapons charge. See *Bradford County Telegraph*, February 6, 1914, 1, February 27, 1914, 1, and March 27, 1914, 1.

29. *Bradford County Telegraph*, December 4, 1914, 1.

30. Mitchell and Moore were most likely hanged on the same scaffold. Mitchell was executed on July 23, 1913, not in 1912, as reported in the paper. Interestingly, Mitchell's execution is listed on the deathpenaltyusa.org database, whereas Moore's is not, but Moore's death warrant is filed in RG156, series 12, box 7, FSLA, and is included in Driggs's "Florida Executions List."

31. *Bradford County Telegraph*, November 6, 1914, 1.

32. *Bradford County Telegraph*, December 4, 1914, 1.

33. Trotti, "The Scaffold's Revival," 201.

34. Readers were then informed—without any hint of irony—that the condemned "seemed to enjoy the occasion better than any person present." See *Bradford County Telegraph*, December 4, 1914, 1.

35. *St. Petersburg Evening Independent,* September 21, 1915, 1, 3. Ebenezer Tobin had been convicted of murdering a local white woman, and his hanging was the first legal execution in Pinellas County.

36. *St. Petersburg Evening Independent,* September 21, 1915, 3.

37. Lawrence M. Friedman, *Crime and Punishment in American History* (New York: Basic Books, 1995), 19; James M. Denham, *"A Rogue's Paradise": Crime and Punishment in Antebellum Florida, 1821–1861* (Tuscaloosa: University of Alabama Press, 1997), 146.

38. James M. Denham and William Warren Rogers, *Florida Sheriffs: A History 1821–1945* (Tallahassee: Sentry Press, 2001), 189, 197–98.

39. The "going rate" for an execution in most US states was $50 to $150. See Gerald D. Robin, "The Executioner: His Place in English Society," *British Journal of Sociology* 15, no. 3 (1964): 239.

40. John C. Weaver, *Crime, Constables, and Courts: Order and Transgression in a Canadian City, 1816–1970* (Montreal, Canada: McGill-Queen's University Press, 1995), 185–86.

41. Charles Duff, *A Handbook on Hanging* (London: Cayme Press, 1928), 26.

42. Dorothy Moses Schulz, *Breaking the Brass Ceiling: Women Police Chiefs & Their Paths to the Top* (Westport, CT: Praeger, 2004), 115–16.

43. *Bradford County Telegraph*, January 7, 1938, 4; Margaret Vandiver, *Lethal Punishment: Lynchings and Legal Executions in the South* (New Brunswick, NJ: Rutgers University Press, 2006), 26.

44. See, for example, Michael J. Pfeifer, *Rough Justice: Lynching and American Society, 1874–1947* (Urbana: University of Illinois Press, 2004); James W. Clarke, *The Lineaments of Wrath: Race, Violent Crime, and American Culture* (New Brunswick, NJ: Transaction Publishers, 2001); Franklin E. Zimring, *The Contradictions of Capital Punishment* (New York: Oxford University Press, 2003); Garland, *Peculiar Institution*, 32–34. Ironically, lynching was also the decisive factor behind the reinstatement of capital punishment in 1918–20 in several states, including Tennessee, which had previously partially abolished the death penalty and where the absence of legal capital punishment and popular resort to illegal executions had seemingly underscored the impotency of the state to punish the most serious offenders. Missouri had also become an abolitionist state in 1917. The death penalty had been reinstated in both Missouri and Tennessee by 1919. See John F. Galliher, Gregory Ray, and Brent Cook, "Abolition and Reinstatement of Capital Punishment during the Progressive Era and Early 20th Century," *Journal of Criminal Law and Criminology* 83, no. 3 (1992): 558, 563–64.

45. Massey and Myers, "Patterns," 474–75.

46. Vandiver, *Lethal Punishment*, 70. The connections between illegal and legal execution are analysed in detail in chapters 4 and 5.

47. It was reported that twelve men had been arrested and were prosecuted at Starke (after a successful change of venue from Putnam County) for firing into an unoccupied dwelling and attacking the Putnam County jail. All were acquitted. When Johnson's lawyer did not file a motion for a new trial, Governor Hardee issued the death warrant on July 9; *Florida Times Union*, July 10, 1923, 4.

48. Pfeiffer, *Rough Justice*, 149; Amy Louise Wood, *Lynching and Spectacle: Witnessing Racial Violence in America, 1890–1940* (Chapel Hill: University of North Carolina Press, 2009), 24.

49. See, for example, "Governor's Message," *Journal of the Senate of the State of Georgia* (Atlanta, GA: Foote & Davies Co. State Printers, 1921), 100–103.

50. Bye, "Recent History," 235; *Augusta Chronicle*, September 24, 1921, excerpt available at www.executedtoday.com (accessed February 19, 2016).

51. Florida, *Seventeenth Biennial Report of Commissioner of Agriculture, 1921–22* (Jacksonville, FL: State Printers, 1923), 13. The third execution was of white mill

worker Robert Backwell on July 23, 1920. According to the tag on the photograph of his hanging, he was executed "for helping in the murder of Uncle Bud and Aunt Nancy Davis in 1917."

52. Pfeiffer, *Rough Justice*, 121.

53. *Florida Times Union*, May 3, 1923, 8, and May 2, 1923, 8.

54. Bill Bond, "Report on Lynchings Details Hideous Chapter in History," *Orlando Sentinel*, January 25, 1987, http://articles.orlandosentinel.com/1987-01-25/news/0100290260_1_lynching-white-man-accused-of-murder (accessed February 19, 2016); Paul Ortiz, *Emancipation Betrayed: The Hidden History of Black Organizing and White Violence in Florida* (Oakland: University of California Press, 2005), 223–24.

55. Ken Driggs, "A Current of Electricity Sufficient in Intensity to Cause Immediate Death: A Pre-*Furman* History of Florida's Electric Chair," *Stetson Law Review* 22, no. 3 (1993): 1205. Florida's first electric chair was placed in a rather rundown room behind the prison hospital; a purpose-built concrete death chamber did not materialize until the early 1930s. See L. F. Chapman, "The Florida Prison—and I," 17, Record Group 900000, M94-2, Leonard F. Chapman Papers, 1933–56, FSLA.

56. Browne had originally been sentenced to death by hanging in 1923 but was sentenced to electrocution after a second trial in 1925. The manner of his execution was subsequently appealed, again successfully, and so he was hanged. See Driggs, "A Current of Electricity," 1188.

57. Vivien M. L. Miller, *Hard Labor and Hard Time: Florida's "Sunshine Prison" and Chain Gangs* (Gainesville: University Press of Florida, 2012), 117–21.

58. Ayers, *The Promise*, 75.

59. Ibid., 72–75, 322–37; David E. Nye, *Electrifying America: Social Meanings of a New Technology, 1880–1940* (Cambridge, MA: MIT Press, 1992); Martschukat, "'The Art of Killing,'" 900–905. Further, the electrical circuit and the telephone were integral features of the modern death chamber.

60. Ring, *The Problem South*, 9.

61. See Florida, Board of Commissioners of State Institutions Minutebooks, vol. 8, p. 562 (August 15, 1924). According to many prison histories, including that of Florida, inmate carpenters routinely built the electric chairs in different states. However, a *St. Petersburg Times* journalist suggests that it was made at "Cook's Cabinet Shop on Newnan Street in Jacksonville." Even if the chair itself was built by inmate carpenters, the electrical circuitry required free-world expertise, although in time, this would move in-house also. See Sydney P. Freedberg, "The Story of Old Sparky," *St. Petersburg Times*, September 25, 1999.

62. Seitz, "Electrocution," 111–12.

63. Florida, Board of Commissioners of State Institutions Minutebooks, vol. 8, p. 562 (August 15, 1924). BCSI members refused Hammatt's second request that Dr. Squires, who performed the autopsies on the executed at Sing Sing, should also be present at the first Florida electrocution.

64. The same Duval County jury recommended mercy and a life sentence for his unarmed accomplice, Eugene Mills, a twenty-three-year-old mechanic originally from

Savannah, Georgia. Mills remained at the state prison farm from April 1924 until he was granted a conditional pardon in December 1933. See Division of Corrections, Prison Registers 1875–1959, Record Group 670, series 500, box 15: Eugene Mills #15935, Frank Johnson #16128, FSLA; *Florida Times Union,* March 19, 1924, 13, and October 8, 1924, 1.

65. Trotti, "The Scaffold's Revival," 208; Wood, *Lynching and Spectacle,* 37.

66. *Richmond Times-Dispatch,* March 6, 1908, 1, 3, quoted in Bessler, *Death in the Dark,* 60.

67. Currently, there is also no public access to Florida's executive clemency correspondence from the 1920s that might offer relevant insights here.

68. J. S. Blitch to Cary A. Hardee, October 8, 1924, Division of Elections, Death Warrants, 1869–1972, Record Group 156, series 12, box 9 (1924–26), FSLA.

69. Ibid.

70. From "List of Executions, 1924–1964," Florida Department of Corrections, www.dc.state.fl.us/oth/deathrow/execlist2.html (accessed August 17, 2017).

71. There were, however, jurisdictional disputes between state and county officials over control of the process. See *Palm Beach Times,* December 20, 1934; and *Sarasota Tribune,* December 21, 1934, MS94-2, Newspaper Clippings 1933–35, Leonard F. Chapman Papers, 1933–56, FSLA.

72. *Atlanta Constitution,* January 5, 1923, 3; James W. Marquart, Sheldon Ekland-Olson, and Jonathan R. Sorenson, *The Rope, The Chair, and the Needle* (Austin: University of Texas Press, 1994), 15. Despite Warden Miller's assertion, performing executions could exact a heavy psychological toll on many individuals, leading to intoxication or alcoholism, even criminal activities, and suicide. In his study of executioners, Gerald Robin noted that J. E. "Crap" Thomas, North Carolina's executioner from 1917, died in 1929 of cirrhosis of the liver, an alcohol-related disease that took several years to develop, but in this case during the period of national prohibition. Robin, "The Executioner," 234; Seitz, "Electrocution," 112.

73. *Florida Times Union,* May 26, 1926, 22, and May 27, 1926, 4. Scrimm had been convicted in Dade County for "criminally attacking a child." He was one of three men executed in successive weeks in May 1926. Across the region, increasing numbers of white southerners were being executed between 1926 and 1945, but African American executions still outnumbered white executions by more than three to one. Allen and Chubb, *Race, Class,* 68.

74. See boxes 9 and 10, Division of Elections, Death Warrants, 1869–1972, Record Group 156, series 12, FSLA.

75. J. S. Blitch to Cary A. Hardee, October 8, 1924, Division of Elections, Death Warrants, 1869–1972, Record Group 156, series 12, box 9 (1924–26), FSLA.

76. Harriet C. Frazier, *The Death Penalty in Missouri: A History* (Jefferson, NC: McFarland, 2006), 101.

77. For example, In re Kemmler, 131 U.S. 436 (1890); Mallory v. South Carolina, 237 U.S. 180 (1915); Hart v. Commonwealth, 131 Va. 726, 109 S.E. 582 (1921); John Dinan, *The Virginia State Constitution* (New York: Oxford University Press, 2014), 60–61; D. W. Denno, "Is Electrocution an Unconstitutional Method of Ex-

ecution? The Engineering of Death over a Century," *William & Mary Law Review* 35 (1994): 551–692.

78. See, for example, Alex Lichtenstein, *Twice the Work of Free Labor: The Political Economy of Convict Labor in the New South* (New York: Verso, 1996); Tammy Ingram, *Dixie Highway: Road Building and the Making of the Modern South, 1900–1930* (Chapel Hill: University of North Carolina Press, 2014).

79. Sarah Haley, *No Mercy Here: Gender, Punishment, and the Making of Jim Crow Modernity* (Chapel Hill: University of North Carolina Press, 2016); Wali R. Kharif, "Black Reaction to Segregation and Discrimination in Post-Reconstruction Florida," *Florida Historical Quarterly* 64, no. 2 (1985): 161–73.

CHAPTER 9

THE MAKING OF THE MODERN DEATH PENALTY IN JIM CROW NORTH CAROLINA

Seth Kotch

Larry Newsome's mother did not record his birth date, but she recalled that he was born in Wilson County, in North Carolina's coastal plain, in November 1904 or 1905. He lived in poverty with his parents and his wife, finding sporadic employment laboring on nearby farms and transporting illegal liquor. His family had a history of mental illness, and after Newsome was arrested on suspicion of murdering a child, he received a psychiatric diagnosis of "subnormal in general intelligence and decidedly psychopathic," according to an evaluation conducted at Raleigh's Central Prison.[1] He was deemed, with remarkable precision, to have an IQ of thirty-four and a mental age of five years and six months. During his 1927 trial for first-degree murder, as he was defended by uninterested attorneys, a small mob led by the victim's father and uncle attempted to drag Newsome from the courtroom, failing only when the presiding judge drew a pistol. With the threat of violence hanging over the courtroom, Newsome received a guilty verdict and with it a mandatory death sentence. In 1928 this grandson of formerly enslaved people was executed in the electric chair.[2]

Newsome's trial received ample coverage in North Carolina's white press, which condoned both the victory of the legal process and its result: a death sentence for an African American man convicted of a crime against a white woman. But the following year, the journalist and activist Cornelia "Nell" Battle Lewis highlighted the case to decry the frequent use of the death penalty against the state's most "friendless" citizens.[3] Lewis was the scion of a prominent North Carolina family who became a widely read columnist for the *Raleigh News and Observer*, using her column, Incidentally, to advocate women's rights, education and labor reform, academic freedom, separation of church and state, and other progressive causes. By the early 1920s, she had made herself a well-established pundit with a track record of advocacy so forceful that her family became convinced she was mentally ill.[4] According to her editor at the *News and Observer*, Lewis was North Carolina's "champion idol-smasher and hell-raiser," and she attacked the death penalty with verve throughout the 1920s, 1930s, and 1940s.[5]

In her columns, Lewis treated the death penalty and its defenders with equal parts ironic disdain and righteous fury, mocking execution as a stupid attempt to control crime and castigating it as immoral and unfair. Embodying what poet Donald Davidson called North Carolina's "agitating and crusading spirit," she rallied her readers around issues still in play nearly a century after she wrote, such as the absence of evidence that capital punishment deters crime, the risk of executing innocents, and its barbarity.[6] Lewis even stepped out from behind her desk to use her law degree in defense of a number of adolescent girls facing death sentences for setting fire to their beds in the Samarcand Manor, a juvenile detention facility.[7]

She also compiled a pamphlet, titled *Capital Punishment in North Carolina*, which was published by the North Carolina State Board of Charities and Public Welfare. In the document, she adopted the restrained language of sociology, a rising field led by the University of North Carolina's Howard Odum. *Capital Punishment in North Carolina* was the first and only comprehensive picture of the death penalty in the state, laying out a powerful argument against the death penalty substantiated with neat, hand-drawn graphs and charts, photographs of death row prisoners, and case histories. It was here that Lewis laid out the details of Larry Newsome's short, troubled life.

Lewis and playwright Paul Green were North Carolina's most vocal death penalty abolitionists in the first half of the twentieth century, becoming part of a modest movement inaugurated by other cultural elites, such as *News and Observer* editor and publisher Josephus Daniels, who before he became Lewis's boss endorsed the creation of the Anti-Capital Punishment League in North Carolina.[8] While Lewis sought to undermine the rationale for the death penalty, Green believed it was appropriate in some cases but decried how it was applied in North Carolina, describing the punishment as "murdering ignorant negroes."[9] Lewis attacked the death penalty's cruelty and ineffectiveness, while Green sought to pluck North Carolinians' heartstrings, imagining himself in one work of fiction as someone whose "sensitive imagination pictures the whole misery of the thing."[10] Their influence is unclear at best. Although no doubt many readers of Lewis's columns and Green's plays understood their position, others wondered why victims of crime did not receive similar sympathy. For instance, in a 1939 letter to the *News and Observer*, one man observed that for victims, as opposed to condemned prisoners, "hurts are caused through no fault of their own and the sob-sisters don't care how much they suffer before they die."[11]

As the above missive suggests, early twentieth-century North Carolina was not necessarily replete with the sensitive imagination demonstrated by Lewis and Green. This was, as historian George Tindall wrote, an era of "business progressivism" during which academics and politicians teamed to rebuild and strengthen essential institutions, not to tear them down.[12] Lewis's fellow reformers aspired, in the words of Governor Angus MacLean, to "efficiency, economy, and rational progress" in all areas of public life, including the death penalty process.[13] In seeking to rebuild and strengthen capital punishment in the state, politicians signaled its importance to a Jim Crow North Carolina in which the race question had been resolved with rigid segregationist laws and well-established customs. In this view, African Americans were intellectually inferior, biologically different, and socially stunted, and while they deserved preservation against wanton violence, they did not merit the vote or protection from widespread discrimination, whether in daily life or in the courtroom.[14]

Published in 1929, *Capital Punishment in North Carolina* appeared amid a series of reforms inspired not by concerns about human rights but by a determination by lawmakers to make the death penalty more efficient and less noisy. The ideal execution would take place, in the words of one optimist, "without howling, without squirming."[15] The speaker in this case aspired for the condemned prisoner to die quietly, but equally if not more important was the desire to stifle and ultimately eliminate the crowds that gathered at public and later semipublic executions. These interracial crowds disrupted the emergent ideal of a modern North Carolina where white supremacy operated with the professionalism of a well-run state agency. This vision rebutted criticism from two fronts: the Agrarians, who bemoaned the urbanizing South's apparent rejection of traditional southern values, and critics outside the region, perhaps most notably the acerbic journalist H. L. Mencken, who helped cement a national consensus around the image of a "benighted" South.[16]

The calcification of the rigid racial control of the Jim Crow era aligned well with the progressive impulses and programs of the New South but cut against the tradition of public execution in the Western world. For much of its history the death penalty operated as a public punishment to be experienced with as much howling and squirming as possible, witnessed by a tractable population. Executions of enslaved persons in North Carolina, for instance, were directed by law to be brutal and visible to other enslaved people.[17] As law enforcement in the South slouched toward professionalization after the Civil War, and as lynchings staged gruesome pantomimes of legal hangings, politicians and other elites grew increasingly uncomfortable with public executions. Public hangings after the Civil War were often hugely popular, celebratory affairs, their center of gravity a hanging that struck many observers, in the words of one editorialist, as a "relic of barbarism."[18] Influential citizens inside and outside government held a dim view of the public who attended them. Their morbid delight and how they expressed it were deeply troubling to elites. And at the heart of that unease was the fact that these crowds were often dominated by African American observers— most importantly, women—intent on honoring the life of African American prisoners.[19]

The technological solution to this social problem arrived in the form of the electric chair. The chair, first used in New York at the end of the nineteenth century, promised to give execution a modern sheen, one contained in a central place. Its many failures only strengthened the resolve of reformers to keep searching for more efficient methods.[20] As they did so they pushed the death penalty out of the public square and onto the fringes of social and political life, eventually to be experienced by most people as a media event and by its participants in a cramped execution chamber in the wee hours of the morning. As the execution spectacle was constrained, the confusing tangle of meanings that freighted public hangings fell away, leaving just one powerful symbolic resonance. The death penalty in Jim Crow North Carolina represented the state's commitment to a criminal justice system that was crafted to control the bodies and lives of African Americans and that included African Americans only as subjects, very rarely as actors.

This chapter argues that the effort to improve the death penalty in North Carolina transformed it from a white supremacist practice that nevertheless accommodated claims to African American personhood into one that starkly expressed and enforced the racial subjugation and exclusion of Jim Crow. African American men subject to public hanging between the end of the Civil War and the early 1900s could expect their executions to be attended by neighbors and relatives and to afford them a measure of dignity in their final moments, as their suffering was interpreted as part of a process that would take them to heaven. After the state of North Carolina took control of this process in 1910, condemned African American men were killed before all-white audiences, their suffering indicative of, according to the perverse rationale of white supremacy, diminished personhood. Crucially, Jim Crow execution protocols excluded African American women, who had played an important role in the public hangings of African American men. This chapter focuses on the state of North Carolina because it displayed notable zeal in both its progressive rhetoric and its frequent use of the death penalty, which made the state among the national leaders in executions for much of its history.[21]

Before the Civil War, the death penalty in North Carolina operated as an arm of the slave regime bent toward subjugation of enslaved persons and the protection of the property of enslavers. Enslaved persons' value as human property did little to protect them, particularly when their enslavers believed that an execution would contribute to controlling the larger enslaved population and received financial compensation for their loss.[22]

Between 1726 and 1860, African Americans, virtually all of them enslaved men, accounted for 74 percent of those executed. During the Jim Crow era, capital punishment grew still more starkly racial, if only slightly. Between 1910 and 1961, 78 percent of those executed were African Americans, most for crimes in which the victims were white.[23] Including American Indians, a full 80 percent of those executed were people of color. In contrast, just one white person was executed for a crime against a person of color.[24] This deeply biased yet performatively modern system represented the New South imagination in North Carolina. In the words of historian David Potter, like the New South itself, the death penalty "could not bear either to abandon the traditions of the Old South or to forego the material gains of modern America."[25]

Executions in the American South between the end of the Civil War and World War I were fairly ritualized, often rowdy, and, like the rest of the criminal justice system, deeply veined with race.[26] Prisoners were transported from a county jail to a usually newly constructed scaffold. Standing on this lethal stage and joining a generations-old tradition that reached back to medieval Europe, the condemned person delivered a speech of some kind, often embracing religion and warning observers against whiskey, women, and other bad habits. Execution rituals carried various meanings beyond the scope of this chapter, but crucially, they drew the condemned prisoner into complicity with his own execution.[27] This complicity and that of the gathered crowd were essential to the state's authority, meaning executions posed risks as well as rewards. Disorder might breed contempt for the state, and the chance for disorder was high when many viewed executions not as grave, quasi-religious shows of state authority but as social events.[28] Unfortunately for state authorities, the latter was often the case.

Between the end of the Civil War and the early years of the twentieth century, even when local law enforcement authorities sought to restrict access, hangings were often hugely popular social events. For instance, as many as ten thousand people attended a hanging in the tiny town of Hillsborough in 1879, dwarfing its total population.[29] An article about the hanging of Tom

Dula, who, in a ballad later recorded by the Kingston Trio, famously hung his head and cried, described large crowds, "males and females, whites and blacks, many being on foot and many in carriages." These people demonstrated a "morbid" fascination with hanging "so general among the ignorant classes of society."[30] The more enlightened classes of society hoped to relieve the less enlightened of their morbidity, not least by barring them altogether from the scene. While public executions drew out the undesirable elements of public society, private ones might inspire, in the words of one editorial, "a great sigh from the waiting crowd and [a] feeling that there is indeed something awful in death and something majestic in law."[31] By the turn of the century, there were few voices willing to defend public hanging and many rising to condemn it, as one editorialist did, as "not in . . . harmony with nineteenth-century civilization."[32]

There were two chords to this apparent disharmony: the gruesome spectacle of poorly conducted hangings, which resulted in protracted and disturbing—exciting to many, of course—death scenes, and the fact that hangings brought crowds into the public square to celebrate the life, death, and afterlife of a condemned person. Numerous protracted and torturous hangings in the late 1800s and early 1900s prompted public calls for central, state-run executions conducted in an electric chair by a professional.[33] Such bungled hangings troubled white elites, but the gathering of substantially African American crowds lurked at the heart of the uneasiness about hanging in the later years of the nineteenth century.[34]

Despite the casual racism of newspaper reportage in white-run papers during this period, it was rare for an editorialist to directly implicate African Americans in the bad behavior they perceived at public hangings, perhaps because lower-class whites appeared equally worthy of disdain. Indeed, white attendance and behavior at public hangings caused considerable concern, as they substantiated some reformers' anxiety about the racial degeneration of poor whites just as the state was trying to draw a stark line between the races.[35] However, at least one piece crossed the line between intimations and outright claims of misbehavior by African Americans. When the county commissioners in Oxford, North Carolina, decided to hold a public hanging for an African American man condemned to death for the rape of a white woman, the local newspaper attacked the decision, complaining that the small town would "be filled to overflowing with negroes from every point on the compass, which to say the least of it will not be of any particular advantage to the place." The piece continued, "Wherefore this mighty concourse of people? To satisfy an idle and barbarous curiosity. We should have passed that stage in social evolution."[36]

One problem with these interracial crowds, white elites opined, was that the African Americans among them offered condemned prisoners the opportunity of a lifetime to take control of their personal narrative and even to critique the criminal justice system in front of an integrated audience. For instance, in 1906, when Henry Bailey, dressed in a neat black suit, delivered his last words from the gallows, a reporter covering the event sought to dismiss them with a breeziness that belied their asperity: "The drift of his remarks was the frequent injustice given in the trials of negroes and [he] said in his own case that had [his white victim] killed him there would never have been a hanging."[37]

African Americans who were receptive to this message might have transformed the scaffold into a surprising gathering site of resistance to the violence of Jim Crow regimes. This element of public executions stood in stark contrast to the sites of lynchings, which were hostile spaces and remained so long after a mob killing.[38] As historian Michael Trotti has argued, public hangings presented opportunities for "subversive moments" that could seem more like revivals than executions, where a mixed-race or predominantly African American crowd enjoyed the equivalent of "a camp meeting at the scaffold."[39] Yet even when African Americans gathered in solemnity and condemnation, they did so as full participants in a racially mixed social ritual, the kind of comingling white supremacist ideology rejected.

White observers mocked the phenomenon. In 1879 one Raleigh newspaper derided what it called the "unctuous goody-goodyness of the 'last speeches' of the condemned, particularly the negroes." In fact, the piece argued, a long criminal career ably prepares bad men to die well and thereafter to be celebrated for their courage and poise; the worse the person, the better their death. Conversely, the innocent, morally upright person was most likely to cower on the scaffold. "Soon, the scaffold will be considered quite the auxiliary to the church," the writer warned.[40] Later that year, one editorialist scoffed at the "halo of renown" on the brows of those condemned men of color who received a kind of undeserved "sainthood" at the gallows.[41]

The primary drivers of this refurbishment of racist public punishment were the African American women who gathered on or around the gallows to pray with condemned men and to demonstrate their enduring value to their families and communities.[42] Evidence of their presence at the public hangings of African American men appears in problematic sources: newspaper articles and editorials in white-owned papers decrying it. An editorial in the *Henderson Gold Leaf* complained about the behavior of African Americans, "especially the women," at one 1897 hanging. Noting that the air "reverberat[ed] with shrieks and shouts as the trap fell and some minutes thereafter," the piece argued that "right thinking persons" must have "felt that such a spectacle was a disgrace to a civilized community."[43] An editorial in the *Wilmington Messenger* escalated this complaint, calling African American women "the most dangerous element in many communities." According to the writer, led by these women, African Americans in attendance at hangings showed a "decided inclination . . . to take sides with rapists and to become turbulent in the expression of their leanings and sympathies."[44]

African American women living in the Jim Crow South endured popular depictions of them as less than human, unbound by moral or sexual strictures, and dangerous to the white household, especially if they were poor. At best, African American women were denied the courtesies and privileges enjoyed by white women. Worse, white society sought to deny them personhood altogether and blamed them for creating the dangerous African American men imagined by white supremacists.[45] Condemning black crime, the writer and reformer Rebecca Latimer Felton sneered at "the Black whore," who, "brazen in her defiance of moral laws," raises her son to be a sexual threat to white women.[46]

Pressure on African American women to stay out of the public sphere did not come only from white supremacist ideologues. Some upper- and middle-class African American women laid a different kind of blame at the feet of poor women of their race, embracing a politics of respectability that urged such women to rise in their wake even as they sought to explain the presence of "depraved" black women by pointing to the violence of slavery and white men.[47] Furthermore, middle-class African American men expressed concerns about African American women leaving the protection of their homes and entering an interracial public sphere, even as their own expulsion from political life had created space for African American women to stake their claim to new civic territory.[48]

In one sense, by leaving their homes, African American women in the late nineteenth and early twentieth centuries indeed threatened mainstream white supremacist society. During this period they were stepping forth into civic life with new vigor, forming mutual aid, suffrage, and uplift organizations, and otherwise asserting their humanity and leadership.[49] Educated middle-class women of color formed groups such as the National Association of Colored Women and joined the Women's Christian Temperance Union. The civic victories of working-class African American women took both overt and clandestine forms, from unionization efforts to work slowdowns at tobacco factories.[50] And some African American women may have seized on public hangings as opportunities for civic engagement outside the home, or perhaps hangings simply offered a public site to gather for social mixing and a bit of drama.[51] However they viewed public hangings, at them, African American women could defend the African American men in their community specifically and generally against assaults from white people and white society, a defense these men were not always able to make themselves.[52] When African American women joined African American men on the scaffold, they rebuffed the notion of their pernicious influence on African American society and asserted their roles as protectors, uniters, and voices for and of the black community. Echoing political activism after the Civil War, these women "participated from the gallery" even as they were excluded by virtue of their sex and, eventually, their race from more direct political participation, such as voting.[53]

Anxiety about African American women taking active roles in public life contributed to sensibility-based arguments for eliminating public hanging. Indeed, constraining the public lives of black women was integral to the Jim Crow experiment. It enthroned white women as the sole public performers of femininity, reflecting not only a white supremacist vision of their social role but also their high value as potential victims of crime.[54] White women, after all, were supposed to be the focus of acts of protection; conversely, African American women needed to know that they could expect no protection. This message was not sent subtly. For instance, in 1913, when industrialist and Lost Cause propagandist Julian S. Carr dedicated "Silent Sam," the Confederate monument on the campus of the University of North Carolina, he boasted of beating an African American woman in the streets within sight of occupying US Army forces.[55] The absence of structural legal protection for African American women made them easy targets for Felton's remarkably cruel antirape campaign.[56] White women, on the other hand, presuming their adherence to certain standards, were the recipients of a great deal of protective energy, sometimes lethally so.[57]

Moreover, the legal designations and hierarchies produced by slavery and reinforced thereafter placed black women, particularly those in the lower classes, at the bottom of the social ladder and vastly diminished their standing as victims under the law.[58] Crimes against African American women were not punished as frequently or severely as crimes against white women, white men, and African American men, in that order, a fact the black-owned press bitterly noted.[59] By expelling black women from the final phase of the death penalty process, elites sought to further rigidify sociolegal hierarchies. If these women held so little value as victims before white law enforcement officers and all-white juries, why should they enjoy such an influential role at executions? With the transition to state-run execution via electrocution, they no longer would. Existing records of executions do not include mention of any African American woman in attendance at an electrocution.

Another white imperative contributed to the move toward state-run electrocutions: lynching. North Carolina was not a high-frequency lynching state, like its southern neighbors, but between the end of the Civil War and World War II, at least 175 African Americans were lynched, nearly all of them by white mobs.[60] As in other southern states, elites decried lynching even as they often blamed its victims and African Americans generally for provoking mob violence with their criminal behavior. More frequently than in other southern states, North Carolina's law enforcement officers occasionally arrested and prosecuted members of lynch mobs. For instance, George Hall, the leader of a mob who perpetrated a particularly gruesome lynching in Salisbury, North Carolina, in 1906 was, with the support of Governor Robert B. Glenn, charged with conspiracy and given a fifteen-year prison term.[61] The relative harshness of this punishment shrinks, however, upon consideration of the fact that Hall escaped after two years of confinement and lived unmolested for some time in South Carolina before being recaptured and pardoned.[62] Despite Hall's experience, and perhaps in recognition of the juries' sympathy for mob members, in the 1920s Governor Thomas W. Bickett began arming National Guardsmen with live ammunition, resulting in the shooting death of two members of a mob.[63]

In the post–Civil War South, lynching and the death penalty were inextricably linked. They were linked in the minds of lynchers who sometimes explained their actions by claiming they acted in response to what they felt was a sluggish or insufficiently retributive legal system. They were linked in the minds of political elites and religious leaders who saw lynching as a premodern form of a perfectible punishment. And they were socially and culturally linked, sharing form and function. "The mob lynches, the State electrocutes," Nell Battle Lewis wrote. "The group mind, expressing through public opinion, acts in both cases, merely with more decency and decorum in the latter, and with cleverer 'rationalization' of the deed. But the results are the same."[64] Yet despite the "decency and decorum" of the formal death penalty process, as lynchings receded in the twentieth century, capital punishment came to resemble them in important ways. Legal hangings under county authority and lynching had less in common than might appear; the state-run death penalty and lynching had more in common than was immediately apparent.

Mass lynching's symbolic power was more stable and complex than that of capital punishment. Like public hangings, lynchings were staged as object lessons for African Americans. But unlike public hangings, the attendees and participants at lynchings rarely included African Americans, and unlike at public hangings, those being killed were rarely given an opportunity for redemption. When they were, their prayers or confessions were cynically used to sanctify the mob's actions. If public hangings were meant to demonstrate the mercy of the state by making prisoners full participants in their own deaths and allowing them a chance to redeem themselves through contrition, lynchings did the opposite: they demonstrated the white community's furious power by torturing, silencing, and displaying black bodies.[65] If the message of a public hanging was delivered by the voice of the prisoner before death, the message of a mass lynching was delivered by the abductee's body after death. The victim's family might wait days to recover the body of their kin, while photographs, postcards, and sound recordings traveled as far as the West Coast, creating indelible images of black bodies in pain. Members of the mob were not just unconcerned with arrest or judgment; they boasted about their participation and took body parts of their victims as gruesome souvenirs.[66]

Many antilynching activists fought lynching because of what it was: systematic white supremacist terrorism often justified with claims of the need to protect white women. Progressive elites in the South, on the other hand, tended to oppose lynching because to them it appeared antistatist at a time of consolidating state control; they believed lynching barbaric not because of its racist character but because of its ostentatious violence.[67] Lynching, even if it required the complicity of state actors such as sheriffs and coroners, dramatized the failures of the justice system to protect its visible boundaries, threatened the state's reputation with external business partners, and too visibly expressed the essential violence at the core of a white supremacist social and political system. Decrying the violence of lynching was an important way of arguing for the inherent legitimacy of the other components of the racial subjugation of Jim Crow. It said to the public, as did one North Carolina Supreme Court justice, that there is a right way and a wrong way to administer criminal justice.[68]

North Carolinians who bore witness to executions conducted under county or state authority, whether in person or in newspaper accounts afterward, viewed them in the context of a lynching society and sometimes compared them unfavorably to lynchings.[69] But despite the fact that lynchings shared a great deal of visual iconography with legal public hanging, they were starkly dissimilar. Lynchings sought to create and disseminate narratives of black pain and silence and to terrorize black communities. Public hangings seemed to send the opposite message—that African American suffering might be redemptive rather than degrading and that viewing a black body in pain might not prompt disgust but empathy or even respect. Public hangings, too, offered their subjects the chance to vocally resist injustices, general and specific. Lynching's power lay in what historian W. Fitzhugh

Brundage has called its "brutal logic" and, as historian Amy Louise Wood has described, its exploitation of technologies of distribution.[70] Lynchings were often conducted clandestinely (though often with wide public knowledge) and with few exceptions they excluded African American participation, especially after 1890. In these ways, lynchings anticipated centralized legal executions.[71] Social scientists have persuasively dismissed the death penalty as a functional replacement for lynchings, but in the early twentieth century, legal execution, with a central African American figure often dying in agony before a gathering of white onlookers, took lynching's position at the apogee of the criminal justice system as lynchings themselves declined.[72]

Spurred on by these many stimuli, in the second half of the nineteenth century lawmakers and their agents waged an ineffective battle against public interest in hangings. As early as 1868, the state's Reconstruction constitution had directed that sheriffs conduct executions behind an enclosure, but adherence was uneven and often poorly implemented. For instance, in 1870 Hillsborough's sheriff constructed a complex mechanism to hang two condemned men in private; outside, a mob raised a "deafening roaring and yelling and hooting" so loud that at least one reporter could not hear the death sentence when the sheriff read it from the scaffold. With the murder victim's father peppering the prisoners with angry questions, with the prisoners crying and praying, and with the crowd surging outside the jail's windows, this was a constrained spectacle but a spectacle still.[73]

In 1901 the General Assembly directed that sheriffs conduct hangings "as much removed from public view as the means within [their] control will allow" in order to invest hangings "with the solemnity appropriate to the final act of penal law."[74] Sheriffs appeared to make reasonable efforts to remove executions from broad public view, but their failures continued to give ammunition to advocates of centralized execution.[75] Lawmakers were listening. In 1908 the state attorney general urged the General Assembly to remove executions from sheriffs' hands, arguing that such a change would not only stifle the "mock heroism" of prisoners but also ensure "a speedy death at the hands of persons familiar with the work, rather than a bungling execution at the hands of sheriffs who are totally unfamiliar with hangings."[76] In response, Assemblyman John Underwood of Cumberland County submitted a resolution in superior court in Fayetteville asserting that electrocution was more humane than hanging. Shortly thereafter he moved to change the state's method of execution.[77] These efforts aligned North Carolina with a trend scholars have called delocalization, or the migration of diverse responsibilities to central governments in the early twentieth century. Delocalization profoundly changed how executions took place in the United States between 1890, when approximately 90 percent of executions were administered by counties, and 1920, when the same percentage was administered by state governments.[78]

In 1909, with an act of the General Assembly, North Carolina became just the sixth state in the nation to adopt the electric chair as its method of execution.[79] The act also directed that the prison warden or a deputy, as well as a physician and at least twelve reputable citizens, attend each execution. It threw open the doors to other visitors as well; the condemned prisoner's counsel was welcome, as were ministers and relatives of the condemned. The law did not make other provisions for attendance, though custom soon dictated that sheriffs distribute tickets to members of the injured community. Thus, even as they lost control over the mechanics of the execution, sheriffs continued to control who could attend executions and, crucially, who could not. The result was the near complete exclusion of African Americans from the death penalty process—they were also by and large excluded from jury service—except as its subjects.[80]

The death chamber was built on the first floor of the east wing of the main building of Raleigh's Central Prison. The hub of the state's expanding penal landscape, Central Prison was a castle-like structure built by convict labor over the course of two decades in the late nineteenth century. The state's zeal for convict labor was such that only a small number of prisoners were actually confined there: seventy-five in 1912, or just 3 percent of the prison population, and just 10 percent by 1940.[81] These prisoners were either too old or too mentally or physically unwell to work, or they were on death row. Not far from death row was the death chamber. According to the *News and Observer*, the chamber was "scarcely as large as an average-sized living room in a well-appointed house." Meager light from six long windows shone on its lime-green walls.[82] There were two doors, one for prison officials and the prisoner and another that opened onto the lawn at the front of the building through which spectators entered. Edwin Davis, the man who built New York's electric chair, also built North Carolina's. Upon completing the work, he asked to perform the first electrocution himself, that of an itinerant laborer named Walter Morrison. The warden denied Davis's request but allowed him to assist in strapping Morrison into the chair.[83]

This first electrocution proceeded fairly well, according to observers, and newspaper coverage reveals the persistence of religious themes in the absence of lengthy professions of innocence, prayer with familiar clergy, or other rituals. Morrison was baptized in a basement bathtub on the day before his execution. The following morning, rather than facing a gathering of curious onlookers, Morrison faced an array of incandescent light bulbs, burning brightly to indicate the electric chair was in working order. Instead of sharing moral and spiritual lessons with his peers, Morrison stared at the ground as the small, all-white crowd looked on, separated only by a chain; an African American minister had sought admittance but was denied entry.[84] The warden would later note that the execution "was perfect."[85] Indeed, the electrocution was sanctified by Morrison's body itself; the 1,800 volts of current caused his arm to rise from his lap. In his hand was a crucifix, given to him by the prison chaplain, which he involuntarily raised above his head as he died.

This transitional moment calcified the death penalty in Jim Crow North Carolina as reserved almost exclusively for African American subjects to be witnessed almost exclusively by white observers. With the exception of black clergy, African Americans made only rare appearances as witnesses to executions. The first African American reporter was not given access to the death chamber until 1934, nearly twenty-five years after executions were first conducted there.[86] The exclusion of African Americans was so complete that rumors began in the black community that death row prisoners were not in fact being killed but instead were being secreted off to work camps.[87] One white prisoner attempted suicide on death row to avoid becoming the first white person to die in the electric chair.[88] Executing white men for rape was so unusual that when the first such person's execution date approached, he enjoyed robust efforts to delay and prevent his death, including an investigation conducted personally by the governor, who visited the victim, a child, to interview her about the crime. After weighing petitions for commutation, hearing posttrial arguments from attorneys, and commissioning a psychological examination, the governor decided the condemned man had to die.[89] Upon his execution he became one of just five white men executed for rape between 1910 and 1960, all of whom assaulted children.

With capital punishment conducted along rigid racial lines, the witnessing of an execution focused on the interests of the white victims of black crime. Most of those executed between the end of the Civil War and delocalization in 1910 were African Americans convicted of crimes against white victims, yet the crowds who gathered to watch the hangings were mixed, focusing the event on the subject of the execution rather than the victim of the crime. When executions were brought under state authority, similarly to lynching, white victims and their families had more opportunity to bear witness to the punishment. For instance, the white survivor of a rape, for which eighteen-year-old McIver Bennett was executed, watched the 1923 electrocution with eighty to ninety others. Asked by another witness if she enjoyed the execution, she replied that she did.[90]

Throughout this period, despite the construction of a dedicated death chamber, executions remained semipublic affairs. Although crowds were far smaller than they were at their peak and dwindled as time passed, the tiny execution chamber in Central Prison could hold up to ninety observers, if they were willing to cram themselves inside. They were: the crowd at one 1922 electrocution was so thick that when a woman fainted she did not fall to the ground.[91] Outside, in the early years of state-run electrocution, people still gathered to try to catch a glimpse of the body's transit. This was where African American prisoners' relatives waited to claim the bodies of their sons and husbands, if they chose to do so. Many prisoners, African American and white, ended up buried in a potter's field or, increasingly, given to local medical schools for dissection. The destruction of the black body would be completed under the scalpel.[92]

Yet over time, the execution witnesses were winnowed down to what reporters would call "the usual crowd," so seasoned that they mocked one newcomer who confessed ignorance of the execution process.[93] What was once unpredictable had become routine. After a series of swift, quiet electrocutions, one reporter complained that a 1912 electrocution was "perhaps the least [of all the executions so far] adapted to feature from the point of view of the chronicler of human events. There was no hitch or delay, was no pitiful loss of nerve, no fainting of spectator or imprecation of prisoner. It was a perfect execution with a big black man as victim."[94] Despite the general success of electrocution, the execution chamber assaulted the senses, however. In warmer months, the stuffy room held the odor of burned flesh from where the chair's electrodes were attached to the prisoner's skin. And the occasional botched electrocution resulted in screaming headlines and calls for further reform.[95]

Even as the number of people actually witnessing executions dwindled, newspaper coverage meant that they remained widely public, though to a more educated and whiter population than those who had access to public hangings. The circulation of the most read paper in the state, the *News and Observer* of Raleigh, grew from fifteen thousand in 1910 to fifty thousand in 1935, eclipsing the crowds and readership of earlier eras.[96] Its coverage of executions reveals a deeply racist mainstream narrative about African American personhood and criminality. The result was twofold: the denial of narrative agency to African Americans and the opportunity to reinforce the worst stereotypes about African American character. Newspaper coverage of the electrocutions, and later the asphyxiations, of African American men was often cruel, depicting some men as childlike (and indeed many were likely mentally impaired) and others as animalistic. For instance, one reporter witnessing the 1920 electrocution of Andrew Jackson, sentenced to death for rape, described Jackson as "a great, stupid, unlettered animal." After the execution, according to this witness, Jackson's "great hulking body was trundled away to do its first service to society in the hands of medical students."[97]

Public hangings in North Carolina between the end of the Civil War and the early twentieth century dramatized the problem of the color line in that region. Black people were disproportionately likely to be executed for crimes against white people, and even if scenes on the scaffold celebrated black personhood, they made black criminality the centerpiece of an important criminal justice exercise. It was the drama and instability of public hanging that drove it indoors, but behind that sense of instability was concern about fraying racial etiquette. When executions were made private despite the desires of the wider public, elites and those in their thrall, crucially, newspaper reporters and editors, had the opportunity to rewrite execution as a punishment reserved for African Americans and conducted and attended by whites. Crucial to this narrowing of public purpose was the idea that execution, with its new technologies, expressed an ascendant white purpose, unknowable and particularly scary to African Americans. On the pages of North Carolina's daily papers, those African Americans in the crucible of the execution chamber revealed not Christian personhood but, through their pain, something less evolved.

Restructured and centralized, the death penalty in North Carolina after 1910 played the same role that lynching did for previous generations: it demonstrated the lethal force of white political and social power. But it did so in a modern setting and with the application of technology rather than brute force. State-run execution, then, evolved not just from the public hangings that were its legal predecessors but from the illegal lynchings that laid its ideological foundation. The new death penalty centralized and professionalized public hangings, rationalizing to some extent their unpredictability and replacing the noose with something more "in the line of progress," as one editorialist put it.[98]

The 1957 execution of Ross McAfee demonstrates the crystallization of Jim Crow justice in the North Carolina execution chamber. By the late 1950s, the number of annual executions in North Carolina had dwindled, thanks to new laws removing burglary from the list of capital crimes and allowing people charged with murder and rape to plead guilty in exchange for life sentences.[99]

McAfee, described as an "itinerant Negro farm worker," was put to death by asphyxiation for "an attack on a young white housewife." In 1936 the state replaced electrocution with asphyxiation with lethal gas. The prison warden attested that McAfee had told him he was "ready to go," and McAfee repeated as much to the prison chaplain. Then, under the gaze of a crowd of reporters, observers, and officers from the scene of the attack, McAfee died. One reporter observed that "there were no Negroes among the spectators."[100] McAfee was among the last men to die in North Carolina's gas chamber; after the 1961 execution of "penniless drifter" Theodore Boykin, an African American man condemned for the rape of a white woman, the state did not execute another person until 1984.

To those sensitive to the image of North Carolina and the American South at large, the chaotic public hangings of the late nineteenth century were intolerably unstable and interracial, both threatening and representing declension rather than progress. Hanging "would naturally suggest itself in the infancy of a State," wrote one editorialist in the *Raleigh Signal*, adding that "the Hottentots" tended to punish miscreants brutally before a populace "who take great delight in their barbarous practices."[101] This practice required a solution that expressed not only the centralizing bureaucratic tendencies of the New South but also the settled nature of its white supremacy. Transforming the death penalty from a fairly inclusive community event expressive of a racist criminal justice system into the systematic exertion of force by whites against blacks settled the death penalty's race problem in the minds of white supremacist reformers. To them, the deep social complexities of death as punishment, in the words of legal scholar Austin Sarat, had been "reduced to a matter of mundane technique."[102]

NOTES

Thank you to Amy Louise Wood, Natalie J. Ring, Sharon Holland, W. Fitzhugh Brundage, and two anonymous readers for their editorial interventions in this chapter.

1. *Capital Punishment in North Carolina* (Raleigh, NC: State Board of Charities and Public Welfare, 1929), 138.

2. Ibid., 133–38.

3. Ibid., 37.

4. Alexander S. Leidholdt, *Battling Nell: The Life of Southern Journalist Cornelia Battle Lewis, 1893–1956* (Baton Rouge: Louisiana State University Press, 2009), 62–64. Leidholdt suggests that Lewis may have suffered from bipolar disorder.

5. Quoted in Darden Asbury Pyron, "Nell Battle Lewis (1893–1956) and the New Southern Woman," in *Perspectives on the American South: An Annual Review Society, Politics and Culture*, ed. James C. Cobb and Charles R. Wilson (New York: Gordon and Breach Science Publishers, 1985), 3:66.

6. Donald Davidson, *The Attack on Leviathan: Regionalism and Nationalism in the United States* (Chapel Hill: University of North Carolina Press, 1938), 287.

7. Susan Cahn, "Spirited Youth or Fiends Incarnate: The Samarcand Arson Case and Female Adolescence in the American South," *Journal of Women's History* 9 (Winter 1998): 152–81.

8. *Wilson Mirror*, January 29, 1890, 4. Articles from this period rarely included bylines; authorship appears in the notes when it appears in the source.

9. *News and Observer* (Raleigh, NC), April 4, 1934, 3.

10. Paul Green, "Work in Progress," November 2, 1953, n.p., series 5: Other Files, subseries 5.3: Capital Punishment, 1947–53, Paul Green Papers, Southern Historical Collection, University of North Carolina at Chapel Hill.

11. *News and Observer*, January 2, 1939.

12. George Tindall, *The Emergence of the New South, 1913–1945* (Baton Rouge: Louisiana State University Press, 1967), 368; Michael O'Brien, *The Idea of the American South, 1920–1941* (Baltimore, MD: Johns Hopkins University Press, 1979), 16, 41.

13. Quoted in Tindall, *The Emergence of the New South*, 227.

14. Ibid., 224; O'Brien, *The Idea*, 17.

15. *News and Observer*, January 21, 1936, 1.

16. Fred Hobson, *Serpent in Eden: H. L. Mencken and the South* (1978; Baton Rouge: Louisiana State University Press, 1995), 60, 83.

17. Michael Kay and Lorin Lee Cary, *Slavery in North Carolina, 1748–1775* (Chapel Hill: University of North Carolina Press, 1995), 91; Alan D. Watson, "North Carolina Slave Courts," *North Carolina Historical Review* 60 (January 1983): 33–34.

18. "Capital Punishment," in *The Encyclopedia of North Carolina*, ed. William S. Powell (Chapel Hill: University of North Carolina Press, 2006), 177. See also *Durham Morning Herald*, February 13, 1949, clipping file through 1975 (Capital Punishment), 41, North Carolina Collection, University of North Carolina at Chapel Hill; Stuart Banner, *The Death Penalty: An American History* (Cambridge, MA: Harvard University Press, 2002), 152; *Asheville Citizen-Times*, January 13, 1909, 4.

19. Seth Kotch, "Unduly Harsh and Unworkably Rigid: The Death Penalty in North Carolina, 1910–1961" (PhD diss., University of North Carolina at Chapel Hill, 2008), 34; Michael A. Trotti, "The Scaffold's Revival: Race and Public Execution in the South," *Journal of Southern History* 45 (Fall 2011): 195–96.

20. *News and Observer*, December 12, 1931, 12.

21. William H. Chafe documents the cultivation of a progressive mystique in *Civilities and Civil Rights: Greensboro, North Carolina, and the Black Struggle for Freedom* (New York: Oxford University Press, 1980). Since the colonial period, North Carolina ranks sixth nationally in number of executions. M. Watt Espy and John Ortiz Smykla, "The Espy File: 1608–2002," www.deathpenaltyinfo.org/executions-us-1608–2002-espy-file (accessed March 20, 2017). Though not without errors, the Espy File is the most comprehensive single record of executions in the United States.

22. Marvin L. Michael Kay and Lorin Lee Cary, *Slavery in North Carolina*, 88.

23. Espy and Smykla, "The Espy File: 1608–2002." Race of victim information was gathered from newspaper reports and is in the possession of the author.

24. Seth Kotch and Robert P. Mosteller, "The Racial Justice Act and the Long Struggle with Race and the Death Penalty in North Carolina," *North Carolina Law Review* 88, no. 6 (2010): 109, 114.

25. David M. Potter, "On Understanding the South: A Review Article," *Journal of Southern History* 30, no. 4 (1964): 460.

26. Trotti, "The Scaffold's Revival," 195–224; see also Seth Kotch, *Lethal State: A History of the Death Penalty in North Carolina* (Chapel Hill: UNC Press, 2019), 61–64.

27. Sharpe, "'Last Dying Speeches': Religion, Ideology, and Public Execution in Seventeenth-Century England," *Past and Present* 107, no. 1 (1985): 152–56; Émile Durkheim, *The Division of Labor in Society*, trans. George Simpson (New York: Macmillan, 1933); Michel Foucault, *Discipline and Punish: The Birth of the Prison*, trans. Alan Sheridan, 2nd ed. (1977; New York: Vintage Books, 1995).

28. For instance, one 1896 editorial described hangings in North Carolina as "festal occasion[s]" (*Charlotte Observer*, February 18, 1896, 2). For more evidence of the social nature of hangings in the South, see Trotti, "The Scaffold's Revival."

29. *Goldsboro Messenger*, May 19, 1879, 3.

30. *Statesville Record and Landmark,* January 15, 1959 (originally published May 1, 1868), 3. For newspaper reportage excoriating "morbid" crowds at hangings, see *Wilmington Morning Star*, August 18, 1885, 3; *Semi-Weekly Messenger* (Wilmington, NC), April 18, 1905, 5; *Wilmington Messenger*, January 11, 1890, 1; *Wilson Mirror*, June 21, 1893, 2.

31. *Carolina Watchman* (Salisbury, NC), November 26, 1885, 1.

32. *Morning Post* (Raleigh, NC), June 8, 1898, 2.

33. See, for instance, *Greensboro Patriot*, May 21, 1879, 2; *Goldsboro Messenger*, May 19, 1879, 3.

34. Trotti, "The Scaffold's Revival," 195–224.

35. Natalie J. Ring, "The 'New Race Question': The Problem of Poor Whites and the Color Line," in *The Folly of Jim Crow: Rethinking the Segregated South*, ed. Stephanie Cole and Natalie J. Ring (College Station: Texas A&M University Press, 2012), 92–93.

36. *Torchlight* (Oxford, NC), May 13, 1887, 4.

37. *News and Observer*, September 1, 1906, 1.

38. Stewart E. Tolnay and E. M. Beck, *A Festival of Violence: An Analysis of Southern Lynchings, 1882–1930* (Urbana: University of Illinois Press), 78.

39. Trotti, "The Scaffold's Revival," 195–96.

40. *Farmer and Mechanic* (Raleigh, NC), July 3, 1879, 5.

41. *Daily Review* (Wilmington, NC), August 20, 1879, 2.

42. See, for instance, *Henderson Gold Leaf*, May 3, 1895, 1.

43. *Henderson Gold Leaf*, September 9, 1897, 2.

44. *Wilmington Messenger*, September 4, 1897, 2.

45. Anastasia Sims, *The Power of Femininity in the New South: Women's Organizations and Politics in North Carolina, 1880–1930* (Columbia: University of South Carolina Press, 1997), 107–8; Evelyn Brooks Higganbotham, "African-American Women's History and the Metalanguage of Race," *Signs* 17, no. 2 (1992): 262–64.

46. As quoted in, Crystal N. Feimster, *Southern Horrors: Women and the Politics of Rape and Lynching* (Cambridge, MA: Harvard University Press, 2011), 115.

47. Ibid., 115; Evelyn Brooks Higganbotham, *Righteous Discontent: The Women's Movement in the Black Baptist Church, 1880–1920* (Cambridge, MA: Harvard University Press, 1993), 96–97, 184–94.

48. Glenda Elizabeth Gilmore, *Gender & Jim Crow: Women and the Politics of White Supremacy in North Carolina, 1896–1920* (Chapel Hill: University of North Carolina Press, 1996), 75–76; Sims, *The Power of Femininity*, 83.

49. Grace Elizabeth Hale, *Making Whiteness: The Culture of Segregation in the South, 1890–1940* (New York: Vintage Books, 1998), 32–33; Mia Bay, "From the 'Ladies Car' to the 'Colored Car': Black Female Travelers in the Segregated South," in Cole and Ring, *The Folly of Jim Crow*, 150–75.

50. Robin D. G. Kelley, "'We Are Not What We Seem': Rethinking Black Working-Class Opposition in the Jim Crow South," *Journal of American History* 80, no. 1 (1993): 75–112.

51. On middle-class women forming and joining groups, see Gilmore, *Gender*, 44–45; Jacqueline Jones, *Labor of Love, Labor of Sorrow: Black Women, Work, and Family from Slavery to the Present* (1985; New York: Vintage Books, 1995), 112.

52. Jones, *Labor of Love*, 149–50.

53. Elsa Barkley Brown, "Negotiating and Transforming the Public Sphere: African-American Political Life from Slavery to Freedom," in *Time Longer Than Rope: A Century of African-American Activism, 1850–1950*, ed. Charles M. Payne and Adam Green (New York: New York University Press, 2003), 76.

54. Sarah Haley, "'Like I Was a Man': Chain Gangs, Gender, and the Domestic Carceral Sphere in Jim Crow Georgia," *Signs* 39, no. 1 (2013): 73.

55. Julian S. Carr, "Unveiling of Confederate Monument at University," June 2, 1913, series 2, subseries 2.2: Addresses, 1896–1923, folder 26: Addresses, 1912–14, Julian Shakespeare Carr Papers, Southern Historical Collection, University of North Carolina at Chapel Hill. See, too, this transcript of an 1889 speech by Carr on the subject: "Col. Carr on the Race Problem," *Farmer and Mechanic*, May 30, 1889, 6.

56. Feimster, *Southern Horrors*, 63–79.

57. The idea that lynching protected white women was behind Jessie Daniel Ames's crusade against it. Jacquelyn Dowd Hall, *Revolt against Chivalry: Jessie Daniel Ames and the Women's Campaign against Lynching* (New York: Columbia University Press, 1979).

58. Feimster, *Southern Horrors*, 40–41; Peter W. Bardaglio, *Reconstructing the Household: Families, Sex, and the Law in the Nineteenth-Century South* (Chapel Hill: University of North Carolina Press, 1995), 66–68.

59. For instance, despite the fact that a rape conviction carried a mandatory capital sentence, no white man was ever executed for committing this crime against a black woman. Kotch and Mosteller, "The Racial Justice Act," 109; *Carolina Times* (Durham, NC), April 15, 1938, 4.

60. The website lynching.web.unc.edu lists these events, many of which were sourced from the data of E. M. Beck, Stewart Tolnay, and Amy Kate Bailey, as well as Vann R. Newkirk, *Lynching in North Carolina: A History, 1865–1941* (Jefferson, NC: MacFarland, 2008). The rare person was lynched by a mixed-race or all-black mob.

61. Claude A. Clegg III, *Troubled Ground: A Tale of Murder, Lynching, and Reckoning in the New South* (Urbana: University of Illinois Press, 2010), 146–62.

62. *News and Observer*, October 8, 1908, 5; *Davie Record* (Mocksville, NC), July 27, 1909, 1; *Gastonia Gazette*, October 17, 1911, 1.

63. Newkirk, *Lynching*, 80.

64. Nell Battle Lewis, "Incidentally," *News and Observer*, September 17, 1922, 6.

65. David Garland, "Penal Excess and Surplus Meaning: Public Torture Lynchings in Twentieth Century America," *Law and Society Review* 39, no. 4 (2005): 6–7. Victims were occasionally given concessions, such as a last request or a less painful death, if doubts about their guilt arose.

66. Amy Louise Wood, *Lynching and Spectacle: Witnessing Racial Violence in America, 1890–1940* (Chapel Hill: University of North Carolina Press, 2009), 71–94.

67. See, for instance, *Daily Tar Heel* (Chapel Hill, NC), December 11, 1931, 2.

68. Woodrow Price, "Negro Facing Life Term Confesses Role in Crime," *News and Observer*, June 28, 1947, 1.

69. "First Lethal Gas Victim Dies in Torture as Witnesses Quail," *News and Observer*, January 25, 1936, 1.

70. W. Fitzhugh Brundage, *Lynching in the New South: Georgia and Virginia, 1880–1930* (Urbana: University of Illinois Press, 1993), 49; Wood, *Lynching and Spectacle*, 71–75.

71. Hale, *Making Whiteness*, 201.

72. Stewart E. Tolnay and E. M. Beck, *Festival of Violence: An Analysis of Southern Lynchings, 1882–1930* (Urbana: University of Illinois Press, 1995), 111; Margaret Vandiver, *Lethal Punishment: Lynchings and Executions in the South* (New Brunswick, NJ: Rutgers University Press, 2006), 14–17.

73. *Daily Standard* (Raleigh, NC), April 5, 1870, 2. For more examples, see *Daily Journal* (Wilmington, NC), November 8, 1870, 1; *Daily Standard*, November 4, 1870, 1.

74. "An Act Requiring the Execution of Capital Offenders to Be Private," chap. 215 in *Public Laws and Resolutions of the State of North Carolina Passed by the General Assembly at Its Session of 1901* (Raleigh, NC: E. M. Uzzell, 1902), 352.

75. See, for instance, *News and Observer*, April 7, 1905, 1.

76. *Biennial Report of the Attorney General of the State of North Carolina, 1907–8* (Raleigh, NC: Edwards and Broughton Printing Company, 1908), 11.

77. Charles K. Craven, "North Carolina's Prison System: A Chronological History through 1950" (MA thesis, University of North Carolina at Chapel Hill, 1987), 30–31.

78. William J. Bowers, with Glenn L. Pierce and John F. McDevitt, *Legal Homicide: Death as Punishment in America, 1864–1982* (Boston: Northeastern University Press, 1984), 38, 63.

79. *Public Laws and Resolutions Passed by the General Assembly of the State of North Carolina at Its Session of 1909* (Raleigh, NC: E. M. Uzzell and Company, 1909), chap. 443, North Carolina Collection, University of North Carolina at Chapel Hill.

80. Kotch and Mosteller, "The Racial Justice Act," 147. There were, of course, exceptions to the general rule of excluding African Americans. "One negro," for example, was allowed to witness the electrocution of Norman Lewis in 1911; *Raleigh Times*, May 12, 1911, 1.

81. Prison Reports (1927–28), 32, Table 1: Movement of Prisoners, in *Report of the Director of Prisons, Biennial Report of the State Highway and Public Works Commission for 1938–39 and 1939–40*, 393, North Carolina Collection, University of North Carolina at Chapel Hill.

82. *News and Observer*, March 19, 1910, 1.

83. *News and Observer*, March 18, 1910, 5.

84. *News and Observer*, March 19, 1910, 3.

85. *Biennial Report of the State's Prison, 1909–1910* (Raleigh, NC: The Prison, 1910), 15. North Carolina Collection, University of North Carolina at Chapel Hill.

86. *News and Observer*, September 22, 1934, 12.

87. *News and Observer*, November 23, 1924, 5.

88. *News and Observer*, February 24, 1914, 2.

89. *News and Observer*, January 13, 1920, 16.

90. *News and Observer*, October 13, 1922, 1.

91. Ibid.

92. The bodies of at least 25 percent of executed people between 1910 and 1961 were sent to medical schools for dissection. This percentage is based on my accounting from hundreds of newspaper reports in this time period.

93. *News and Observer*, November 23, 1924, 5, November 15, 1918, 8, September 21, 1920, 16, and December 8, 1923, 9.

94. *News and Observer*, May 18, 1912, 5.

95. *News and Observer*, May 28, 1921, 3.

96. Numbers taken from *News and Observer* front pages, February 12, 1911, March 16, 1935, and May 2, 1953.

97. "Long Battle with Law Brings Death," *News and Observer*, November 6, 1920, 10.

98. *Morning Post*, November 8, 1904, 1.

99. "Survey of Statutory Changes in North Carolina Law in 1941," *North Carolina Law Review* 19, no. 4 (1941): 444.

100. *Statesville Record and Landmark*, November 22, 1957, 1.

101. *Raleigh Signal*, August 18, 1887, 1.

102. Austin Sarat, *When the State Kills: Capital Punishment and the American Condition* (Princeton, NJ: Princeton University Press, 2001), 66.

CONTRIBUTORS

PIPPA HOLLOWAY is a professor of history at Middle Tennessee State University. She is the author of *Living in Infamy: Felon Disfranchisement and the History of American Citizenship* (Oxford University Press, 2013). She is also the author of *Sexuality, Politics, and Social Control in Virginia, 1920–1945* (University of North Carolina Press, 2006), which won the Willie Lee Rose Prize from the Southern Association for Women Historians, and the editor of *Other Souths: Diversity and Difference in the U.S. South, Reconstruction to Present* (University of Georgia Press, 2008).

TAMMY INGRAM is an associate professor at the College of Charleston, where she teaches courses on the modern South, twentieth-century US politics, urban history, and film and history. Her first book, *Dixie Highway: Road Building and the Making of the Modern South, 1900–1930* (University of North Carolina Press, 2014), has been awarded an Excellence in Research Award by the Georgia Historical Records Advisory Council and the 2015 Malcolm Bell, Jr., and Muriel Barrow Bell Award by the Georgia Historical Society. It was named a 2014 Book of Interest by the Business History Conference. She has also written blogs and op-eds for outlets such as the History News Network, Like the Dew, the Huffington Post, and the *Atlanta Journal-Constitution*. Her current book project is *The Wickedest City in America: The Rise and Fall of Organized Crime in the Jim Crow South*, a case study that explores the links between corrupt Jim Crow regimes and white criminal networks in the Deep South.

BRANDON T. JETT earned his PhD from the University of Florida in 2017. He currently teaches at Rollins College, Florida. His research focuses on the effects of demographic shifts, urbanization, and economic diversification on criminal justice in the twentieth-century South. He has published award-winning articles exploring issues of extralegal violence in East Texas and homicide trends in Memphis. His current manuscript is under contract with LSU Press and will be published as part of the Making the Modern South series. In 2017 the American Society for Legal History awarded him the William Nelson Cromwell Foundation Early Career Scholar Fellowship.

SETH KOTCH is an assistant professor of digital humanities in the Department of American Studies at the University of North Carolina at Chapel Hill. He conducts research at the intersections of a number of fields and disciplines, most prominently, modern American history, digital humanities, and oral history. He is the coauthor of "The Racial Justice Act and the Long Struggle with Race and the Death Penalty in North Carolina" (*North Carolina Law Review*, 2010). He also served as coprincipal investigator of Media and the Movement, a project sponsored by the National Endowment for the Humanities that explored the role of journalists and the media in the civil rights movement during and after the 1960s. He served as project supervisor and PI on the Civil Rights History Project, a nationwide oral history project administered by the Smithsonian's National Museum of African American History and Culture and the American Folklife Center in the Library of Congress. His first book, *Lethal State: A History of the Death Penalty in North Carolina*, will be published by the University of North Carolina Press in January 2019.

TALITHA L. LEFLOURIA is the Lisa Smith Discovery Associate Professor in African and African-American Studies at the University of Virginia. She is the author of *Chained in Silence: Black Women and Convict Labor in the New South* (University of North Carolina Press, 2015), which has won numerous awards, including the Best First Book Prize from the Berkshire Conference on the History of Women, Genders, and Sexualities; the Philip Taft Labor History Award from the Cornell University School of Industrial and Labor Relations & Labor and Working-Class History Association; the Letitia Woods Brown Memorial Book Prize from the Association of Black Women Historians; and the Darlene Clark Hine Award for the best book in African American women's history from the Organization of American Historians. Professor LeFlouria's research was featured in the Sundance-nominated documentary *Slavery by Another Name,* as well as C-SPAN. Currently, she serves on the board of directors for Historians Against Slavery and the Association of Black Women Historians. She also serves on the editorial board of the *Georgia Historical Quarterly* and *International Labor and Working-Class History* journal.

VIVIEN MILLER is an associate professor of American and Canadian studies at the University of Nottingham UK. She is the author of *Hard Labor and Hard Time: Florida's "Sunshine Prison" and Chain Gangs* (University Press of Florida, 2012), which merited an honorable mention in the BAAS Book Prize 2013, and of *Crime, Sexual Violence, and Clemency: Florida's Pardon Board and Penal System in the Progressive Era* (University Press of Florida, 2000), and she is the coeditor of *Transnational Penal Cultures: New Perspectives on Discipline, Punishment, and Desistance* (Routledge, 2015). Her articles on Florida crime and punishment cover murder, rape, kidnapping, and theft, convict leasing, chain gangs, and prisons. She is currently working on a project about capital punishment and the emergence of death row in the post-1945 American South.

SILVAN NIEDERMEIER is an assistant professor (*wissenschaftlicher Mitarbeiter*) of history at the University of Erfurt, Germany. He received his PhD from the University of Erfurt in 2011 and has worked as a postdoctoral fellow at the Graduate School of Cultural Encounters and Discourses of Scholarship at the University of Rostock. He is the author of *Rassismus und Bürgerrechte: Polizeifolter im Süden der USA 1930–1955* (Hamburger Edition, 2014; the English translation, *Racism and Civil Rights: Police Torture in the American South 1930–1955*, is under contract with University of North Carolina Press). He also coedited *Violence and Visibility in Modern History* (Palgrave Macmillan, 2013). He is currently working on a project about the role of photography in the Philippine-American War.

K. STEPHEN PRINCE is an associate professor of history at the University of South Florida. He earned his PhD from Yale University in 2010. His first book, *Stories of the South: Race and the Reconstruction of Southern Identity, 1865–1915* (University of North Carolina Press, 2014), was selected as runner-up for the 2014 Society for U.S. Intellectual History Annual Book Award. He is also the author of *Radical Reconstruction: A Brief History with Documents* (Bedford–St. Martin's, 2015). He is currently at work on a study of Robert Charles and the 1900 New Orleans riot.

NATALIE J. RING (coeditor) is an associate professor of history at the University of Texas at Dallas. She is the author of *The Problem South: Region, Empire and the New Liberal State, 1880–1930* (University of Georgia Press, 2012), which was a finalist for two prizes: the Best First Book Award from the Berkshire Conference of Women Historians and the TIL Award for Most Significant Scholarly Book from the Texas Institute of Letters. She is the coeditor of *The Folly of Jim Crow: Rethinking the Segregated South* (Texas A&M University Press, 2012), as well as the author of several articles in journals and edited collections. Currently, she is working on a history of Louisiana State Penitentiary, commonly known as Angola Prison, and a coedited collection titled *The Lost Lectures of C. Vann Woodward*, which will be published by Oxford University Press. In 2015 she was appointed an OAH Distinguished Lecturer by the Organization of American Historians.

AMY LOUISE WOOD (coeditor) is a professor of history at Illinois State University. She is the author of *Lynching and Spectacle: Witnessing Racial Violence in America, 1890–1940* (University of North Carolina Press, 2009), which won the Lillian Smith Book Award and was a finalist for the Los Angeles Times Book Award in History. She is also the co–guest editor of a special issue of *Mississippi Quarterly* on lynching, representation, and memory (2008) and the editor of *The New Encyclopedia of Southern Culture: Violence* (University of North Carolina Press, 2011). Her article "Killing the Elephant: Murderous Beasts and the Thrill of Retribution," published in the *Journal of the Gilded Age and Progressive Era,* won the Best Article Prize in 2013 from the Society for Historians of the Gilded and Progressive Era. She is currently working on a book project entitled "Sympathy for the Devil: The Criminal in the American Imagination."

INDEX

Abbeville, Alabama, 73
Adams, Joe, 162
Adler, Jeffrey S., 17
African American women, 8, 10, 35, 45, 45, 50, 130–34, 140, 141–42, 144n10, 162, 195, 198–200. *See also* prisoners
African Americans, 1–2, 3; and assistance with police investigations, 35, 43–47; and capital punishment, 173, 195–96; clemency for, 160–63; criminalization of, 5, 8, 7, 30, 37, 39, 81, 82, 83, 99, 122, 149n93, 199, 206–7; as eyewitnesses to crime, 7, 39–47, 55n30; and interactions with police, 35–36, 38–41, 43–47, 51–52, 53n6; middle-class, 37–38, 199–200; as police officers, 17–19, 28–30; and support for increased policing, 37–39; and surrender to police, 36, 47–52; as victims of police violence, 35, 59, 61, 72–74; working-class, 39, 133, 134, 199. *See also* Jim Crow; parole; prisoners; public executions; white supremacy
Alabama, 8, 12n7, 61, 72, 73, 75n13, 79–80, 81–83, 86, 87, 94–95, 101n19, 115, 138–42, 170; Beverage Control, 93; Board of Administration, 142; Civic League, 70; common law in, 114; contract labor in, 130–32, 135, 139–40, 146fn29; convict leasing in, 131, 135, 138, 139, 146fn29; National Guard, 86, 98; politics in, 84, 89, 96–99, 103fn47, 104fn64; Supreme Court of, 71, 72, 96, 114; testimonial incapacity in, 114, 119–20. *See also* Abbeville, Alabama; Montgomery, Alabama; Phenix City, Alabama; Russell County, Alabama
Alabama Tribune, 70
Alachua County, Florida, 174, 177
alcohol, 21, 88, 89, 190
Alexander, Early, 40
Alexander, Michelle, 2
Alexander, Will, 66
Allen, John, 161
Allen, T. T., 71
Alston, Tommy, 46
American Civil Liberties Union, 66
Ames, Jessie Daniel, 211
Anderson, Elijah, 54
Anderson, John, 159
Anderson, William D., 65, 66
Anti-Capital Punishment League, 193
appellate courts, 109, 127n53
Arizona, 12n7
Arkansas, 12n7, 61, 75n13, 170; common law in, 117; Supreme Court of, 117, 119; testimonial incapacity in, 117, 119, 120
Association of Southern Women for the Prevention of Lynching, 67
Athens, Georgia, 60
Atlanta, Georgia, 58, 59; District Court of, 73; Juvenile Court of, 58; Police Department, 58, 59
Atlanta Constitution, 58–59
Atlanta Daily World, 59
Augusta, Georgia, 60,

Bailey, Henry, 198
Bama Club, 79, 97

Banks, Henry, 49
Barnes, George, 157
Beachie's Swing Club, 85, 89
Beckham, J. C. W., 170
Bell, Ed, 50
Bennett, McIver, 205
Benson, J. D., 47
Bentham, Jeremy, 157
Bentley, Hugh, 94, 96
Berry, James, 46
Bessler, John, 172
Bethea, Rainey, 177
Bible Belt, 79
Bickett, Thomas W., 201
Bilbo, Theodore, 66
Birch, Alex C., 71
Black Belt, 87
Blease, Cole, 9; background of, 149–50; and
    chain gangs, 152–53; criticism of, 148,
    158–59, 160; as defender of lynching,
    147, 148, 155, 162; and executive clem-
    ency, 148, 151, 153–58, 160–62, 163;
    and penal reform, 148–9, 151, 156, 158,
    163; support for, 148–50, 152, 159–60.
    See also executive clemency; pardons;
    parole; South Carolina
Blitch, J. S., 180–82
Bond, Bate, 130
Borders, A. S., 90–92
Boykin, Theodore, 208
Bradford County, Florida, 174, 175, 177,
    179; Circuit Court of, 174; Jail, 174, 179
Bradford County Telegraph, 174, 175
Brandon, William M., 139
Brassell, Jabe, 92
Bratton, Theodore D., 67
Brent, A. O., 139
Brewer, Earl, 66
bribery, 93, 159
Briceville, Tennessee, 107
Brooks, George, 34
brothels, 79, 85, 86, 89. See also prostitution
Brown, Costie Louis, 44
Brown, Ed, 63, 64, 66, 67, 71, 72
Brown, H. H., 107
Brown, James, 44
Brown, Michael, 75n18
Brown, Ruth, 140–41
Brown, Walter, 49
Browne, Charles, 179, 189n56
Brown v. Mississippi, 63, 67, 70

Brundage, W. Fitzhugh, 202–3
Bullock, Rayfield, 44
Bullock, Virginia, 44–45
Buren, Martin Van, 120

California Supreme Court, 120
Cambria Coal Company, 107
Canty, Dave, 68–72
capital punishment, 2, 3, 6, 9–10, 174, 176–
    77, 178–84, 195–96, 185n7, 188n44,
    201; and asphyxiation, 175, 206–8;
    criticism of, 193, 197; and death war-
    rants, 175, 179, 182; and gas chamber,
    184n6, 208; and lethal injection, 2; and
    modernization, 171–73, 180–81, 183–84,
    189n59, 194–96, 207; reform of, 9, 170,
    172, 178–79, 194; and white supremacy,
    175, 195, 201–2, 204–5, 207. See also
    electrocution; Florida; Georgia; Jim
    Crow; North Carolina; public execution;
    prisoners; Tennessee; United States
Carlton, David, 150
Carr, Julian S., 200
Carter, William A., 130
Central Prison (North Carolina), 192, 204,
    206
chain gangs, 6, 132, 151, 152–53, 155, 159,
    161, 162, 163
Chambers v. Florida, 71
Charleston, South Carolina, 19
Chattahoochee River, 79, 83, 86, 87
Chicago, Illinois, 10, 37, 79, 81, 95
Child Welfare Association (Georgia), 58
Christianity, 151, 156, 207. See also clergy
civil rights activism, 8, 59, 60, 62–63,
    65–67, 71, 72. See also Civil Rights
    Movement
Civil Rights Act of 1866, 120
Civil Rights Movement, 8, 59, 98
Civil War, US, 5, 79, 83, 120, 195, 196, 200,
    201, 205, 207
Clark, John, 65–66
Clark, Susie, 45
clergy, 88, 94, 112, 157, 175, 180, 204, 205,
    208
Cleveland, Ohio, 10
Cobb, Homer, 88
Cobb Memorial Hospital, 91
Colbert, Georgia, 95
Cole, Cora, 46–47
Coleman, R. F., 182

Columbia, South Carolina, 147, 161
Columbus, Georgia, 79, 82, 83
Columbus Ledger-Enquirer, 80, 90, 94
Commission on Interracial Cooperation, 66
common law, 108–12, 114, 118, 127n53.
    See also Alabama; Arkansas; Florida;
    Georgia; South Carolina; Tennessee;
    Texas
Congress, US, 1, 62, 113
Connecticut, 112
Constitution, US, 72, 116, 147, 157
contract labor, 8, 130, 135, 137, 151, 152;
    and the apparel industry, 5, 131–32,
    138–40. *See also* Alabama; Tennessee
convict labor, 5, 6, 131, 132, 137, 138, 204.
    See also chain gangs; contract labor;
    convict leasing
convict leasing, 4–5, 121–22, 138–39,
    151–52, 176; abolition of, 131, 135, 151,
    172; opposition to, 131, 146n29, 152.
    See also Alabama; Tennessee
Cooper, W. L., 159
Costello, Frank, 95
Coward, John, 46
crime syndicate. *See* organized crime
Cummings, Jim, 20

Dade County, Florida, 182, 190n73
Daily Picayune (New Orleans), 23–25, 27
Daily States (New Orleans), 23–28
Daniel, Pal M., 84, 96
Daniels, Josephus, 193
Davidson, Donald, 193
Daviess County, Florida, 177
Davis, Annie, 142
Davis, Edwin, 180, 204
Davis, Fred H., 172, 178, 179
Davis, Godwin, 97, 98
Davis, Natalie Zemon, 161
death penalty. *See* capital punishment
Democratic Party, 24, 80, 159
Democrats, 121
Denmark, S. B., 175–76
Dial, Cliff, 64
disease, 6, 86, 148, 155, 190n72
disfranchisement, 4, 7, 83, 93, 101n19; of
    convicted felons, 1, 2, 5, 8, 10, 12n8, 83,
    101n19, 110, 117–18, 121–22, 129n93.
    See also voting rights
Division of Negro Economics, Department
    of Labor, US, 133

DNA testing, 2
Dowling, W. H., 182
Doyle, George, 7, 19; accusations against,
    21–23; and assault charge, 20; back-
    ground of, 19–20; and false imprison-
    ment charge, 20; murder trial of, 18,
    22, 25–28; Police Board trial of, 18, 19,
    22, 28–29; police career of, 20–21; and
    removal from duty, 18, 28–29
Draper, Hamp, 142
Du Bois, W. E. B., 60, 129n93
due process, 4, 63–67, 116, 121, 163, 171,
    177, 183
Dula, Tom, 197
Dulaney, W. Marvin, 18, 19
Duncan, Robert, 40
Duplantier, Leonce, 20
Duval County, Florida, 173, 177, 181, 182,
    187n28

Eddyville Penitentiary, Kentucky, 170
Edwards, Lula May, 142
election fraud, 93, 97, 103n47
electrocution, 9, 69–70, 72, 163, 166n21,
    170–73, 178–84, 184n6, 189n56,
    189n63, 192, 195, 197, 200–201, 204–6,
    208; as more humane, 170, 203; and role
    of electrician, 180; witnesses of, 170,
    179, 205, 207, 213n80. *See also* Florida;
    North Carolina
Ellington, Arthur, 63, 64, 66, 67, 71, 72
Ellis, Joe, 49
Ellis, Simeon, 161
Ellison, John, 155
El Salvador, 10
Episcopal Diocese of Mississippi, 67
eugenics, 181
Evans, Howard, 47
executive clemency, 9, 141, 148, 151,
    153–55, 158, 160–63, 168n69, 190n67;
    criticism of, 157, 159–60; and mercy,
    153, 157, 161; as premodern, 156–58;
    and reform, 148, 151, 153–54, 157–58.
    See also Blease, Cole; pardons; parole

Fair Sentencing Act of 2010, 1
Federal Bureau of Investigation, 2, 73, 87,
    90
federalism, 10, 89
Felton, Rebecca Latimer, 199, 200
female prisoners. *See* prisoners

Ferguson, Billy, 116
Ferguson, Missouri, 10, 75n18
Ferguson v. State of Georgia, 116, 124n10
Ferrell Jr., Arch, 92, 93, 96, 97, 98
Fifth Amendment, 113
Fisher, George, 109, 128n85
Flores-Robert, Vanessa, 18
Florida, 9, 12n8, 19, 71, 75n13, 173; common law in, 111, 116; convict leasing in, 172, 176; electrocution in, 170–72, 178–83; Federation of Women's Clubs, 178; penal system in, 170, 179, 183; public executions in, 173–78; state legislature, 111, 115, 116; state penitentiary, 171, 176, 179, 180, 182; testimonial incapacity in, 115–17. *See also* Alachua County, Florida; Bradford County, Florida; Dade County, Florida; Daviess County, Florida; Duval County, Florida; Jacksonville, Florida; Liberty County, Florida; Miami, Florida; Okaloosa County, Florida; Pinellas County, Florida; Putnam County, Florida; Starke, Florida
Folsom, James, 81, 91, 92, 93, 94, 97, 103n47
forced confessions, 7–8, 50, 59, 62, 67; activism against, 60, 62–63, 66–67, 70–73; admissibility as evidence, 62–63, 65, 67, 69, 71–72; courtroom testimony about, 64, 68–69, 73; and police interrogation methods, 58, 64–65
Fort Benning (Georgia), 79, 83, 85, 86, 87, 89, 92, 96
Fourteenth Amendment, 62–63, 65, 66, 67, 72, 120
Frazier, Harriet, 183
Friedman, Lawrence, 176
Fuller, Albert, 88–89, 93, 97, 98
Fulton County Criminal Court (Georgia), 59

Gadsen, Josh, 161
Galveston, Texas, 98
gambling, 8, 21, 79, 82–83, 85–86, 88–92, 95, 96, 98, 144n10
Garrett, Silas, 96–98
General Electric Company, 180
Georgia, 12n7, 58–59, 60–61, 75n13, 79, 82–84, 89, 92–93, 95, 132, 190fn64;

Association of Women Lawyers, 58; Bar Association, 115; and capital punishment, 170, 173, 177; common law in, 116; Court of Appeals, 115; Humane Association, 58; testimonial incapacity in, 115–16; Women's Democratic Club, 58. *See also* Athens, Georgia; Atlanta, Georgia; Augusta, Georgia; Colbert, Georgia; Columbus, Georgia
Glenn, Robert B., 201
Glover, William, 34, 35, 48
Golden, Bertha Lee, 142
Gordon, George, 34–35
Governors' Conference: (1912), 147; (1915), 148, 156, 158
Graham, William, 45
Graves, Bibb, 141, 42
Green, Paul, 193–94
Green, Willie, 182
Greenleaf, Simon, 110
Greenville, South Carolina, 159–60

Haberland, Michelle, 132
Hackney, Sheldon, 84
Hall, Felix, 87
Hall, George, 201
Halladay, Donald, 122–23
Hammatt, C. S., 180, 189n63
Hardee, Cary A., 181, 188n47
Hardie, Dan, 182
Hargrett, Guy, 88
Harris, Sylvester, 49
Harrison, Mrs. C. E., 58
Hart, Moses, 46
Hartsfield, William B., 58
Hay, Douglas, 156
Hays, Arthur Garfield, 65
Haywood County, Tennessee, 130
Henderson, Charles, 84
Henderson Gold Leaf, 198
Hill, Virginia, 95
Hillsborough, North Carolina, 196, 203
Hilton, Otis, 154
Holloway, Pippa, 101n19
Holt, Linnie, 141
Houston, Charles, 62
Houston, Texas, 19
Howard, Beachie, 85. *See also* Beachie's Swing Club

Hoyle, Walter, 49
Hudson, Arcarrie, 46–47
Huntsville, Texas, 182

Illinois, 10, 61, 75n14, 133. *See also* Chicago, Illinois
immigrants, 84, 102n28, 111, 122
Indiana, 75n14, 112, 133
industrialization, 5, 6, 132, 134, 170
Ingram, Tammy, 152
Iowa, 12n8, 112

Jackson, Andrew, 207
Jackson, Charles, 49
Jackson, Clara, 142
Jackson, E. C., 70
Jackson, Mary, 141
Jackson, Mississippi, 65, 67
Jacksonville, Florida, 19, 89, 173, 180, 182, 187n28, 189n61
Jim Crow, 2–3, 6, 18, 80, 81–82, 87, 108, 149, 163, 202; and capital punishment, 2, 9–10, 184, 194, 195–96, 198, 205, 207; and the criminal justice system, 2, 3, 6, 69, 82, 160, 184; and incarceration, 2, 8–9, 131, 132, 133, 142; laws, 5, 7, 8, 83, 194; and policing, 2, 7, 18, 19, 23, 27, 29–30, 36, 60, 74; and politics, 3, 82, 95, 99, 194; and segregation, 4, 7–8, 17–18, 42, 60–61, 81, 93, 98, 133, 194; and white supremacy, 3–4, 10, 60, 74, 199, 200. *See also* capital punishment; disfranchisement; lynching; police; voting rights; white supremacy
Johnson, Arthur, 177
Johnson, Dorothy, 44
Johnson, Frank, 180–83
Jones, Buster, 40
jury tampering, 90, 93

Kansas, testimonial incapacity in, 118; Supreme Court of, 118
Kantrowitz, Stephen, 30
Kefauver, Estes, 95
Kefauver Committee, 95
Kentucky, 12n7, 12n8, 75n13, 127n54, 170, 177, 185n7. *See also* Eddyville Penitentiary
Key, V. O., 84

Kilby Prison (Alabama), 68, 72
Klarman, Michael J., 62
Knoxville, Tennessee, 19
Koen, Walker I., 46
Ku Klux Klan, 87, 185n10

Lamb, Otis, 93
Leeburn, Fayette, 90
LeFlouria, Talitha L., 132
Lewis, Cornelia Battle, 192–94, 201, 208n4
Liberty County, Florida, 178–79
Life magazine, 80
Lightweis-Goff, Jennie, 19
Link, William, 149, 150
Litewear Manufacturing Company, 139–40
localism, 4, 8, 9, 10, 82, 84, 89–91, 94, 96, 101n20, 149, 150, 172, 179
Look magazine, 80
Looney, Bill, 45
Los Angeles, California, 81
Lost Cause, 200
Louisiana, 4, 12n7, 26, 29, 60, 75n13, 113, 170, 178, 184n6; common law in, 113; constitution of, 17; Supreme Court of, 112. *See also* New Orleans, Louisiana
Love, Jimmie, 40
lynching, 2, 3, 4, 10, 47, 50, 87, 173–74, 178, 179, 195, 198, 205, 207, 212n60; activism against, 62, 202; decline of, 64, 171, 177, 188n44, 201; defense of, 147–48, 155, 162, 201, 202, 211n57; and lynch mobs, 62–65, 201; opposition to, 62, 67, 202, 211n57; photographs of, 62, 177, 202; as spectacle, 201–3. *See also* North Carolina

MacLean, Angus, 194
Maine, 1, 113
Malone, Isaac, 47
Mann, F. K., 139
Mann, William Hodges, 118
Mann Act of 1910, 89
Marshall, Thurgood, 62, 70, 71
martial law, 98
Martin, Jake, 178
Martin, Logan, 84
Martschukat, Jürgen, 180
Maryland, 127n54, 170, 184n6
Massachusetts, 112, 172

Massey, James, 173, 177
mass incarceration, 1, 2, 10, 11n6, 12n10, 81, 86, 99
Mathews, Ralph, 88, 92–93, 94, 95–96
Matthews, Jimmy, 84, 85–86, 88, 91, 97, 98
May, Jacob, 135–36
May Hosiery Mills. *See* Rock City Hosiery Mills
McAfee, Ross, 207–8
McAllister, Franklin, 161
McFarland, Conteller, 45
McKinney, Ike, 46
Meek, Walter, 45
Memphis, Tennessee, 7, 34, 42–43; homicide rates in, 36–37; middle-class African Americans in, 37–38. *See also* Memphis Police Department
Memphis Police Department, 7, 35, 54n21, 55n30; African American cooperation with, 35–36, 38–41, 43–47, 51–52, 53n6; African American surrender to, 57–49, 50, 51, 52, 56n65; and brutality, 35–39, 46, 48–51; and homicide rates, 36–37, 38, 42, 53n11, 55n30; and policing of African Americans, 37, 40–43
Memphis World, 47, 50
Mencken, H. L., 194
Mercer, Jeanette, 90
Meridian, Mississippi, 63, 66, 67
Meridian Star (Mississippi), 64
Merriweather, Hannah, 130
Miami, Florida, 89, 95, 182
Michigan, 61, 75n14, 112, 133
Miles, Sherman, 35
Miller, Kelly, 129
Miller, Vivien, 4, 168n59
Miller, Walter Monroe, 182
Mills, William, 160
Minnesota, 75n14
Mississippi, 4, 12n7, 60, 63–68, 75n13, 83, 127n54, 170, 184n6; Supreme Court of, 65, 66. *See also* Jackson, Mississippi; Meridian, Mississippi
Missouri, 10, 12n7, 75n14, 75n18, 183, 184n6, 188n44
Mitchell, Hersey, 174f8.1, 175, 176, 187n30
Monkkonen, Eric, 35
Montana, 127n55

Montgomery, Alabama, 68–72, 79, 81, 87; Bus Boycott, 73; Circuit Court of, 70, 72
Montgomery Advertiser, 69
Moore, Abe, 35
Moore, Fred, 137
Moore, Leonard N., 18
Moore, Will, 174–75, 179, 187n28, 187n30
Morrison, Walter, 204–5
Moss, Charlene, 46
Muhammad, Khalil, 86
Myers, Fredonia, 51
Myers, John, 51
Myers, Martha, 173
Myrdal, Gunnar, 61, 62

NAACP. *See* National Association for the Advancement of Colored People
Nashville, Tennessee, 130, 135
National Association for the Advancement of Colored People, 8, 62–63, 65–67, 70–73, 99
National Civic League, 81
Native Americans, 111, 122
Nebraska, 126n53
Nevada, 126n53
New Deal, 62, 72
New Orleans, Louisiana, 7, 17–19, 23, 37, 89, 95; Board of Police Commissioners, 18, 20, 22, 28–30. *See also* Doyle, George; New Orleans Police Department
New Orleans Item, 23, 24, 27–29
New Orleans Police Department, 17–19, 22, 26; African American officers in, 17–18, 23, 25, 32n18; exclusion of African American officers from, 28–30; resistance to African American officers, 23–25, 28; reform of, 25
Newsome, Larry, 192–93
New South, 7, 9, 184, 194, 196, 208; boosters, 150, 158
New York, 111, 133, 172, 180, 195, 204. *See also* New York, New York
New York, New York, 37, 62, 65, 70, 79, 81, 95
New York Evening Post, 147
North Carolina, 9, 75n13, 111, 133, 170, 180, 184n6, 190n72, 194–96; black women's political activism in, 199–200; electrocution in, 200, 204–5; lynching in,

201–2; National Guard, 201; State Board of Charities and Public Welfare, 193; Supreme Court of, 202; University of, 193, 200. *See also* Hillsborough, North Carolina; Raleigh, North Carolina; Oxford, North Carolina; Salisbury, North Carolina; Wilson County, North Carolina
Nye, David, 180

Obama, Barack, administration of, 1
Odum, Howard, 193
O'Hara, John Grady, 107
Ohio, 10, 75n14, 127n54, 133, 172. *See also* Cleveland, Ohio
Okaloosa County, Florida, 176, 178
Oklahoma, 12n7, 75n13, 170
Oliveri, Maud. *See* Stark, Maud
organized crime, 8, 79, 85, 88, 89–90, 93, 95; historical study of, 81; and politics, 80, 82, 92, 93, 97; and white supremacy, 82, 95. *See also* gambling; Phenix City, Alabama; prostitution
Oxford, North Carolina, 197

pardons, 9, 71, 111, 118, 148–49, 153–54, 160, 163, 190n64, 201; critiques of, 157–58; history of, 156; and penal reform, 151–52, 155, 163; petitions for, 154, 159, 161, 168n59. *See also* Blease, Cole; executive clemency
Parker, John M., 29
parole, 1, 9, 98, 148–49, 151, 153–54, 157–59, 162–63; and African Americans, 160–62; and penal reform, 155, 157. *See also* Blease, Cole
paternalism, 149–50, 160–62
Patterson, Albert, 94–95; law career of, 90–92, 96; murder of, 80–82, 97, 99; political career of, 80, 92–93, 96–97, 99
Patterson, John M., 98–99
penal reform, 1, 8–10, 135, 149, 151, 156–57, 163, 166n21, 167n30. *See also* Blease, Cole; capital punishment; pardons; parole
penitentiaries, 1, 3–6, 8–9, 12n10, 151, 158, 172, 180, 183; chaplains in, 180, 205, 208; physicians in, 137, 155, 161, 181, 204; solitary confinement in, 1, 142. *See also* Eddyville penitentiary; Florida;

Georgia; Kilby Prison; penal reform; prisoners; Raleigh, North Carolina; South Carolina; Speigner Prison; Tennessee; Wetempka; Walls
Pennsylvania, 126n35, 127n54, 133
peonage, 92, 159
perjury, 108, 110–11, 114, 116–17, 124n3
Persons, Gordon, 94, 98
petit larceny, 114, 119–22, 129n93
Pfeifer, Michael, 177
Phenix City, Alabama, 8, 94–96, 99; Citizens Committee, 94; end of organized crime in, 80–81, 98; history of, 79–80, 82–84, 90; law enforcement in, 86, 88, 90, 96; local politics in, 80, 90, 93, 96–97; racketeering in, 80, 82, 84–85, 87, 89–91, 95, 97, 101n23. *See also* brothels; gambling; organized crime; prostitution; Russell County, Alabama
Phillips, W. W., 179
phrenology, 181
Pinellas County, Florida, 175
police, and brutality, 2, 7, 10, 34–36, 38, 49–52, 60–61, 73; departments of, 4, 6–8, 60, 90; and shootings, 10, 13n24, 17, 61, 75n18; and white supremacy, 7, 30, 73–74. *See also* African Americans; Atlanta, Georgia; Doyle, George; forced confessions; Memphis Police Department; New Orleans Police Department; white supremacy
Ponsell, Putnam, 178
poor whites, 92, 150, 197
Porter, Lee, 96–97
Porter, William G., 70–71
Potter, Albert, 21–28
Potter, David, 196
Power, Tyrone, 82–83
prisoners, 1, 118, 138–39, 149, 151, 176, 179; African American women as, 8, 131–34, 136, 138–42; corporal punishment of, 61, 142, 149, 151, 153, 156, 161, 172, 183; on death row, 2, 180, 193, 204; and vocational training, 183; white women as, 132–33, 140–42. *See also* chain gangs; contract labor; convict labor; convict leasing; executive clemency; pardons; parole, penal reform; penitentiaries; probation

probation, 1, 98, 149, 151, 155
Progressive Era, 149, 156, 180
progressive reform, 6, 148, 157–58, 192, 194, 196, 202; southern progressivism, 9, 149–52, 163. See also penal reform
prostitution, 8, 85, 88–89, 92–93. See also brothels
public executions, 4, 9, 10, 64, 166n21, 172, 179, 194, 201–2, 205, 207; African American presence at, 175, 198–200; criticism of, 171, 178, 194–95, 197, 208; rituals of, 174–76; role of sheriffs in, 4, 9, 171, 173, 175–77, 203; as spectacles, 195–97, 203. See also capital punishment
Putnam County, Florida, 177, 188n47

Raleigh, North Carolina, 198, 204; Central Prison, 192, 204
Raleigh News and Observer, 192, 206
Raleigh Signal, 208
rape, 73, 137, 162, 173, 182, 186n20, 186n23, 197, 200, 205, 207, 208, 212n59
Raper, Arthur, 61, 75n13
Reconstruction, 4, 7, 19, 24, 30, 60, 108, 122, 160, 184, 203
Reese, Elmer, 90
Republican Party, 95
Republicans, 120
Revel, Clarence, 84, 92, 98
Revels, Lawrence, 179
Richmond, Virginia, 147, 148
Richmond Times-Dispatch, 181
Robinson, Gracie, 40, 49
Robinson, Jerry, 40
Rock City Hosiery Mills, 135–37
Rosewood Massacre, 172
Ross, Will, 45
Rousey, Dennis, 18
rules of evidence, 109, 119–20, 123, 128n81, 129n93
Russell County, Alabama, 79–80, 83–84, 86, 88–93; Russell Betterment Association, 95; Draft Board, 92, 94. See also Phenix City, Alabama

Salisbury, North Carolina, 201
Sarat, Austin, 208
Scheer, Bernard W., 139

Scott, Walter, 45
Scrimm, Henry Harry, 182, 190n73
Scroggins, Ben, 93
segregation. See Jim Crow
Seibel, W. T., 68. 72
Seneca, South Carolina, 95
Shepherd, Grady, 90
Shepherd, Hoyt, 84–86, 88, 90–92, 97–98
Shields, Henry, 63–64, 66–67, 71–72
Simpson, Mabel, 44
Sing Sing Prison, 180, 189n63
slavery, 3–5, 60, 111, 199–200
Smith, Harvey, 154
Smith, Quintell, 40
social Darwinism, 181
South, Quintar, 58–59, 73
South, Rosa, 58
South Carolina, 9, 60, 75n13, 147, 151–52, 154–55, 164n12, 170, 186n17, 201; Board of Charities and Corrections of, 151, 153; Board of Health, 155; Board of Pardons, 153–54; common law in, 117; penal system in, 148, 151, 158; state legislature, 149, 151; state penitentiary, 147–48, 151–53, 155, 159–62, 166n21, 167n30; Supreme Court of, 117, 119; testimonial incapacity in, 117, 119–20. See also Charleston, South Carolina; Columbia, South Carolina; Greenville, South Carolina
southern exceptionalism, 3, 108
Speigner Prison (Alabama), 139–40
Stark, Bertha, 21–23, 27
Stark, Maud, 21–23, 27–28
Starke, Florida, 174
The State (Columbia, South Carolina), 159
State of Louisiana v. Albert Potter and George Doyle, 22
Steven, J. Morgan, 67
St. Petersburg (Florida) Evening Independent, 175
Strickland, Lena May, 40
Stuart, Henry Carter, 118
Stuart, Raymond, 63
Sturdivant, J. I., 64
Suggs, Estelle, 45
suicide, 87, 190n72, 205
Sutherland, W. F., 58–59
Sykes, Bernard, 98

Taggart, E. W., 70
Tapping, Thomas Lee, 44–45
Taylor, Philip, 182
Taylor, Recy, 73
Taylor v. State (Alabama), 114
Teaster, George, 107–8, 122
Tennessee, 8, 75n13, 95, 133–34, 136, 138,
   143; Board of Prison Commissioners,
   135–37; capital punishment in, 170,
   177, 188n44; common law in, 111, 117;
   contract labor system in, 130–31, 138;
   convict leasing in, 131, 135, 138; state
   penitentiary, 130, 135–38, 143; state
   legislature, 111, 122–23; Supreme Court,
   107; testimonial incapacity in, 107–8,
   117–18, 122, University of, 122. *See also*
   Briceville, Tennessee; Haywood County,
   Tennessee; Knoxville, Tennessee; Memphis, Tennessee; Nashville, Tennessee
Tennessee Law Review, 122
testimonial rights, 8, 126n35, 154; expansion
   of, 112–14, 123; restrictions on, 108–11,
   114, 116–17, 119, 122, 124n3, 124n10,
   126n53, 129n93; and white supremacy,
   111, 120–22; *See also* Alabama; Arkansas;
   Florida; Georgia; Kansas; South Carolina,
   Tennessee, Texas; Virginia
Texas, 11n6, 12n7, 75n13, 170; common
   law in, 116; Supreme Court of, 117;
   testimonial incapacity in, 116–17. *See
   also,* Galveston, Texas; Houston, Texas;
   Huntsville, Texas
The Walls (Alabama). *See* Wetumpka
   Women's Prison
Thirteenth Amendment, 120
Thompson, Florence, 177
Thompson, Heather Ann, 3
Tillman, Ben, 149, 159, 164n12
Times-Democrat (New Orleans), 23–25, 28
Tindall, George, 194
Tobin, Ebenezer, 175–76, 187n35
*Tom Love Grocery Co. v. Maryland Casu-
   alty Company*, 122–23
Trotti, Michael, 175, 181, 198
tuberculosis, 148, 155
Turk, Ethel May, 140–41

Underwood, John, 203
Underwood v. State (Texas), 117

Union v. State (Georgia), 115
United Mine Workers, 107
United States, 30, 53n9, 61, 75n13, 84,
   101n20, 133, 170, 180; Army, 83, 86, 200;
   criminal justice system in, 1–3, 10, 12n10,
   204; Department of Justice, 73; executions
   in, 172, 176, 187n39, 204; Senate, 62, 95,
   164n12, 164n13; Supreme Court, 62–63,
   65–67, 69, 71–72, 83, 116; testimonial
   rights in, 108–12, 119, 126n39
Upper South, 133
Utah, 185n7

Vance v. State (Arkansas), 117
Vandiver, Margaret, 177
Vaughn, Thurston, 159
Vermont, 1, 127n54
Virginia, 12n8, 61, 75n13, 76n52, 129n93,
   133, 170; testimonial incapacity in,
   118–19. *See also* Richmond, Virginia
voting rights, 62, 110, 121, 194, 200. *See
   also* disfranchisement

Wade, Pauline, 40
Wadsworth, Edward W., 71
Walls, Thomas A., 142
Ward, Eunice, 68
Ward, Lillian, 68
Washington, Annie B., 50
Washington, D.C., 80
Washington, Mason, 50
Washington Post, 13n24
Washington Times, 147
Watkins, Garland, 58
Weaver, R. H., 178–79
West Virginia, 133, 184n6
Wetumpka Women's Prison (Alabama), 130,
   139–43
Whitaker, Edward, 20–21, 26, 28, 29
White, Walter, 70–71
white supremacy, 3–4, 6, 8, 18, 23, 60, 84,
   86, 120, 155, 177, 194; and capital pun-
   ishment, 184, 195, 208; and organized
   crime, 82, 92–93; and police brutality,
   60, 72, 74; and police departments, 19,
   25–26, 28–30; and progressive reform,
   150–51, 160n30. *See also* capital punishment; Jim Crow; organized crime; police;
   testimonial rights

white women, 28, 89, 147, 169n81, 177, 199–200, 202, 211n57. *See also* prisoners
Whitfield, Genie May, 39
Whitfield, John, 39
Williams, Arthur, 182
Williams, Charlie, 47
Wilmington (N.C.) Messenger, 199
Wilson County, North Carolina, 192
Women's Bureau, Department of Labor, US, 133–34
Women's Christian Temperance Union, 199

Wood, Amy Louise, 181, 203
Woods, Walter, 45
Woodward, C. Vann, 18, 150
Wooten, John Henry, 39
World War I, 94, 133, 170, 171, 196
World War II, 11n6, 12n10, 18, 86, 89, 201
Wyoming, 147

Yarbrough, Clyde, 90–91
Young Men's Democratic Association, 25